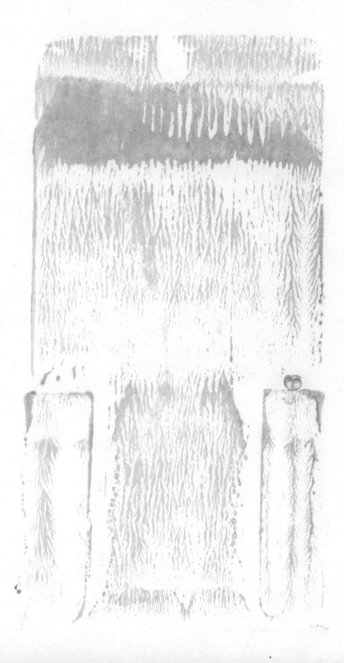

ROADS TO AGREEMENT

Roads to Agreement

SUCCESSFUL METHODS IN THE SCIENCE OF HUMAN RELATIONS

STUART CHASE

In Collaboration with

MARIAN TYLER CHASE

GREENWOOD PRESS, PUBLISHERS
WESTPORT, CONNECTICUT

Originally published in 1951
by Harper & Row, Publishers, New York

Reprinted with the permission
of Harper & Row

First Greenwood Reprinting 1970

Library of Congress Catalogue Card Number 71-109287

SBN 8371-3830-2

Printed in the United States of America

Instead of looking into the causes of conflict that we hear so much about, we ought to try to discover how much peace there is, and what makes peace.

—Clinton S. Golden

The day will come . . . when the human race will allow itself to be happy and will decide to have done with . . . outworn enmities. . . . We ought to feel a new sense of human power, of capacity to master a reluctant environment, and to learn the difficult art of living together in the same world without mutual hatreds.

—Bertrand Russell

In a time when change in certain aspects of "human nature" has become necessary to the survival of our species, it is comforting to know that it can be done and has been done. The problem of the scientist is to find out how.

—Ralph Linton

CONTENTS

CONTENTS

FOREWORD

THIS book grows out of its predecessor, *The Proper Study of Mankind*, published in the fall of 1948. The relation is something like one of those maps in the papers which has a circle drawn around a given area where the news is coming from. Then a larger scale map is shown of the circled area. The earlier book was an attempt to map the social sciences, and establish interconnections and lines of progress in the study of human relations. The question of conflict and agreement, noted there briefly, is shown here on a considerably larger scale.

Anthropologists, sociologists, psychologists, semanticists, are actively trying to find the principles by which people get along together or do not get along. Meanwhile, a number of practical methods have been developed over the years—such as the conciliation of labor disputes and the unanimous agreement of a jury. We shall bring both the science and the art of agreement into this survey, while pointing out that the science is destined to become increasingly important, reliable and available. As the reader will see, not only are the universities full of interesting new experiments, but industry, government, international bodies like UNESCO, are setting up laboratories and observation posts.

I have been thinking about the subject of this book for a long time, and have repeatedly touched on it in personal experience. For instance, I happened to attend one of the early seminars in conference methods with E. C. Lindeman in the 1920's—which started me wondering about group behavior. As a staff member of the Labor

Bureau, Incorporated, in New York, I had an opportunity to look rather closely at techniques in collective bargaining, conciliation and arbitration, and joint production programs of management and labor.

Later, I made a special study of the famous Hawthorne plant experiments of Elton Mayo, with their surprising conclusions about morale and productivity. I published a book describing these, and also analyzing the Training within Industry program in World War II, where some of the Hawthorne findings were taught to more than a million foremen. I reviewed at first hand the program of the Labor Management Production Committees which Donald Nelson set up in war plants.

This in turn led to an independent examination of labor-management relations in the refineries of the Standard Oil Company of New Jersey, where there had been no strike for thirty years. As a member of the National Planning Association's Committee on Conditions of Industrial Peace, I have been associated with Clinton S. Golden and others in looking for the "universals" which underlie good labor relations everywhere.

In Paris in 1949 I had the honor to be a delegate to one of UNESCO's "tension project" conferences, in which social scientists from nine different countries tried to assess the effects of the machine age on frustration and aggression. If the mechanical impact could be lessened, would war be less likely? We concluded that it would. Meanwhile, ever since 1936 I have been interested in the new discipline of semantics, about which I wrote a book, *The Tyranny of Words*. Semantics aims at analyzing and preventing linguistic misunderstandings, and thus promoting agreement.

Through all these activities, I began to feel, ran a common factor, which might emerge if one could arrange them in some sort of pattern. Instead of one common factor, I found, as you will see, at least five.

But I suppose the most compelling reason for undertaking this study was the natural anxiety of a citizen, watching the spiraling disagreements of the "cold war," with two stockpiles of fissionable material rising in the background. Collecting techniques of agreement seemed to relieve the anxiety a little, even if the direct applicability in international relations was not always clear. One has to begin somewhere.

In spite of these various personal contacts with the subject matter, your author is not expert in all branches—nor, so far as he is aware, is anybody else. I have tried to keep the reports simple, informal, and as clear as possible without sacrificing accuracy. Technicians in any one field will probably wish for more detail, but that would embark us upon an encyclopedia. The selected bibliography at the end of the book will direct the reader to more complete treatment of the various fields.

An inventory of this nature is not an encyclopedia, but neither is it a primer. What is it? the critic may ask. I offer it, as I did the *Proper Study*, as an experiment in *integration*. Specialists "know more and more about less and less" as science advances, and a liaison service is needed to keep them in touch with one another. Even more, perhaps, a service is needed to keep the intelligent layman in touch with the advancing front. The "integrator," like a walkie-talkie operator, is a communications man.

There are no specialties in nature. In the space-time world the subject matter of physics flows into the subject matter of chemistry into biology into medicine into psychiatry into psychology into economics, by "insensible gradations." The divisions are in our minds, a function of the language structure by which we think. The integrator cannot rise above his language, but he can try to see how the various subjects are related to form a process and a whole. He can try to get the picture puzzle together. So far as I know, this is the first attempt to integrate techniques of agreement from widely distant sources. I hope it may serve as a useful map for better equipped expeditions in the future.

This is an exploration, not a handbook. We shall probably raise as many questions as we answer. But I think the study helps to indicate a point of view, an orientation, which can prove useful in a variety of day-to-day situations. Just digging out and assembling the

material has markedly improved my own human relations. I am sure
that I do not look for nearly so much trouble from my fellows as I
used to, and when I unexpectedly find it I can often manage to
resolve it. Most of us could probably improve our human relations—
which are a good deal more important than our public relations.
I believe that much of the material can be applied quite widely, but
that is for the reader to determine.

As for the international disagreements which are threatening to
destroy large areas of civilization, if not man himself, we shall find
here some tools to begin work on a long-range program, but no
complete blueprints for abolishing war, or inaugurating One World.
Proven techniques for agreement have not yet progressed to such
global proportions. But perhaps the reader will find in Chapters 19
and 20 some approaches to the problem.

A recent poll by Elmo Roper asked Americans: *Why send the
children to high school?* The largest vote was, of course: *To get
them ready for a job.* But next came: *To teach them to get along
better with other people.* It is a little surprising and very encouraging to find American public opinion so solidly behind the subject
of our inquiry!

Many persons have helped at various stages in this experiment
in integration. My wife has been partner, research assistant and
operator of a sort of literary Geiger counter. "That's fine," she would
say, "but what has it got to do with agreement?" Or, "This monograph is tough but important." Or, more simply: "Too global."
Mrs. Russell A. Loring was ready to type or retype manuscript at
any hour of the day or night, and I am very grateful to her.

I have had aid and advice from friends and specialists who helped
with the outline in its various metamorphoses, or corrected sections
where their own work was cited, or took me around the shop to see
the experiments. They are not responsible for the conclusions—
except in the special sense that everyone now stands on everyone
else's shoulders, so vast is the cultural accumulation to 1950. I am
deeply grateful to them all, and especially to the following: Gordon

Allport, Charles Ascher, Leland Bradford, Charles Dollard, John Dollard, Leonard Doob, Charles Estes, John Fischer, Stuart Grummon, Pendleton Herring, William Hodson, Jr., Harold E. Jones, Clyde Kluckhohn, Irving Knickerbocker, Charles Krutch, Irving Lee, Rensis Likert, Charlotte Lochhead, George A. Lundberg, Douglas McGregor, Alfred Norris, William Ogburn, Milo Perkins, Joseph Scanlon, Benjamin Selekman, Henry Lee Smith, Jr., Herbert Thelen and Donald Young.

STUART CHASE

Redding, Connecticut
December, 1950

ROADS TO AGREEMENT

CHAPTER ONE

The Price Is High

BACK in the days of World War I, workers and managers in the Standard Oil refinery at Bayonne, New Jersey, were carrying on a war of their own. In the summer of 1915 there were pitched battles in the streets, with strikers throwing bricks and stones, police and guards shooting revolvers. Fires were set, tank cars of oil, box cars of merchandise, once even the company pump house, went up in flames. At least one striker was killed and many on both sides were wounded.

The men complained that foremen mistreated them cruelly, especially by keeping them too long cleaning the hot stills, where temperatures ran up to 250 degrees. They demanded a fifty-hour week and time-and-a-half for overtime. An agent from the Industrial Workers of the World tried to get them to join his union but without success. The men preferred their own local organization.

Trouble flared again the following year. Then suddenly it stopped. Since that bloody period more than a generation ago, there have been no strikes and no violence at the Bayonne refinery, nor at any large plant of the company's nationwide organization. Why? What happened to the hot tempers, so hot indeed that men and managers were ready to kill one another? Human nature cannot have changed in a generation. The country as a whole has not achieved a society without strikes. The oil industry has seen many labor conflicts;

in 1945, for instance, practically all refinery workers were out on strike except those of Jersey Standard.

What did unions and managers do in this company to bring such a long era of peace? The company, as we shall see in more detail later, made one of the first scientific studies of human relations in industry, and as a result drastically changed its policy in the direction of more trust, more security for workers, better communication between men and management, more participation in company affairs. The men responded. A time of violent conflict gave way to a time of accommodation, and after a while to co-operation.[1]

Two Billions of Us

What men and management did at Bayonne needs to be done all over the country in situations of every scale. What they did in a small way needs to be done by Homo sapiens in a big way. There are something over two billions of us on the planet, faced not only with labor battles but with more serious conflicts between East and West, between nations, cultures, races, ideologies, religions. Asia, as I write, seems to be one huge conflict.

The whole earth in 1950, in terms of the time to ride around it, is no bigger than a Texas county in 1850, while applied science in transport and communication shrinks it day by day. We may or may not be our brothers' keepers, but we are increasingly in our brothers' laps. Some progress has undoubtedly been gained through strife and conflict in the past, but a heavy price has been paid for it. Today the price has risen sharply, perhaps to the point of survival itself. The A-bomb gives way to the H-bomb, and presently the Z-bomb. Dr. Enrico Fermi is now speculating about a super H-bomb.

To expect people to abandon their right to quarrel with the neighbors, however high its price, is of course Utopian. But the mounting cost of belligerency is causing thoughtful observers to look around for ways and means to reduce it. Perhaps it is none too

[1] This story is taken from my report to the company in 1947, called *A Generation of Industrial Peace*. It was about this time that the idea of a book on the techniques of agreement took shape in my mind.

soon to take an inventory of those techniques—such as the labor policy of Jersey Standard—which could be used to reduce the area of conflict and make us less vulnerable to outbreaks of our own belligerency. When we begin to look, a surprising number of methods come to light. Some, like the new principles of "group dynamics," have been deliberately investigated by social scientists; some have just grown, like the Quaker business meeting with its principle of unanimity.

Here are samples of the kind of material which an inventory of agreement should contain:

Race Distinctions in the Army

Dr. Samuel A. Stouffer of Harvard was in charge of a research project that sampled the opinions of some millions of soldiers during World War II.[2] One of the studies dealt with the attitude of white G.I.s toward Negroes. After many tests, some astonishing conclusions were recorded. The question, "Would you like to be brigaded with Negroes?" was asked of white enlisted men with the following results:

Those who had no experience with Negroes in the Army voted more than 90 percent against being brigaded with them.

Those who had limited contact voted 67 percent against it.

Those who were used to Negroes in the same regiment, but not in the same company, voted 50 percent against it.

But white soldiers who had fought in the same company side by side with Negroes, were 86 percent in favor of continuing the arrangement.

Where there was intimate contact, there was confidence between the races. Said a white platoon sergeant from South Carolina: "When I first heard about it, I'd be damned if I'd wear the same shoulder patch they did. After that day when we saw how they fought, I changed my mind. They're just like any other boys to us." A company commander from Nevada reported on his mixed group in these words: "We found good co-operation between both races in combat.

2 *The American Soldier*, 2 Vols. This and other references are listed in the Selected Bibliography at the end of this book.

They have their pictures taken together, go to church services, movies, play ball together. For a time there in combat, our platoons got so small that we had to put a white squad in the colored platoon. You might think that wouldn't work well, but it did. The white squad didn't want to leave the platoon. I've never seen anything like it."

Elmo Roper, summarizing Stouffer's findings, notes that the races worked together well because they had a common enemy and had to depend on each other in the heat of battle. Nobody was trying to conduct a moral crusade in race relations but rather to win a war against very tough opposition. "The results indicate," says Roper, "as clearly as anything which has ever been done before, that prejudice is something which grows out of the environment in which people live."

Quaker Meeting

We were very divided about the possibility of lending the Meeting House to relieve the acute shortage of places where men and women— particularly those in the Armed Forces—could go for rest or a social time in the evening. There was a great doubt whether the Meeting House should be used for such a purpose. . . . But after a period of silence, there appeared to be unanimous feeling that we should make the offer of the Meeting House whatever was entailed.

Thus the Society of Friends in Reading, England, resolved a potential conflict among its members during the Blitz. Quakers are pacifists, and to use the Meeting House for the entertainment of the armed forces was in a way against their principles. But obviously the need was great. The business meeting discussed the matter and found the members, as the Pollards say in their book, "very divided."

For almost three hundred years, whenever members find themselves very divided at Quaker meetings, a period of silence is declared. After it, if the division persists, the clerk postpones the question to a future meeting. No vote is ever taken; nothing is ever decided except *unanimously*—according to the "sense of the meeting." Time and time again after the silent period, unanimity comes.

Why? What keeps the Society of Friends from the wrangles, the bitterness, the recriminations, the splits between majority and minority which characterize so many other meetings and so many other churches? A procedure which has been delivering unanimous agreement for three centuries belongs well up in the inventory, and we will go into it more thoroughly in Chapter 6.

Lebanon Village

Communities in Lebanon have a tradition of dreadful feuds, sometimes lasting for generations. The members of two opposing clans, though meeting constantly in the streets and market, may not speak during their whole lives. An American social scientist, reared in Syria, decided to make an experiment. He organized a game of volley ball in one of the villages torn by feuds. Young men became interested in the sport, and presently the whole village gathered to watch them play. Members of opposing clans began to talk to one another in the excitement of the game.

The scientist then arranged a match with a neighboring village which already had a volley ball team. "Our" village turned out to a man to root for "our" team. Old crones, long feudists, congratulated each other as "our" boys scored a point.

In due time, the pattern of feuds collapsed, and the village returned to more normal behavior. Observe, however, that conflict did not necessarily disappear. It was transferred to a higher level, against the people of the neighboring village, and in a considerably less dangerous form.[3]

Cocktails for Two

Here is a simple technique with a semantic angle for avoiding misunderstandings and stopping quarrels. I have borrowed it in part from S. I. Hayakawa, who uses it very skillfully. It takes a bit of practice and is worth it.

Someone deliberately tries to provoke you into an argument, for reasons of his own. The time, place, and subject vary; in our example

[3] This story comes from Stuart C. Dodd, University of Washington.

a total stranger approaches you at a cocktail party after a drink or two and fixes you with a stern eye.

"I hear you like labor unions," he says belligerently. "Well, they are nothing but rackets."

This is pretty close to an insult, in view of your past record. You can hit him, or you can turn your back and walk away. You can contradict him and spend the rest of the afternoon deadlocked in a verbal battle. But this time you are experimenting, and you stand your ground and wait.

"Pegler is dead right," the man goes on, "when he says they are nothing but rackets."

You continue to control yourself. The essence of the method is refusing to argue on a generalization.

"Well, that's one point of view. Tell me more." It is a real effort to bring this out, but you are rewarded at once. Your assailant, slightly disconcerted, clears his throat.

"Well, Pegler ought to know, oughtn't he?" he inquires, on the defensive now. If you are tempted to pursue, resist it.

"Go ahead," you say. "I'm listening."

The chances are that the stranger's offensive will soon fizzle out for lack of facts to support it. Or he may produce an authentic case of labor racketeering. In either event you have established a communication line. You may agree that his case is outrageous and should be stopped, after which he may admit that such cases are not universal, or even that Westbrook Pegler occasionally shows a little prejudice. Since you have listened to him, he is willing to listen to you. Conflict gives way to an amicable discussion from which both parties can profit. You have proved again that it takes two to make a quarrel.

Children Making Masks

Our next exhibit is a classic in the new discipline called "group dynamics," which is the study of interactions between individuals in groups and the special energies released in group action. The exhibit demonstrates that the form in which a group is set up has a lot to do with the way members behave. This case bears somewhat the same relation to group dynamics that the famous Hawthorne experiments of Dr. Elton Mayo bear to the scientific study of labor-management relations. Both inaugurated fruitful inquiry in a new and important field; both throw a flood of light on how conflict can be reduced.

Dr. Kurt Lewin, the noted psychologist, working with Ronald Lippitt and R. K. White at the Iowa Child Welfare Station in the late 1930's, studied groups of children ten to twelve years old, making masks in handicraft classes. The groups included both boys and girls; they were tested and found to be comparable in size and membership.

One group was given an *autocratic* structure, where an adult leader made all the decisions. He specified who worked with whom, how the masks were to be made, what rules were to be followed.

A second group was organized on a *democratic* basis. There was an adult leader, but now it was his business to encourage the children themselves to make the decisions and plans, and to suggest and guide rather than direct them. Strict rules were avoided; the atmosphere of the class was relaxed and free.

A third group, set up somewhat later, was given an *anarchistic* or *laissez-faire* pattern. There was a nominal leader but he did no leading. The children were asked to work everything out for themselves —a little along the lines of the early progressive schools.

When the results were compared, the children in the *autocratic* group were found obedient enough to the commands of the leader, but they took it out on each other. Twice a member was so picked upon he had to leave the group. Members were apathetic and uncooperative, showing considerable tension, and what Lewin calls "I-feeling." When the leader left, the group rapidly disintegrated, for it had no inner strength.

The children in the *democratic* group were more co-operative, were keen about their tasks and showed little tension. They showed a pronounced "we-feeling" and ran nobody out of the class. After the leader left, the group continued on its own momentum. It had plenty of inner strength.

The *anarchistic* group hardly functioned at all. It was rife with "I-feeling"—every child for himself. As mask-making demands teamwork, naturally very little was done of a purposeful nature.

Then the structures were reversed. Lewin, in commenting on the change from the democratic to the autocratic method, observes:

> There have been few experiences for me as impressive as seeing the expression on the children's faces change during the first day of "autocracy." The friendly, open and cooperative group, full of life, became an apathetic gathering without initiative. . . . Autocracy is imposed upon the individual; democracy he has to learn.

A Matter of Taste

Captain James Saunders, U.S.N., retired, teaches the principles of agreement in a graduate class in Washington, D. C. One of his illustrations is to give each member a piece of white paper about the size of one's little finger and then ask him to chew it up and report the taste—sweet, sour, bitter, what? The paper (wrapped in cellophane) has been treated with phenyl-thio-carbamide. The class chews thoughtfully. Some say "bitter"; some say "sweet"; some say "no taste at all." Arguments break out; voices are raised: "It certainly *is* sweet." . . . "You're crazy, it's sour!" . . .

Captain Saunders then appoints two leaders, one for the group reporting no taste, the other for the group reporting various tastes, and asks them to reach some kind of agreement. Pandemonium results. "The talk and confusion," says the Captain, "remind me very much of the conferences at Lake Success where statesmen seek to settle the affairs of the world." Eventually the two groups are completely deadlocked.

At this point the Captain calls for order and explains the scientific *facts* about phenyl-thio-carbamide. It is a chemical which tastes different to different people. The reactions have been statistically analyzed and grouped. Three people out of ten, on the average, cannot taste anything, while the other seven experience a variety of

tastes. As the class grasps this scientific explanation, the arguments
and shouting disappear. Everyone now understands that in this situation it is possible to lift the dispute to a higher level, where personal
opinions, feelings, prejudices have no place at all. The class can
reach unanimous agreement on the basis of scientific facts.

The conclusion raises an interesting question for our study. In
how many cases can solid agreement be reached by bringing in the
facts? Unfortunately, we do not always have a Captain Saunders
around to find them for us so neatly. Unfortunately, too, some people
will move heaven and earth to prevent facts being known.

The Pattern We Shall Follow

I have given seven cases, counting the trouble in Bayonne, which
illustrate techniques for getting on better with people. They range
all the way from two private citizens at a cocktail party to that
considerable section of the American army where race prejudice is
a serious problem. They constitute the raw material of our inventory
and give the reader a preview of what he will find, in more detail
and better ordered, throughout the rest of the book.

In studying conflict and agreement, four main questions presently
emerge. Three we shall discuss only briefly; the fourth will demand
most of our attention. The questions are:

1. *Areas of conflict.* What are the classes of human quarrels? In
Chapter 2 we will picture them as a kind of skyscraper of conflict,
with a fight on every floor.

2. *Roots of conflict.* Where does this quarrelsomeness come from?
Is it all due to the "cussedness of human nature"? Is it imposed by
the culture? Is it personal frustration? What? These questions we
will examine in Chapters 3 and 4, with the help of some good scientific testimony.

3. *Natural offsets to conflict.* If Homo sapiens is a social animal,
as the scientists say, there must be limits to his quarrelsomeness or
he would be as extinct as the tyrannosaurus. In Chapter 5 we will
note some obvious limits and some less obvious ones.

4. *Techniques to lessen conflict and promote agreement.* This is

the heart of the inquiry. It starts with the analysis of the Quaker business meeting in Chapter 6 and goes on to the last page, broken only by various summaries as the cases accumulate.

One feels a little like Diogenes with his lantern. We are looking not so much for an honest man as for one who has learned to get on with his fellows and can tell us how he does it. (He is probably an honest man, too.) We will look under any promising bush for such men and women, whether they do it by science or by intuition, for we need all the help we can get. We will look for little personal things as well as for big global things, expecting to find more dependable aid, on the whole, from the former.

The case of Captain Saunders' impregnated paper, simple as it is, demonstrates the scientific method for reducing conflict. The quarrel is halted by a statistical report on individual differences. Although the class has not studied the physiology of taste perception, it accepts the findings of biology and drops the quarrel.

The application of the scientific method has cleared up mystery after mystery in the last three centuries. Before Galileo, the causes of events were mostly mysteries to be explained by supernatural happenings. How milk turned sour might be laid to goblins and was a deep mystery until bacteria were discovered. How witches rode broomsticks was a pseudo-mystery, but endless hours of acrimonious debate were devoted to it by minds as good as yours or mine. An electric flashlight would have been sheer black magic to our forebears.

No one debates any longer what water is or whether it is possible for men to fly or what causes yellow fever. For educated people, these questions and thousands like them are no longer open to argument.

The scientific method is, I believe, our best hope for analyzing the roots of conflict and finding ways to resolve it. The science of human relations is growing fast, and already gives us three useful tools in (1) the study of group dynamics; (2) the study of semantics; and (3) the culture concept borrowed from anthropology. The last is somewhat more complex than the others but perhaps the most fruitful of them all. The culture concept gives us leads not only on how to get along with the neighbors but on how to come to terms with the members of the Out-group—"those foreigners" whose words and whose habits so often repel or infuriate us.

It is hoped, finally, that all sorts of people can find useful some of the methods now to be described—teachers, conference leaders, public speakers, writers, Congressmen, diplomats, business managers, labor leaders, club directors, lawyers, parents. But I doubt if there is much profit in it for communists, demagogues, ardent propagandists, debaters, cultists, stern ideologists, or those who are sure they have all the answers.

CHAPTER TWO

Levels of Conflict

SUPPOSE we pick up the morning paper for the headlines of the day's quarrels and conflicts. Here is the New York *Herald Tribune* for May 4, 1950, the day I began to write this chapter. It was supposed to be in peacetime.

U.S. HALTS SALE OF ARMED SHIPS TO EGYPT

IVES JOINS FIGHT TO SLASH ECA FUNDS

TYDINGS WARNS OF WAR

REDS TIGHTEN BERLIN CONTROLS

ALBANIA DENIES HELPING GREEK REDS

RUSSIA BLOCKS ATOM CONTROL

TRYGVE LIE GOING TO RUSSIA, SEEKS COLD WAR END

RUSSIA CHARGES U.S. REBUILDS JAPANESE BASES

LOSS OF HAINAN BY CHIANG CONFIRMED

LUCAS CRIES LIAR IN CLASH ON MC CARTHY

REPUBLICANS HAIL BLOW TO TRUMAN IN FLORIDA

TOBIN ASSAILS STASSEN ATTACK

O'CONOR CHIDES BUSINESS

UNION SUES OIL COMPANY

HALF-HOUR STRIKE THROUGHOUT ITALY

CHRYSLER STRIKE IN 99TH DAY

OHIO COURT BANS RACIAL BIAS AT POOLS

RENT GOUGE CHARGED

ACCUSES SLAIN MAN'S PREDECESSOR

12

POLICEMAN SHOT TO DEATH IN SUBWAY
SAYS SON HIT HIM

A fair day's budget, but nothing out of the ordinary—except possibly the lonely odyssey of Trygve Lie to Moscow. Granted that the
press always prefers a fight to a settlement, enough remains in these
headlines to give us plenty of concern, from international crises
down to the man hit by his son.

SKYSCRAPER OF CONFLICT

One might erect a figurative skyscraper of disagreements in the
world today, with a fight on every floor. We begin with two people
and work up to two billion. It might look something like this:

1. *Personal quarrels,* between husband and wife, for instance, or
employer and servant. Many people cherish personal enemies, dark-
ening their lives for years on end.

2. *Family against family.* The Smiths do not speak to the Robin-
sons. Small towns are more burdened with this kind of conflict than
large cities.

3. *Feuds,* or quarrels between family groups or clans. They were
once rife in Kentucky, as they are in Lebanon today. In the case of
the Hatfields and McCoys, the battles were often lethal. Mark
Twain in *Huckleberry Finn* describes a feuding clan in which practically all the members were killed off.

4. *Community quarrels.* These move feuds up to embrace a whole
town against a neighboring community. In the U.S. they are mostly
non-violent squabbles over the population count or ball teams. Between states there are sharp disputes over such issues as water rights
and resources. One is now raging between Arizona and California
about the Colorado River.

5. *Sectional quarrels.* Still higher we find deep antagonisms between different sections within a given country, often going back
to armed conflict, civil war, or a change of sovereignty. The South
still resents the North, though the war between the states ended
more than eighty years ago. The Mid-Western states, with the Chi-

cago *Tribune* as their champion, resent the effete East. Southern Ireland hates Ulster, the Ukraine is none too fond of Great Russia, and so it goes.

6. *Workers against managers.* This is a major conflict found in all countries, with sub-stories of its own. Here we note foremen's unions which tend to split management, jurisdictional disputes between trade unions, the A.F. of L. versus the C.I.O., and John L. Lewis against the field. We used to be plagued with left-wing unions versus right-wing, but that struggle is abating as communists are purged from the American labor movement. In France and Italy, among other countries, the conflict still rages.

7. *Political parties.* This is an oververbalized, slanderous, and depressing area of conflict, but nobody has yet found a way to maintain political democracy with a single ticket on the ballot. One-party government, whether in Germany, Russia, or the Deep South, is the symbol of a totalitarian regime, with minorities suppressed and often ill-treated. France, on the other hand, has too many parties, a condition which frequently turns the Chamber of Deputies into an irresponsible mêlée and undermines democracy from the other end. At least two strong parties seem to be indispensable if power is to be diffused.

8. *Conflicts between the races.* Here we find a very serious category. The worst conflict is white man versus black; but white versus yellow and red and brown are bad enough. In this country the position of Negro citizens is steadily improving; in South Africa it is said to be growing worse.

9. *Religious conflict.* This area of strife has narrowed in Western countries since the days of the Inquisition and the persecutions of the Quakers. But in India, Hindus and Moslems recently slaughtered one another by the thousands, while Jews and Moslems carried on organized warfare in Palestine. In the United States, few are killed or wounded because of their religion, but strife and bitterness between Catholic and Protestant sects are often serious, while the Ku Klux Klan still lurks in the shadows.

10. *Anti-Semitism,* which deserves a category by itself. It is a

worldwide conflict compounded of racial, religious, and cultural antagonisms.

11. *Ideological quarrels,* of which "communism" versus "capitalism" is the outstanding one at the moment. There are plenty more: "business" versus "government," "free enterprise" versus "planned economy," "democracy" versus the "police state," "labor" versus "capital," and even "communism" versus "socialism"—a very bitter quarrel, especially in Europe.

12. *Occupational conflicts* between farmer and industrial worker, between white-collar man and blue-collar man, and the like.

13. *Competition within a given industry,* where the price-cutter and "chiseler" are denounced and fought.

14. *Competition between industries* for sales and markets. This provides some notable battlegrounds, as in the cases of waterways versus railways, trucks versus freight cars, oil versus coal, rayon versus silk.

15. *National rivalries,* endemic among all the sixty-five sovereign states of the world. Nationalism in the modern sense is only about three hundred years old, according to Beard and other historians. It may be a type of conflict not grooved so deeply as some of the others, but the energy and power it commands make it a major problem today.

16. *Conflicts between cultures*—which are deeply grooved enough. Perhaps for the long run they are the most serious problem which mankind faces. A culture may coincide with national boundaries but often does not. It can be distinguished by four things: (1) a common language; (2) common ways of behaving; (3) common systems of belief and ethics; and (4) common artifacts—tools, houses, clothing, machines. A culture pattern is a custom which, if you fail to follow, you ask yourself: What will the neighbors say?

Every newborn child is molded by his culture until he becomes a living part of it and passes it on, in turn, to his children. This vital process is also at the root of what social scientists call the "In-group"—our kind of folks—as against the "Out-group"—those foreigners talking gibberish. The prime obstacle to achieving One

World is that there is as yet no world culture upon which to build it.

17. *Cold war*—Russia and her satellites against the democracies. It is a most serious conflict today, but has come suddenly and may not continue indefinitely. Only a few years ago, in 1942, we were praying that the Russians would hold at Stalingrad. Russian belongs to the Indo-European language system, along with English, French, and Spanish. Russia was our ally in both World War I and II, and grows closer to Western culture as her heavy industry develops. For the long swing I doubt if this quarrel is as deep as some now believe.

18. *East versus West*. Here the deep cultural differences are emphasized by the fast, dynamic expansion of machine civilization.

The skyscraper of conflict has at least eighteen stories, with many sub-stories and considerable overlapping. We have omitted some classes—for instance, the struggle for "success" which filters through the whole structure in some cultures—but enough remains to give us a measure of our problem.

Roots of Conflict

To gaze up at the edifice, story by story, is both impressive and depressing. How can it ever be by-passed, much less demolished? The first task is to analyze it further. What are the roots of conflict, and can anything be done on the ground? Are there any natural offsets, a kind of counter-skyscraper?

In the next two chapters we shall try to show, in a different frame of reference, how conflicts often arise from causes far below the surface. Social scientists, for instance, have demonstrated that frustration often leads to aggression, thus adding a whole new dimension to a quarrel.

Again, a prime source of conflict, as noted on floor sixteen, is that everyone of us is "culture-bound" and disposed to look with suspicion at people in the Out-group, especially if they do not speak our language. We need constantly to remind ourselves that this truculence is learned, not inherited.

Much trouble comes too from what might be called "cultural

islands," an alien group within the boundaries of a larger culture. Sweden today has no such islands, but America has been full of them—"little Italies," "little Polands," "little Irelands." Gradually they are melted down, although some, like Harlem, continue to be areas of potential strife.

Another root of conflict is the language we learn. Human languages vary in precision, but all are imperfect vehicles for clear communication unless the speaker understands how they work, especially how to handle abstract terms. Semantics is the science which helps him understand, but it is a young science with a long way to go. When Green does not know what White is referring to, he may suspect the worst.

Finally, there is a marked accent in Western civilization on competition for a limited number of places at the top. This is especially acute in our country today and promotes a good deal of additional tension and conflict. The fact that many cultures do not have it at all indicates that it is not an inherited human drive.

A Cheerful Note

Looking up again at the skyscraper, there are at least three offsets which should be considered. In Chapter 5 we will give them some attention; here they will only be mentioned for reference.

The first is that, up to a certain point, some conflict, argument, competition are healthy both for the individual and society.

The second—and it cuts deep—is that man is a group animal. Co-operation within the group is necessary for the rearing of children and for survival itself.

The third is allied to the second. When any given culture is analyzed, it is found that the habits and customs which can be classed as co-operative far outweigh the belligerent, disrupting habits. Such things as the devision of labor, the rules of hospitality, the care of the young, of the disabled and the aged, are all on the side of mutual aid.

Our morning paper is full of fights, but it seldom mentions how many hundreds of writers, editors, compositors, drivers, postal clerks and others co-operate to get the same paper on our doorstep.

CHAPTER THREE

Blocked Goals

A NEW YORK bookbinder walked out of his house in Queens on a fine spring morning in 1950 and proceeded to punch the first man he saw on the nose. "Possible fracture," said the newspaper story. The victim, who happened to be a police department detective, recovered sufficiently to arrest his assailant and call the patrol wagon. Asked what was the big idea, the bookbinder said, "I had a misunderstanding with my wife and felt like belting someone."

Though he picked an unfortunate someone to belt, the story illustrates an important point. A good deal of human conflict is due to something else. A person is frustrated by other causes, feels like belting someone, and does not particularly care whom. This is useful to know in our search for methods of agreement. Forestalling a disagreement is at least as good as settling it, and settling it is easier if we understand how it began.

Town Meeting

A small town in New England is considering a zoning law. A committee has been appointed to bring in a proposal to the town meeting. Their report is read to a packed town hall—a reasonable enough proposal, providing full safeguards for the *status quo* of property owners. Only future activities will be zoned, with plenty of opportunity for appeal.

As the chairman finishes reading the report, a dozen people leap up and begin to shout. The atmosphere at once becomes electric; the moderator bangs his gavel in vain. Those opposed to zoning do most of the talking, or shouting, but presently those in favor begin to contradict. Apparently the opposition has not read the committee's report as mailed out earlier or listened to the reading tonight from the floor. The issue of zoning seems to have been forgotten.

One furious anti-zoner sees a plot to wreck the town and charges that the whole thing has been hatched in secret "just like Hitler." A pro-zoner reminds him of some well-advertised open hearings while the plan was being drafted. Another anti says he speaks for the little man, and if a little man needs a dollar to feed his children, he ought to have the right to earn it! A third man says it is the thin, entering wedge of tyranny. "Pretty soon they'll be telling us when to blow our noses!" The stamping and shouting rock the old town hall.

Where does this gale of emotion come from? Enough energy has been generated to run all the washing machines in the county, and generated by something quite apart from zoning. By what? Many good citizens are enraged about some other issue—so aggrieved that they feel the need of "belting somebody." What is it?

It is not hard to find a grievance for the opposition. In their section of the town many people feel discriminated against by the tax rate, the school situation, and various other conditions. The zoning meeting gives them a chance to work off some of their aggressiveness on the rest of the town.

Even if it was deserved, this is hardly the way to decide important public questions. Yet how often is the incident paralleled in all kinds of meetings, the world over?

Belting a Tennis Ball

Once in Southern California I played a couple of sets of tennis with the late Richard C. Tolman, who had taught me physics at the Massachusetts Institute of Technology. He was over sixty and did not seem to be enjoying the game greatly. "Why do you keep it up?" I asked. "To work off my aggressions!" said the great physicist, taking a vicious swipe at the ball.

Think of all the balls being viciously swiped at throughout the republic at this moment—baseballs, golf balls, footballs, hockey pucks, basket balls, polo balls, ping pong balls. Is it perhaps a great national safety valve?

Trouble in Seattle

In 1948 a housing project in Seattle fell suddenly into turmoil. More than a thousand families, three hundred of them Negro, were packed into temporary barracks designed for war workers. Two white women were alleged to have been attacked by Negroes; a stabbing was reported, guns were oiled and loaded, and tension ran high. The police and the Urban League feared a race riot.

Hastily they called in the Public Opinion Laboratory of the University of Washington to conduct a survey. Within a week, 308 field interviews by 25 trained interviewers from the Laboratory had been assembled and tabulated. The results surprisingly showed little racial antagonism. Ninety per cent of those interviewed reported that they felt either "more friendly" or "about the same" as when they moved in. (This checks with Stouffer's findings set forth in Chapter 1.) Race feeling was present but decidedly minor compared to resentment over the condition of the buildings, the heating and cooking equipment, the bad roads. Also a strike at the Boeing aircraft factory, which affected a third of the families, made for a good deal of unrest.

Here was a case where a series of frustrations from other causes could have brought about a serious race riot. Fortunately, the grievances were discovered in time, and the authorities immediately took steps to correct them. Repairs were made, the kitchen equipment was improved, and the crisis passed. A similar survey a year later showed a marked decrease in irritations about buildings, roads, and kitchen sinks, while racial antipathy was lower than before.

Modern Tempo

E. B. White, in *Here Is New York*, gives us a vivid picture of New Yorkers caught in the frustration of a traffic jam—now practically a national neurosis.

New York has changed in tempo and in temper during the years I have known it. There is greater tension, increased irritability. You encounter it in many places, in many faces. The normal frustrations of modern life are here multiplied and amplified. A single run of a cross-town bus contains, for the driver, enough frustrations and annoyance to carry him over the edge of sanity; the light that changes always an instant too soon, the passenger that bangs on the shut door, the truck that blocks the only opening, the coin that slips to the floor, the questions asked at the wrong moment. There is greater tension and there is greater speed. . . . Hackmen used to drive with verve; now they seem to drive with desperation, toward the ultimate tip.

How much does this tension increase the city's violence and conflict?

From New York we cross the ocean to Germany. Stephen Spender, in analyzing the Fuchs case, where a German-British physicist gave important atomic bomb information to Russia, finds Fuchs a product of mass frustration. The Germany from which he emerged was marked by the ruin of the middle class, by unemployment and despair. It offered no hope to young people—except by political revolution. Fuchs was a brilliant physicist, but his political ideas were infantile. His hate and resentment may have done terrible harm to the whole world. Other infantile Germans ran the concentration camps. Many of their frustrations erupted in the persecutions of the Jews and later in the sweep of Panzer divisions in aggression against the world.

The Theoretical Case

A group of scientists from the Institute of Human Relations at Yale produced a book in 1939 called *Frustration and Aggression,* which has run through many editions and become a classic in this field.[1] It begins by assuming that aggressive behavior presupposes frustration, while frustration leads to some form of aggression. The authors are careful to point out that this hypothesis has not been finally tested and proved, but that it may explain forms of human behavior "which have hitherto been considered more or less isolated . . . and lightly dismissed as irrational, perverse or abnormal."

Frustration is defined as interference with the achievement of a goal, and illustrated with the following case: Jimmy, aged four, hears the bell on the ice cream cart out on the street, and runs to his mother. "I wanta cone," he says and tugs at her skirt. The cone and its ultimate consumption are Jimmy's goal. "No, dear, you won't eat your dinner if you have ice cream now" is the interference with the goal. Frustration follows instantly, as Jimmy sets up a howl.

Aggression is defined by our authors as an attempt to injure the person who blocks the goal. It can take many direct forms—physical violence, verbal abuse, spreading malicious rumors, elaborate plans for getting even, and so on. Jimmy's frustration turns immediately into two kinds of direct aggression. He says to his mother, "I hate you!" and then tries to kick her in the ankle.

Suppose that Jimmy's goal is a cone of *vanilla* ice cream, but that no vanilla is left in the cart. Frustration will occur in this case too, but before aggression results it may be possible to set up a substitute goal, say a *chocolate* cone. Frustrated people finding substitute goals are all around us—the childless woman and her poodle, the sworn-off smoker chewing gum, the jilted lover marrying somebody, anybody, on the rebound.

Aggression may also be displaced to a different object. Instead of kicking his mother, Jimmy may kick the baby or the nearest chair. Aggression may take the form of swearing-in-general, as when one hits his thumb with a hammer. It "may be displaced to some altogether innocent source, or even toward self, as in masochism,

---

[1] Members of the team were John Dollard, Leonard W. Doob, Neal E. Miller, O. H. Mowrer, Robert E. Sears, Clellan S. Ford, Carl I. Hovland, R. T. Sollenberger. Yale University Press was the publisher.

martyrdom and suicide." It may produce useful work with a spade or a saw, in tasks where energy is more important than direction.

On the other hand, aggression may be indirectly expressed in fantasy or dreams or even in a carefully thought-out plan of revenge which is never executed. A mild form, which I sometimes use, is writing long, abusive letters to people who have thwarted or unjustly criticized you, and tearing them up next morning.

The Yale hypothesis, you will note, is a roomy one, with much flexibility in finding substitute goals and objects of aggression. William James was aware of the sequence, as was McDougall. Freud developed it into a well-rounded theory, but later discarded it in favor of the theory of the "death wish." Our authors go back to Freud's earlier conception and build from there. This makes sense to laymen as well as to social scientists. A so-called "death wish" or death instinct is in direct conflict with survival, and if man were normally a prey to it, he would hardly be around today.

Jimmy with his ice cream cone is the first case in the Yale study, but there are many more. A tragic one describes the man admitted to a mental hospital because of his overpowering fear that he would kill his wife and children. It first appeared in dreams and then became a conscious desire. The cause was clear in his particular case. He dared not, for financial and status reasons, have another child; for religious reasons he could not practice birth control. His sex goal was solidly blocked, and impulses of aggression followed the frustration. This conflict is a common one and is often, of course, solved in less tragic ways.

Criticisms of the Theory

The Yale hypothesis has not escaped without some challenge. One comes from Norman Maier of Michigan in his laboratory report, *Frustration*, published in 1949. In his experiments rats are given an insoluble problem, like jumping against a firmly closed door, after being conditioned to jump freely to get their food. This seriously frustrates the rats, but they do not always turn aggressive. They may freeze up in a neurotic stupor, or a "fixation," or go back to earlier trial and error—a "regression," or accept their defeat in "resignation."

J. H. Masserman has done some famous experiments with cats and immortalized them in a documentary film. They are nice normal cats, some brighter than others, until they are subjected to severe frustrations in the laboratory by crossing up their patterns for getting food out of a box. The poor cats show many symptoms of a man with a nervous breakdown—rapid heart, full pulse, catchy breathing, high blood pressure, sweating, trembling, rising of hair. They may become aggressive, or they may lose all interest in mice, or put their heads in the empty food box in utter despair, or try to shrink into the walls of the cage.

Masserman says that his clinical observations support the general conclusions of the Yale scientists. Like them, he thinks Freud was wrong in the later hypothesis of an inborn "death instinct."

That frustration leads to some form of aggression is generally true, but the process is more complicated than first appears. Aggression can be displaced onto other people, as when the bookbinder from Queens, instead of belting his wife, which a gentleman in our culture does not do, had the misfortune to belt a policeman. It can be transferred to inanimate objects, such as tennis balls and parlor furniture.

Sometimes, despite frustration, aggression does not seem to take place at all, as with some of the thwarted rats and cats, and probably with people, who may fall prey to psychosomatic disorders instead. Organized aggression, say that of a well-disciplined army in combat, may utilize the effects of many individual frustrations—including the draft law.

Neurotic People

Some individuals are under such emotional tension all the time that they leave a trail of quarrels behind them—chronic "trouble-makers." A mild case may reveal disturbance by showing off in company or on the job, always demanding admiration. Another man may be oversensitive and demand continual reassurance. Another may be suspicious, always looking for plots and frame-ups. He may be full of self-pity and martyrdom, the early beginnings of paranoia. The world is against him; the man at the next desk is slandering him to the boss.

Perhaps most neurotics are products of insecurity. There is more insecurity in today's world to produce them, due to recurring waves of unemployment and war. Parents are worried and insecure in their livelihood. Children are worried and insecure about their parents' affection. In war zones nearly every citizen is insecure, having been bombed out or expecting to be next time. An insecure person may be a frustrated one, spoiling for a fight.

One neurotic individual can disrupt an office, an assembly line, a town meeting, or a classroom. A neurotic in a position of power can disrupt all the activities under his direction, whether he is a petty tyrant in the shipping room or the dictator of a nation, such as Hitler.

Paris Conference

Twelve men are sitting around a big square table in the Majestic Hotel in Paris, once the headquarters of the German General Staff, now the home of UNESCO. There are three from Britain, two from the United States, and one each from France, Norway, Canada, the Netherlands, Australia, China, and Czechoslovakia—nine nations altogether. One is a physicist by profession, the rest are social scientists, and they have met to discuss the tensions and frustrations generated by modern technology. The question before the meeting is whether or not aggressive acts, and ultimately war, flow from machine-age tensions.

It is spring in Paris; through the window comes the roar of traffic as every conceivable shape and size of motor car goes swerving around the Arch of Triumph. The men sit at their big table all day long concentrating on their problem. English is the language of the conference, though not all the members speak it readily. Everyone has to be patient and listen carefully, remembering how much time is saved if translators can be dispensed with. Fortunately, all are deeply concerned with their subject and have a similar orientation toward it. They all believe that the machine does promote tensions and frustrations.

After four days I am asked, as a member from the United States, to summarize the conclusions. My draft receives some amiable discussion, a few small amendments, and is accepted. We agree that technology creates tensions in three major ways: (1) by mass unemployment; (2) by pressures on the worker at his bench or desk or home; (3) by undermining the culture and way of life of colonial peoples. We agree that statesmen must look carefully at these three world trends, for they help to create mass frustrations, and ultimately war. The report amplifies the trends as follows:

First, as the machine takes over more jobs, people lose their work and often have trouble finding new occupations. Millions of manual tasks, both heavy and light, are now done by inanimate energy. Computing machines of an incredible virtuosity are now invading office work. In the United States upward of 90 per cent of all energy consumed comes from coal, oil, and falling water, not from human and animal muscle. "When established patterns are shattered at this abnormal rate, frustrations are bound to result." Technology has raised living standards and promises some day to lift the curse of Adam. One of the first results, however, is to spread unemployment and insecurity. An insecure person, like an unvaccinated one, can be a threat to the community.

Second, said our report, even when a man has a job, mass production can do strange things to him. The conveyor belt sets the tempo to which he must adjust. Maybe his particular nervous system is not geared to that tempo. Never mind, get that right rear fender on in twenty-one seconds flat!

The worker at his post—often including the foreman—finds many of his hours filled with a sense of discontent if not futility, damaging to his morale and a drag on production, no matter how efficient the machine. He is mostly unconscious of the reasons for such feelings, but they may result in antagonisms against his employer, against racial minorities, against other nations, against society as a whole, against any group or ideology to which chance or propaganda may direct his aggressive feelings.

The *third* cause of frustration that we discussed was modern imperialism. Technology, expanding around the world in a search for markets and investments, has had a disastrous effect upon native cultures. Societies in Latin America, Africa, Asia, the Pacific have been thrown out of balance. "The multiplying tensions are now evident in all the continents."

Technology spreads faster as well as farther. "Diffusion" is the anthropologist's term for the process of introducing new customs and artifacts from one culture to another. The machine sharply steps up the diffusion rate, giving colonial peoples cultural indigestion—especially as they try to absorb cheap whisky, machine guns, canned goods, radios, patent medicines, and 100-horsepower motor cars upon roads designed for one-donkey-power carts.

The twelve men in Paris made it clear that inanimate energy, among many substantial gifts, has bestowed machine-made frustrations on untold numbers of human beings. People in many cultures no longer know where they belong or what their rights and duties are; economic and social insecurity have become worldwide. Following the thesis of the Yale scientists, one is not surprised to find aggressive symptoms in industrial workers, in members of a depressed middle class as in Germany, in a billion aroused people in Asia.

CHAPTER FOUR

More Roots of Conflict

WHEN a goal is blocked, frustration begins in people as well as in laboratory cats and rats. Trouble lies ahead. There is enough unavoidable frustration for every person on earth to fill at least a basement full of conflicts. Above this level, however, a good many frustrations might be removed, and if they were, the skyscraper of conflict would look less formidable.

Authorities point to various other conditions which tend to stimulate conflict and which if they could be reduced would also help. In this chapter we have four of them to consider, the last at some length:

1. Truculence against foreigners—what anthropologists call the In-group–Out-group struggle.
2. Islands of strangers inside a parent culture.
3. Communication failure.
4. Overstimulation of the competitive spirit.

On Human Cussedness

First a word, and a reasonably cautious one, on "human nature"—that inconclusive phrase which defeats so many arguments.

What the original nature of man may be is still a mystery to scientists and perhaps always will be. Man cannot be studied, so to speak, undressed without his cultural clothes. As cultures vary, so human nature seems to vary; but every society in training its children has to discipline and frustrate them to varying degrees. Some experts think this process of socialization is enough to account for most of the quarrelsomeness of Homo sapiens. Others note that his physical equipment is admirably suited to help him express his bad temper, wherever it comes from.

The individual seems to have a kind of fuse in him, perhaps inherited from his Stone Age ancestors, which causes him to flare up under provocation or stress. Once he flared to fight a bear or get away fast from an enemy; now he flares to outshout an opponent on the school committee. What this fuse is specifically the psychiatrists and the biochemists will some day tell us. One biochemist friend of mine thinks that humans are "overadrenalized" for civilized life. The rush of energy, the pounding pulse, may be fine for an encounter with a bear but not so fine for an argument with the boss or with the diplomat across the table. These inconvenient reactions do not specifically afflict neurotics. Normal persons, according to studies at the New York State Psychiatric Institute, actually get angrier than abnormal ones.

As we proceed to look at conflicts which seem unnecessary, we must not forget this fuse, which can be so easily interpreted as human cussedness or even original sin. Conflict can certainly be reduced by understanding and by methods we shall examine later, but some explosiveness will always remain. If we undertake to suppress it altogether, there is a good chance it will break out again, perhaps in a more dangerous place.

Conflict with the Out-group

Along the Arctic coast of North America, travel is difficult and dangerous, and the various tribes of Eskimos and Indians are comparatively isolated from each other. Anthropologists who studied the area some years ago reported that the natives were co-operative and honest in their own communities, but in their dealings with other tribes they were full of suspicion, violence, and fear. One tribe warned the scientists that their neighbors had long claws instead of hands, ready to tear strangers to pieces!

Each little society felt that only *their* members were human, the others being something less than man. "We are good people, we never steal. It is the Coppermine River people who steal." Both statements were true. There was no stealing inside a given tribe, but no tribe hesitated to steal from the people of another.

These Arctic customs, however, are only an extreme case of what the members of every society believe. Are we not all confident that, in the last analysis, wisdom and virtue rest with our way of life and are not to be found among the outlanders?

Some of the crew who sailed with Columbus believed in dog-faced men over the rim of the world and expected all kinds of anatomical marvels when landfall was made. People of the West no longer hold such expectations—although some of us seem ready to believe in 30-inch men on flying saucers from other planets. Science has dissolved a good deal of tribal intolerance, but the progress of the U. S. Army through North Africa, the Mediterranean, and Western Europe shows how much remains. Ask almost any G.I. of the second war what he thought of the *A*-rabs. Of all the tribes he met, he seemed to like the Germans best because their taboos about cleanliness came closest to his own.

On the other side of the world, Americans had little difficulty in equating the Japanese with "yellow monkeys." In 1950, all Korean natives, North and South, were called "gooks" by the G.I.s, which caused the State Department much diplomatic pain. A glance at the cartoons in Russian, Polish, or Chinese papers leaves no doubt what people of those societies are taught to think about Americans.

So far as we know, however, this kind of prejudice is purely cultural. We may be born with a fuse in us but not with fear and suspicion of foreigners. This is built in from early childhood. Must it be built in? A comparatively easy way to make children co-operative in the home is to give them some *outside* object for their hostility—those rude children across the tracks, or the West Side gang. Thus an Out-group is deliberately fostered to help build loyalty to the In-group. As the child grows, his Out-group becomes farther and farther removed, and in war time it may be on the other side of the globe.

Teachers and parents do not intend to build in prejudice, but it results from this process, as well as from imitation. Children absorb it from parent, teacher, schoolbook, older children, politician—practically everyone they meet. By the time they are ready for high school, tests show that their dislike of foreign nationalities is strong and well rationalized, and while still transferable from one Out-group to another, it is difficult if not impossible to remove entirely.

Yet a different kind of upbringing could be devised, educators agree, which by emphasis on security and special attention to language would greatly reduce the hostility. It must be reduced before any kind of world state becomes possible, for a world state can only be effectively operated by men with a world point of view. Somehow, we have to learn to believe in people, not just our people. And we need to learn it fast. Instead of a slow evolution toward the goal, aided by science and education, the atomic bomb has suddenly called for an overnight conversion.

Islands of Alien Cultures

Feeling this hostility to an Out-group, or to a "scapegoat" of some kind, many people go through life without ever meeting a member of the despised group. Others are thrown into constant and irritating contact with aliens. Sometimes an Out-group is encircled in pockets, or islands, within a larger society—after wars of conquest, for instance, or through colonization, or when slaves or immigrants are imported in large unassimilated numbers. The United States has had many such islands, large and small. They have brought us plenty of conflict, as compared for instance with France or Sweden, where one culture and language predominate.

Given tolerance and time, assimilation usually takes place, and this is happening rapidly in America for there has been little immigration since 1913. Yet many nationalities in the U.S. still have pressure groups and lobbies, which grow no weaker with assimilation but indeed stronger as their local techniques improve while their foreign goals persist. Negroes, largely descended from African slaves, have not been assimilated in America, at least by the scientists' test of assimilation, which is intermarriage.

In South Africa, the races are numerically reversed, and thus the situation is more difficult. Whites are in the minority by four to one, surrounded by frustrated black natives. The conflict potential is alarmingly high. In a recent novel, *Cry the Beloved Country,* the personal tragedy of the characters arises from this conflict, as it drives a black boy to murder. The boy's father, an old Zulu parson, meets the father of the murdered man in one of the great tragic scenes in English literature. The dark and smoldering background of the "beloved country" is manifestly the result not of human depravity but of a cruelly twisted social structure.

To live and let live must thus be far harder in Johannesburg than in Stockholm. It is harder in New York, too, but our social structure is less rigid than the Rand's and tends to improve as the melting pot melts year by year.

Communication Failure and Semantics

Another common source of conflict is the language we learn. Even while it binds us together, it throws up formidable barriers to understanding. When Smith and Robinson discuss that new Ford there, or those cigars in that box, they may not always agree, but they can follow one another closely and the communication line is open and clear. When they use abstract terms, however, like "Wall Street," "Bureaucrats," "Labor," "The Bosses," "Socialized Medicine," Smith and Robinson can get into serious difficulties.

Suppose Smith says: "Big Business is the backbone of American prosperity," with a mean look at Robinson. Robinson replies: "Big Business is un-American." They might as well stop right there, for nothing but a bitter quarrel lies ahead. If, however, Smith says: "From where I sit, Big Business seems to be the best solution to the problem of production," and Robinson says: "From where I sit it looks like a pretty unreliable institution, but I may be wrong"—the communication line is still clear, and temperate discussion, perhaps even agreement, is possible.

People hungry for power, suffering from enlargement of the ego, like Hitler, Mussolini, and Stalin, specialize in *deliberately* fouling communication lines. Some trial lawyers are not without skill in this direction too, while political demagogues thrive on public confusion, building chains of verbal guilt-by-association against which the ordinary citizen is often helpless. (In Chapter 18 we will give some illustrations.)

Up to now the role of language as a stimulant to non-rational responses has scarcely been recognized. Within a culture, or between people of different cultures, most agreements must be reached through the spoken or written word. It is vitally important to keep the words clear so that both speaker and listener may see the same event in the same way, or at least as closely as their past experiences permit. But this the demagogue will try to prevent at all costs. He will insist that all Hindus are "niggers" or that all Americans are "imperialists" or that "socialism" and "communism" mean the same thing. Good communication is a function of group living, in one sense the most important function. To foul and distort it is as evil and destructive a thing as one can do.

Semantics is the science which deals with communication, language, and meaning. It has nothing to do with the origin of words but only with live meanings. The following dialogue is credited to Charles Lamb:

"See that man over there?"
"Yes."
"Well, I hate him."
"But you don't know him."
"That's why I hate him."

Before I studied semantics I used to hate quite a lot of people I had not met, and even classes of people, such as "absentee owners" and "intellectuals." I made Absolutes out of them. But semantics helped me to see that the classes are inside one's head; everybody is different in the real world—Adam$_1$ is not Adam$_2$. One stops hating until he knows more about the circumstances. When he knows the circumstances, the chances are he will not hate at all.

COMPETITION IN AMERICA

North American Indians, says Ralph Linton, consider the rest of us North Americans slightly crazy because of our aggressive, driving, competitive behavior. In many tribes the aim of the individual is to merge himself as completely as possible into the group. But the Indians regard mystical ecstasies and the receiving of visions as quite normal, where we would call for a psychiatrist if not for a mental hospital.

A *Fortune* poll published in September, 1949, asked: "Why send your son to college?" Sixty-six per cent replied that a boy goes to college for a "better job and greater earning power." Of course. Only 15 per cent think he goes to college to acquire knowledge not to mention understanding. The goal of the American belief system is to get ahead, get more money, be a "success," not a failure. Of course.

We find the competitive spirit in school grading, in sports, debates, the star system in Hollywood, and Chamber of Commerce drives to make Jonesville the best little city in the state. We find it in rivalry between churches and clubs for membership, in struggles to reach the top in business, to outdo rivals in the professions, to make the best-seller list, to beat out the filling station across the street, to sell more soap than the other fellow, to show that women are just as smart as men.

Remembering that no man is an island unto himself, do we carry the competitive struggle too far in America? Have the Indians some reason to think us slightly cracked? Competition is present in greater or lesser degree in every society, while common sense tells us that in certain situations it can be a useful stimulant to action. Do Americans get too much action and not enough reflection? The standard credo says no, competition is fine and there should be more of it. But a good many observers, who are not Indians, are not so sure.

They point out that it often makes a man feel he is surrounded by rivals or enemies, rather than by friends. Society is not something to trust, it is something to lick.

Morton Deutsch of Harvard has made a study of these standards, and begins by defining them.[1]

A *competitive* situation is one which stimulates an individual to strive against other individuals for a goal of which he hopes to be the sole or principal possessor.

By way of contrast:

A *cooperative* situation is one which stimulates an individual to strive with other members of his group for a goal which is to be shared equally.

In real life, of course, the two situations are often mixed. Members of a football team co-operate to win games but compete for publicity as the star performer. Two professional tennis players will co-operate to put on a good show for the customers but may compete strenuously to see who can win more matches on the circuit. Republicans co-operate to beat the Democrats but compete bitterly for the Presidential nomination.

Primitive Peoples

Melville Herskovits, in his *Economic Life of Primitive Peoples*, finds on the whole more co-operative than competitive activities. He says:

One of the most striking aspects of primitive labor is the cooperation which characterizes it . . . the voluntary association of a group of men or women whose objective is the completion of a specific, definitely limited task. . . . Work organizations of this kind, free or compulsory, temporary or permanent, organized or informal, are found everywhere in the primitive world; for everywhere man has apparently recognized the efficacy of group over individual effort.

He cites the husking feasts of Hidatsa Indians, the communal buffalo-hunts of the Plains Indians, co-operative farming in New

[1] *Human Relations*, Vol. II (1949).

Mexico pueblos, and many others. "The data amply prove that man works neither by nor for himself; that a spirit of mutual aid and of a kind not unlike that suggested by Kropotkin does exist."

But Herskovits shows that altruism seldom goes to the lengths practiced by such a tribe as the Arapesh.[2] He finds competition within co-operative work groups for the prestige of being the best performer. Group may compete with group in a spirit of rivalry which is by no means always friendly. Co-operation does not exclude individual effort, especially where the concept of wealth is well developed. "There is no society which does not know both the shirker, and the man who abstains from co-operating with his fellows, to go his way alone."

School and College

The authors of *Frustration and Aggression* note that American school children throw aside whatever co-operative habits they are taught as soon as the bell rings for dismissal. They begin to scuffle or to compete directly in sports or indirectly by identification with radio heroes. Later on, the boys will be employing every method, some of them pretty dubious, to outwit their competitors and push to the top.

Deutsch, running controlled experiments with college students, found greater facility in problem-solving if the groups were set up on a co-operative rather than a competitive basis. Friendliness, harmony, free communication of ideas abruptly ceased when the boys left the class where they worked jointly for the solution of a problem and entered the class where they had to scramble for mutually exclusive goals. Deutsch found evidence, too, of greater personal insecurity, together with fear and hostility, under the competitive pattern. In discussing school marks he says: "One may well question whether a competitive grading system produces the kind of interrelationships among students, the task efficiency, the per-

[2] Reported by Margaret Mead in her book *Sex and Temperament*. These New Guinea people give away most of the food they grow, hoping somebody will give them some!

sonal security, that are in keeping with sound educational objectives." I hasten to add that this is not an advertisement for progressive schools or any other kind, for nobody has yet found the system which will adequately prepare youngsters for the modern world. Indian children are well prepared for Indian life but not our children for our life.

Locked In

Lawrence K. Frank, an expert in the behavior of young children, is outspoken about the harm done by competitive standards. "Competition," he says, "means striving to defeat or outdo others in a narrowly restricted pattern of activity." A boy so trained, far from developing that robust individuality which the American code calls for, may actually become regimented. "The price paid for competitive success may be the abandonment of individuality, and the acceptance of fashion and social norms for living." John Marquand's novel, *Point of No Return,* offers an eloquent illustration.

There is a circular effect, too, says Frank. Our young American on the make achieves no real security of status, for there is no terminus to his striving. After the vice-presidency, he must try for the presidency. After the presidency, a bigger presidency in a bigger company. It is an endless spiral, with ulcers and heart attacks waiting around the curves. "When those who come out on top make such enormous sacrifices and gain so little, we can but add the human wastage of the successful to what we see in the mass of men, and reach a staggering total of human frustration. . . ."

Dilemma

Dr. Gordon Allport of Harvard poses a dilemma, in an unpublished manuscript he allowed me to read. All normal people, he says, want warm, close relationships with their fellows. At the same time, many of them are very sensitive about slights to the ego. Indignity to one's self-esteem quickly generates hatred, if not violence. "Neither our economic nor our political life is arranged to accommodate this dual need." Sometimes we get both affection and esteem inside the family, but the protection of a man's self-respect is not a particular concern of business, industry, or government. The American credo calls more for running people down than for building them up.

Meanwhile, since the need for warm relationships is met so indifferently, we should not be surprised, says Allport, to find anxiety, insecurity, hostility, and aggression as the commonest by-products of our social relationships. His study of prejudice, with B. M. Kramer, indicates that 80 per cent of all adult Americans have marked prejudice against various groups of their fellow citizens. Yet all the time the need for close human contacts remains unchanged.

Another bad habit in Western culture comes from our training in aggressive refutation, while the techniques of agreement are often looked down upon as "appeasement," or "knuckling under," or "cowardly compromise."

Competition in Business

My friend Milo Perkins contends that a great deal of American business is on what he calls a "killing" basis—get the order somehow, anyhow. After the order comes the check, and that is the end of the story.

When Perkins sold burlap bags out of Houston, Texas, many years ago, he worked on a different basis. Although the books all said: "Brush up your arguments when you hit the road," he avoided arguments; he tried to find an area of agreement. Sometimes, for instance, he would sit down with a buyer and figure out the trend of the market. Were bags going up or going down? Sometimes he would even advise the customer *not* to buy until the market turned. His eye was on the long view, looking for enduring mutual advantage, not a "killing."

Perhaps the competitive spirit has been overdone in America from the standpoint of the good society. How deeply it is now embedded in our cultural standards is another matter.

CHAPTER FIVE

Solid Ground

WE NOW turn to what might be called the assets in the theory of conflict and agreement. Three natural offsets to conflict will be discussed:

1. A certain amount of argument must precede agreement in order to bring out the issues involved.

2. Man is a social animal, which sets a kind of biological limit to his quarrels. And as a corollary—

3. Any given culture is a network of co-operative habits, mostly unconscious.

Necessary Arguments

If your opponent says: "You're crazy; you don't know what you're talking about; any fool knows better"—there is little to do but mount a counteroffensive. But if he says: "I'm afraid I can't agree with you, what are your facts?"—it may well be that a thorough discussion will educate you both. In this case the door between you is left open; in the first case it is slammed in advance.

Often it is better to work out varying interests between people than to clamp the lid on them. Reconciliation can be overdone, as in the case of those determined negotiators who would "unite Heaven and Hell by combining the best features of both." Some students go so far as to say that if a serious conference lacks preliminary disagreement and strong discussion, something is wrong.

The best solution may be found by fusing several points of view. The fusing process is bound to include some heat.

Compromise may be all we can hope for in many cases, but compromise is not true agreement if the parties remain unconvinced, especially if they have been forced into it. That is why so many strike "settlements" do not settle anything. One side or the other—perhaps both—will continue to feel aggrieved. In true agreement everybody gets up from the conference table feeling good, even if he does not receive all he originally asked for. At least his point of view has been considered. We shall look at this procedure again in more detail.

If all disagreements were outlawed we would have no political parties, possibly no political democracy at all. Parties thrive on pointing out one another's mistakes, thus keeping the majority in a state of wary suspense. The one-party system, among other evils, deprives the majority of necessary criticism. There is a great difference between suppressing a conflict, as the totalitarians do, and working it out, as the democracies try to do, and as the Quakers almost invariably do.

Scientific findings usually go through a stage of disagreement, proceeding by criticism and skepticism. Though purely verbal arguments have little or no place in science, theories and hypotheses must meet rigorous objective tests in laboratory, clinic, or observation post before they are accepted and added to the storehouse. It took physicists almost twenty years to accept Einstein.

In short, we are not questioning the value of discussion, argument, skepticism in human affairs. We might call it another case of relativity. Beyond a certain point—often to be noted by a person's emotional reactions—a search for facts and a higher synthesis may degenerate into a name-calling contest and the end of all agreement. Up to that point, the threshing out of differences can be helpful, sometimes cardinal.

Social Animals

Our second offset to conflict goes back to fundamental biology. When we cite the proverb that man is one of the social animals, we

rarely stop to think of other social animals. Yet scientists have recently learned a good deal about them. Conflict in nature, as in
man, is neither so universal nor so instinctive as the Victorians believed. Co-operation is far commoner than we realize. The anthropologist, Ashley Montagu, in a recent book, *On Being Human*, cites
many experiments and observations of co-operation among animals.
Often it serves survival better than aggressiveness. Chimpanzees
often pass each other food through the bars of cages. White mice
grow faster and stronger in groups than when isolated; if they are
injured they lick each other's sores. Goldfish get on better in groups,
and so do sea gulls, tadpoles, and sea urchins. Even the lowly worm,
exposed to ultraviolet rays, lives longer when surrounded by his
fellows than alone—twelve times as long in one experiment.

Almost no animal except man systematically kills its own kind.
As between different species, killing is not often wanton; it is usually
only for food. A gorged lion will trot through herds of easy game,
paying no attention to them. Cats have to learn to kill rats. The
idea of "hereditary enemies" is modified by scores of exceptions.
The Sunday magazines show us photographs of cats nursing pup-
pies or a goat and a rhinoceros on most amiable terms in the zoo.
T. H. Langlos of the Ohio Bureau of Fish Propagation has trained
bass to abandon cannibalism by clearing out the weeds in a pool
and giving everybody plenty to eat.

All this evidence, Montagu tells us, tends to support Kropotkin's
thesis of "Mutual Aid," first published in 1902. In man, the case for
co-operation is especially strong. The human infant has so long a
period of helplessness compared with other creatures that he needs
not only a mother but a group to prepare him for adult life. He
must have food, protection, emotional security; he must be shown
step by step the rules and habits of his culture, from learning to talk,
to learning to be a doctor or a pipe fitter.

No person, says Montagu, has ever been reared without a group;
indeed, it is possible to define a person as "a set of social relationships"—which is what group dynamics is all about.[1] Binding the

---

[1] Some sensational and possibly unreliable reports describe lost children living
alone on roots and grubs. When found they gibbered like idiots.

individual to the group represents some loss in personal freedom but a much greater gain in personal development through identification with his society. Says Erich Fromm in *Escape from Freedom*:

> Unless the person feels that he belongs somewhere, unless his life has some meaning and direction, he would feel like a particle of dust and be overcome by his insignificance. He would not be able to relate himself to any system which would give meaning to his life; he would be filled with doubt, and this doubt would eventually paralyze his ability to act—that is, to live.

Montagu believes that human relations should be taught as the fourth "R" in school. He thinks our competitive spirit is out of line with biological and anthropological facts. If it could be brought into line, through education or otherwise, a large amount of mental disorder and conflict would disappear.

In her book, *Sex and Temperament,* Margaret Mead describes the Mundugumor, a New Guinea tribe on the ragged edge of survival. They are so truculent and competitive that children are reared only with great difficulty. Having no emotional security in childhood, the youngsters who do grow up become fantastically aggressive. The logical end to such a vicious cycle would be self-extermination, but under British rule the remnants of the tribe have been saved. In the Mundugumor and the Arapesh—who were mentioned earlier—we span the whole gamut of human adaptability. These two tribes, of similar original stock, living only one hundred miles apart, represent the extreme limits of competitive and cooperative behavior. Neither makes much sense.

Group feeling comes out strongly in crisis behavior—the way people meet fires, floods, hurricanes, blizzards. One day in spring a hundred New York stevedores pushed a big freighter away from a dock with their bare arms and shoulders. They strained every muscle to make enough room for a living ladder of men to climb down into the water forty feet below and rescue a little girl who had fallen between ship and dock. When her mother called for help, the men came running from all the nearby piers, and the little girl was saved.

This makes us swallow hard, but it is really not abnormal behavior; it is natural behavior.

A Network of Agreement

"What we call society," says Hayakawa, "is a vast network of mutual agreements . . . without them all of us would be huddling in miserable and lonely caves, not daring to trust anyone." It is this network which the sour old gentleman in the cartoon completely overlooked—the gentleman who sat cramped in his cake of ice, saying "people are no damn good."

The network is of course the culture. Although conflict *between* cultures may be mankind's gravest problem, *inside* any given culture the rules for agreement are innumerable and intricate. The fact that the rules are mostly followed unconsciously does not make them less binding—on the contrary. Any society would collapse like the deacon's one hoss shay without the thousands of unwritten rules and customs which members share in common and automatically obey. Like the bones under flesh and muscle, they hold the structure together.

The behavior patterns of our American culture are so familiar and automatic that it is an effort to identify them. A little reflection discloses such habits as passing cars on the right, standing in line to wait one's turn, not taking things without giving money, women and children first, monogamous marriage, respecting other people's property, paying taxes with only verbal protest, accepting conscription and military service.

Meanwhile we cheerfully trust our lives to total strangers in the persons of locomotive engineers, subway motormen, airplane pilots, elevator boys, steamship captains, taxi drivers, traffic cops, and unhesitatingly consign all our worldly goods to bankers and insurance companies.

I asked a hotel manager, with experience in both Florida and New England, to estimate how many of his patrons turned out to be dead beats. "Oh, a quarter of one per cent," he said. If this proportion were as much as 10 per cent, society would rock; charge accounts, installment buying, even ordinary banking would be im‹ possible. If it were 25 per cent, society would explode. Yet how many of us cherish the delusion that "you can't trust anybody these days"? If you couldn't, it is safe to say you wouldn't be here.

In general, the rules of American culture are less intricate than those of many other societies. The family system, for instance, is said to be much simpler than that of the Australian bushfellows. At a rough guess, 90 per cent of the average man's behavior, in any culture, is automatically determined for him by the local mores. Even when he personally decides to go here or go there in his society, when he gets here or there he follows the behavior patterns customary in that location—whether it is an automobile assembly line, a wedding, or a crap game.

Thus below all the conflicts that divide individuals, families, clans, political parties, religions, pressure groups, lies this broad foundation of common agreements due to a shared culture. On this level, people accede, accommodate, move over, co-operate, and get on. Even safe blowers behave themselves in hotel lobbies, and a non-conformist in a bus gets harsher treatment than an unbeliever in church.

So much for some general considerations of our subject. It is apparent that there is solid ground to stand on, both in human nature and in human culture. Now let us go on to an account of specific techniques for agreement, beginning with the remarkable case of the Quaker business meeting.

CHAPTER SIX

Quaker Meeting

THE Society of Friends was founded by George Fox in England about 1650, in protest against Christian formalism. The Protestant revolution had been leveled against the worship of saints and the ceremonials of "popery," but the Quakers leveled their reforms against the ceremonials which the Protestants had retained in their flight from Rome.

The individual Quaker was bidden to seek a light within and forego creeds, hymns, sermons, collection boxes as well as saints, confessionals, vestments, and incense. Protestants took half the color out of worship; the Society of Friends took it all out. When one thinks of a Quaker, the prevailing note is gray.

The worship was based, according to the Book of Discipline, "on common religious ideals and experiences, rather than on a common creed or liturgy of worship." The Quaker needed no vicars to show him how to talk to God; he needed only to search his own soul.

When William Penn was won over by Fox to the new faith, he belonged to the gentleman's caste. A prominent part of a gentleman's costume was his sword. Quakers, however, were pacifists, and Penn began to feel a little uncomfortable about the sword. He asked Fox what he ought to do.

"Wear it as long as thou canst," said Fox, tolerant of the very symbol of conflict.

Penn, as all American school children know, brought the faith to America and founded the City of Brotherly Love. Other converts took the faith around the world. On the Continent it was fiercely persecuted at first but now has won the respect of nearly everyone and the gratitude of sufferers from wars, famines, droughts, and plagues. In the persecution times, "meetings for sufferings" were organized so that members might face their tormentors fortified by group solidarity. These meetings have evolved into help for sufferers everywhere—displaced persons, disaster victims, even alien enemies. When one contributes to Quaker relief projects, he knows that every penny will be well and faithfully spent.

The layman in America thinks of the Quakers not only as kindly people in gray but as extreme exponents of the doctrine of self-help. F. S. C. Northrop, in *The Meeting of East and West*, calls the early Protestants in England pretty good individualists. "But the Quaker, sitting in silence without a professional preacher in his unadorned meeting house, most perfectly represents the credo of individualism" —that credo celebrated by John Locke and immortalized by Jefferson in the Declaration of Independence.

When, however, one begins to examine the actual behavior of Quakers in their unadorned meeting houses, he finds what one historian calls "the happy paradox." Their individualism remains unquestioned, but it is nourished by an unusual system of group participation. The Friends' weekly, monthly, and yearly meetings are like humming generators from which the psychological batteries of the members are charged and from which much of their strength as individuals seems to be drawn. As the Pollards put it:

The most rebellious soul can joyfully accept a discipline which respects him so completely as an individual. Conversely, the Quaker can afford his freedom, because he is strengthened by a profound union, ever renewed in the life of the meeting.

Inside the Meeting House

Quaker meeting houses vary in size but are always plain, and many are ancient. Benches face a low gallery where some older members sit. There is no organ, no choir, baptismal font, stained glass, pulpit, or altar. Perhaps this is why they reject the name "church." There is no doxology, no sermon in the traditional Friends' meeting, no supplication, collection, or benediction.

What does one find then? "The effective worship of Almighty God," says William Wistar Comfort. "No other form of worship makes such demands upon the spiritual resources of those present." Ambition, self-seeking, ideas of power and domination are resolutely put aside. The meeting for worship on Sunday morning opens with a period of silence, lasting several minutes, while members seek the inner light, purging their minds of outside matters. This concentration, they feel, gives the silence a special vitality. "Dead" silence, says Comfort, where people are merely quiet but not concentrated, is valueless.

In Britain, the business meeting usually follows Sunday morning worship, but in America it may be held on a weekday once a month. It is the business meeting which primarily interests us, for here mundane matters are discussed and agreements reached—sometimes very difficult and far-reaching agreements, as when the Philadelphia Yearly Meeting had to decide whether members should own slaves.

Typical Business Meeting

Suppose we look in at a typical monthly business meeting, described by the Pollards. As it takes place in England and in the afternoon, it begins of course with tea. The only officer for this executive group of men and women is the Clerk. He is the only officer in any Quaker meeting though sometimes he may have assistants. He bows his head, and the regular period of silence opens the meeting. He then reads the minutes, and if there are no corrections, proceeds to a report on deaths, marriages, transfers, and appointments. A list of applicants for membership usually brings out the first discussion.

After everyone has had his say, the Clerk drafts a minute—the famous "sense of the meeting" minute in which group opinion is summarized. He reads it to the members for their assent or modification. *There is no formal voting.* Nobody, I am told, has voted in any Quaker meeting, in any country, in three hundred years—except where the law requires it on specified documents. The challenge of the Clerk to the members on the minute, and their response, can perhaps be interpreted as a kind of voting. But when a policy or an action is decided upon, there is no division between majority and minority; the decision is invariably unanimous.

Next on the agenda, at this particular British meeting, is a statement of the group's opinion about atomic energy. Discussion is general and prolonged. Finally, the Clerk sums up the sense of the meeting in a minute which is accepted by all. Shall the resolution be given to the Member of Parliament representing the district? Would a letter to the press be better? Or should a public meeting be called? More discussion, and then a unanimous decision in favor of a letter to the press.

The Clerk proceeds to ask a member to give his ideas on the closed shop in union contracts. The others listen carefully; there is no discussion. Another member describes relief work in Greece, again without action by the group. These are apparently reports for information only. The agenda completed, the Clerk bows his head for a final period of silence, and the meeting stands adjourned.

I had the privilege of attending a Friends' business meeting in a neighboring town in Connecticut. Except that it was held in one of the community centers instead of a meeting house, the procedure followed the pattern just described. Perhaps fifteen members were present. The Clerk was a local physician, tired that evening but alert. He kept his voice clear and low as he read the minutes and invited comment on the agenda. He scrupulously refrained from imposing his own views; never once did he say, "I think we should do this, or that." From time to time, in the same low voice, he carefully summarized other people's views.

I found the atmosphere peaceful, almost relaxing. One or two of the older women were knitting industriously—even while they talked. No emotions came to the surface. Committees reported on foreign relief, on a delegation to Hartford, on applications for membership, on a public meeting to present the Quaker plan for the control of atomic energy. The Clerk called members by their first names, and so did all the others—which seemed a curious touch of informality in a procedure so dignified and ancient.

After the period of silence and adjournment, the Clerk told me that a really stirring issue divided the group, though no visitor could have guessed it. The issue was whether or not to build a meeting house. "We have had to ask for periods of silence when that comes up," he said. "Feelings are strong; but it will be settled, and settled right."

"Unanimously?" I asked.

"Unanimously," he replied with the utmost confidence.

Burial Ground

Some years ago, the Pollards tell us, the burial ground of an English meeting house filled up. The business meeting had to decide where to inter the rest of the congregation when their turn came. Certain members wanted to enlarge the present ground to give everyone a fair chance to be buried comfortably close to the meeting house. Others observed that if this were done it would cut down the playground area of the Quaker school. Deep feelings were aroused—school and children versus a resting place for loved ones, a theme to engage a Thomas Hardy.

As emotions flared in the first meeting, the Clerk called for silence, and then, when he found the atmosphere still electric, held the matter over for a month—put it, as it were, into the refrigerator to cool. The second meeting showed little sign of cooling, however, and back to the icebox the subject went. It took six months for temperatures to get suitably low, but agreement when it came was unanimous, with no resentful minority or jubilant majority. The solution followed a pattern common in Quaker business meetings and profoundly significant to our study. *The issue was not compromised but moved up to another level where a new plan was evolved—a plan in nobody's mind at the beginning of the discussion.* The bury-

ing ground was enlarged but in a special manner which did not
limit the playground or the school. A good many technical facts had
to be brought out and digested before the solution was found.

Casebook

Quakers have the usual business problems which confront all
churches: budget, upkeep of property, trust funds, charities, new
members. They also have special Quaker schools, and they have their
extraordinary missions of relief and social service here and abroad,
including at least one experiment with psychiatric treatment of
delinquents. In wartime, conscientious objectors are a special concern. The Friends look after boys of other pacifist organizations as
well as their own.

The Society was early interested in prison reform and in the
improvement of intolerable conditions in insane asylums—movements which later became worldwide. It helped to set up Utopian
communities, like Robert Owen's "New Lanark." It was one of the
first to take an interest in the condition of American Indians.
William Penn was always their friend, treating them as fellow human
beings, not "savages."

The Society has never hesitated from the beginning to take a
position, often an exposed position subject to much crossfire, on
highly controversial matters. The London Meeting raised the red-
hot question of peace with France in 1802, as Napoleon soared up
the horizon. (Our feelings for Stalin in 1950 were relatively amiable
compared with British feelings toward Napoleon in the early 1800's.)
More than a century later, in 1920, the same Meeting called on
British dock workers to stop the help they were giving to Soviet
Russia; the next year the American Friends' Service Committee
was aiding victims of the Russian famine. Today the Society is
deeply interested in better American-Soviet relations. Quakers are
always concerned with disarmament and peace, and always oppose
conscription.

At any time a meeting may have to consider such questions as
these:

Shall we take government grants for Quaker schools? What shall be the testimony on Palestine and the Arabs? How shall we assess the proposed bill to nationalize the land of Britain?

I mention these subjects to show the variety of thorny problems which a meeting may be called upon to handle. The Society of Friends does not hide its light under a bushel and never has.

Quaker Principles

At least nine major principles and procedures appear in Quaker business meetings, though not necessarily all in any one gathering. I saw perhaps half of them in the meeting I attended. All nine are directed to a specific goal, namely: *How can we settle this problem so that it will stay settled, so that it is settled right?* "Right" to the Quakers always has a deeply religious significance. We must not forget that they start on the basis of an ethical "inner light."

Here are the principles; as in most categories, there is some overlapping.

1. *Unanimous decisions.* There is no voting, no minority to nourish grievances and so prevent a real settlement.

2. *Silent periods,* always at the opening and closing of meetings, and whenever two opposing parties begin to clash.

3. *A moratorium* (or cooling-off technique) for questions where agreement cannot be reached unanimously, where opposing parties start to form. If they are important questions, they will come up again at future meetings until disagreement ceases and unanimity is found. Slavery kept coming up in the Philadelphia Meeting year after year.

4. *Participation* by all members who have ideas on the subject. Experience has demonstrated, says the Book of Discipline, "that the final decision of the group is usually superior to that of the individual." Members pool their knowledge and experience.

5. *Learning to listen.* Again to quote the Book of Discipline: "It behooves them in their meetings to hear with attentive and tolerant minds the messages and views of all members present." Quakers do not go to meetings with minds made up; they go to

learn, expecting the right solution to crystallize from the experience of all.

6. *Absence of leaders.* The Clerk does some steering, but he must not interpose his ego or take a dominant role.

7. *Nobody outranks anybody.* Rich and poor, men and women, old and young, have equal status and are expected to participate equally. Everybody has had past experiences, and so everybody has something to give.

8. *Consider the facts.* As emotions are at a minimum, facts and their cool consideration can be at a maximum.

9. *Keep meetings small.* The best size for solving problems is a face-to-face group of not more than twenty persons. Yearly meetings of several hundred, however, are able to use the method.

From the beginning, Quakers have realized the conflict and trouble which a human ego on the loose can raise. Their meetings are specifically designed to keep the ego in its place, to encourage "we-feelings," discourage "I-feelings." Members try to think about the reaction of the group to the problem rather than about their personal reaction to it.

Cross Check with the Psychologists

The Pollards in their book have raised some interesting questions about the relationship of Quaker methods to recent findings in psychology and social science.

Take the matter of ego, for instance. Many of us find it difficult to accept other people freely, but this is often much easier, psychologists say, than accepting oneself. Organized into small, permanent groups, Quakers have gone far to help one another face the reality of oneself—to stop fighting one's ego, trying to escape from it. After this internal conflict diminishes, it becomes easier to get along with other people.

Again, the Quakers recommend an attitude they call *"integration,"* rather than dominating or submitting to domination. Most of us are prone to one extreme or the other—indeed, there is a pre-human parallel. Psychologists describe the famous "pecking order" found in barnyard fowl as evidence of domination—who pecks whom. They compare it with the behavior of humans in a so-called "dominance-submission scale"—who outranks whom. By integration, of course, the Quakers do not mean submission but rather the power to co-operate, to act together in groups without domination. Integration implies even more: "a growth phenomenon that involves a change in the functions of an organism through the confronting of differences." Fusing differences may result in new and sounder conclusions all around.

Such "integrative" or "permissive" behavior by X is likely to be contagious. It also tends to make Y and Z feel more secure, as they recognize that X accepts them as they are, with no desire to dominate them. "The Friends' witness," say the Pollards, "has always been against dominative relationships of all kinds." People are accepted for themselves, not for pictures of themselves, and that makes for friendly relations. The Society of Friends has tried to live up to its name.

A Special Case?

The Quakers have found a road to agreement and obviously a wide one. You can use some of their methods in the next meeting you attend, in every meeting for the rest of your life. But before you can use the total approach, a definite structure must be in place.

To begin with, Quakers are like-minded people, coming mostly from the same sub-culture in society, the "upper-middles" and the "lower-uppers," as W. Lloyd Warner might classify them. They know each other well; many are born in the faith—"birthright" members. They are not in so much of a hurry as most Americans; they can afford to let the right decision make itself known in due time. Their motto seems to be: When in doubt, Wait!—while the American hustler counters with: When in doubt, Act! And as we said earlier, Quakers begin with a religious conviction that it is their duty to find agreement.

Quakers meet usually in small face-to-face groups—a great help in problem-solving. As we have seen, they have learned a high degree of control over their egos and have all but banished from their gatherings the loud-mouthed, dominating type. They know how to listen, a function much neglected by most Americans. They respect the judgment of others, hoping to find there a new dimension for group judgment. This is not so much neglected by the rest of us as unheard of.

Wider Applications

The most suitable bodies to make use of Quaker methods, say the Pollards, are executive committees, boards of directors, meetings of not more than a score of persons whose personnel remains fairly constant. One can call to mind various groups which already practice the rule of unanimity and others that have used silent periods. Comfort reminds us, for example, of the international conference in San Francisco in 1945, where the United Nations was born. The Secretary of State opened this conference by asking for a period of silence. With more than fifty nations represented, many of them non-Christian, any spoken prayer would have been out of place.

In February, 1950, a regional conference of fifty-five non-governmental bodies was held in Bangkok, the capital of Thailand. Representatives came from Australia, Burma, India, New Zealand, Pakistan, the Philippines, and other eastern countries. They adopted a resolution "recognizing the value of periods of silence as a spiritual force in the solution of controversial issues."

The General Assembly of the U.N. also favors a short period of silence to begin its sessions. If the international delegates are also able to empty their minds of preconceptions and prejudices, as the Quakers try to do, this should be a valuable device. The Quakers, incidentally, in spite of being Christians, are less culture-bound than other religious groups and almost free from national prejudices. Their sympathies are worldwide, going out to all mankind.

As for the rule of unanimity, I know of one board of directors that tries to practice it—the Standard Oil Company of New Jersey. The twelve directors meet once a week, and the executive board of five within the larger board meets every business day. All twelve are drawn from the active operations of the company—production, sales, personnel, but not the legal department. They seldom take a vote. If disagreement develops—say over a project to build a new refinery —the technical staff is called in, equipped with charts and statistics. The board listens to the facts. When the final decision is made they are all in it. Nobody says later on, "I told you so."

The anthropologists have some testimony running parallel to the Quaker method. Clyde Kluckhohn tells me that a Navaho community will fiddle around all day discussing a matter which any up-and-coming business executive would settle in fifteen minutes. It seems to Western eyes like dawdling nonsense. But when the Navahos finally settle the matter, the whole community has participated, *and it stays settled.*

Councils of the Solomon Islanders do not vote but come to unanimous agreement. William Penn wrote that Indian councils in America forego formal rules of order and "do not speak two at a time, or interfere in the least, one with another." George P. Murdock, who developed the famous Cross-Cultural Index at Yale, says that unanimous agreement is the rule in the councils of many primitive societies. The ancient Russian village organization, the *Mir*, used to hold open discussion of community problems and in some cases insist on unanimous agreement for a new policy.

The Quaker meeting is thus not an isolated case. It follows a deep groove, carved by many cultures, ancient and modern. But no other modern group of men and women has developed methods of group consensus to a comparable extent, while applying them so long and so successfully.

CHAPTER SEVEN

Groups in Action

ALL of us, unless we are practicing hermits, take part in group activities every day of our lives. W. Lloyd Warner, studying Newburyport, Massachusetts, in the 1930's, when it had a population of seventeen thousand, found about eight hundred formal organizations in existence—churches, clubs, lodges, unions, and the like. There were also some four thousand families, each a functioning group, and heaven knows how many informal associations, like boys' gangs, "our set" on Laurel Avenue, work teams in factory and office, the "drug store crowd," and so on.

In all American communities such groups form and reform, change and disappear. Group dynamics is the term applied to the study of this very human activity. It has at least two meanings: the observable energy generated by the interaction of people in groups; and, secondly, the scientific study of this interaction.

Behind such familiar slogans as "two heads are better than one" and "many hands make light work" is an energy potential which often exceeds the possibilities of the same people working as individuals. The phenomenon, though it seems to border on the miraculous, has a simple explanation. When a number of individuals combine for a common purpose—whatever it may be—new patterns of activity arise from the interactions of the members to each other. Working to the same purpose individually, obviously there are no such relationships.

It could happen, and sometimes does, that the new energy is destructive. A theater panic might be such a case, with members fighting for the exits. A gang organized for crime is another. Fortunately in most cases the new energy takes a constructive course, at least for the members of that group.

Let us look at a few groups in our society which have functioned constructively, to illustrate the point.

Drafting the Lilienthal-Acheson Plan

Following the holocaust at Hiroshima in 1945, the President of the United States asked five men to try to work out a plan for the international control of atomic energy. They labored for many weeks, and their report is an outstanding document in human history. We are all familiar with its fate, but the story of its drafting, although it was reported in the *Saturday Review of Literature*, is not so familiar.[1]

The five were all strong and independent men, not too fond of committee techniques. Early in their deliberations they decided to by-pass the old devices that led to the usual compromise report and seek a bold new approach. The subject was too important to be left to the hazards of the usual push and pull. "We studied committee techniques, and why the system fails so often or comes up with sterile compromises. We discussed semantics, dialectics, the art of persuasion. . . ."

The group observed that many committees fail because members arrive with their minds made up. They spend the committee's time fighting for preconceived theories, and a struggle between personalities usually develops. So the five resolved to divest their minds, so far as they were able, of any previous thoughts on what should be done about atomic energy and try to start with a clean sheet. They would then carefully assemble the available facts and let the plan grow out of them.

They agreed that questions coming up were to be considered the

1 June 15, 1946. The five men were David E. Lilienthal, J. Robert Oppenheimer, Chester I. Barnard, Charles A. Thomas and Harry A. Winne.

product of the group, not of the member introducing them; not "my idea" but "our idea." If somebody had an objection, it was to be considered a difficulty troubling the group. There was to be no log-rolling and no trading—a bold new approach indeed! They found it difficult at first, but gradually preconceptions were laid aside. Some of the best discussions, as it turned out, took place on long plane trips to the laboratories in the South and West.

The group avoided incomplete discussion, sporadic meetings, erratic attendance, personalities, and the common practice of turning undigested material over to a secretary to work out a statement which would offend nobody. "Each of us was pledged to emancipate himself from the tyranny of his own ego. We were trying to create a collective wisdom." The report was not to be a list of individual ideas tied together with rhetoric but a real synthesis. Note how close this comes to the Quaker goal of "integration."

All the world knows how well they succeeded. The report which came out of this unique process was not final, and was not meant to be, but it provided a solid foundation on which to build. It went further than representatives of one nation had ever gone before in limiting national sovereignty in the interest of all mankind. One reason for its rejection by the Russians was that the Kremlin could not believe the surrender of sovereignty had been made in good faith; anything so generous must have a catch in it. There was no catch in it.

After some years of the so-called Cold War, people began to call for a new plan. When one is made it will be the stronger because of the work of these five men. Their method sets an historic pattern for other committees which need unanimous agreement on high and dangerous subjects.

The Jury System

The Anglo-Saxon jury system has an even longer history than the Society of Friends. Some centuries ago, the principle was established that the opinion of jurors, instead of being formed before the trial begins, should be formed by a kind of group dynamics in court.

Ever since, jurymen have been isolated from the rest of the community throughout the trial and expected to empty their minds of
preconceptions about the case.

When the trial draws to its close, it is the duty of the judge to sum
up the evidence—evidence which is now subject to strict rules as to
what is a fact and what is not. Hearsay evidence, though admitted
by other groups—for instance, Senate committees investigating the
loyalty of government employees—is thrown out of court. The judge
is also careful to discount the verbal tricks of trial lawyers who are
primarily concerned with winning a fight. The twelve good men and
true retire to render their verdict, *which must be unanimous.* If it
is a hung jury, a new trial is in order. It consistently happens that
these twelve men and women, selected by lot, will come to a
unanimous decision covering a question which would hopelessly
divide them in the outside world. Often the judge, for all his legal
training and experience, is stumped by the question. But the jury,
deliberating as a group, is very generally right. This applies more to
criminal cases than to civil. As we shall see later, many civil cases
can be handled more expeditiously by arbitration.

Learning in Groups

The ancient tutorial system in Oxford and Cambridge broke
down because of the number of students admitted after World
War II. Tutors, instead of concentrating on *one* boy at a time, were
forced to impart knowledge to groups of five or six. To the surprise
of all it was found that the students learned more this way! "There
is a distinct gain in meeting with more than one student; students
engage in mutual discussion, often continued beyond the session with
the tutor," says a report to the Rockefeller Foundation by Robert T.
Crane.

Following the same line, ski instructors usually find that private
lessons are not so successful as group lessons. Similarly with music
teachers. Says one of them in a magazine called *The String Player*:

Violin students should be taught in groups. . . . Children not only
derive a great deal of pleasure from this approach, but they learn much

more rapidly by watching one another, hearing one another, and by making comparisons. . . . The strong points of the student should be emphasized in front of the class in order to build confidence.

The most common result of courses in English composition, says Hayakawa, is not the creation of good writers but a lifelong fear of grammatical errors.[2] Many a freshman theme is a literary shipwreck, not because the student is stupid or ignorant, but because the line of communication is so artificial and meaningless. The student is writing on a subject not of his own choosing, aware that whatever he writes will be met with a hostile eye.

Hayakawa proceeds to make a startling suggestion based on his own teaching experience. Let freshmen write for each other, *not* for the teacher! Modern ditto machines and projectors can easily make a theme visible to all in the class. Its merits will be judged by classmates, not by the teacher—who will now act as group leader.

Language in freshman English classes—and elsewhere for that matter—has two functions: communication and status—placing the speaker in the social scale. Communication is more important by far, but many English teachers, says Hayakawa, are chiefly concerned with the latter. If a boy's theme tells the reader clearly how to clean ignition points so that a competent job can be done it is good communication—no matter what the spelling or the grammar. The latter Hayakawa compares to "paper panties on one's mutton chop." Students writing themes for their classmates soon feel the need for linguistic decorum and get the paper panties in place. "They fear the ridicule of their classmates more than low grades from the teacher."

Group Theses

A psychologist, Hubert Coffey, at the University of California had three brilliant students. He put them to work as a group on a Ph.D. thesis. They produced an excellent monograph—better, he is sure, than any one of them could have written alone. The academic authorities, however, were baffled by the idea of a group thesis, no

[2] *ETC.* (Winter, 1950).

matter how brilliant. They had no way of giving doctorates to groups; tradition holds that degrees can be awarded only for individual work. . . . But some day a college is going to recognize the group thesis and perhaps dramatically raise its academic output.[3] Another professor in a far Western university found, logically enough, that he could not grade individual students but only the whole class when he used group dynamics as a teaching method. This brought the university practically to a standstill! A badly shaken dean said it must be stopped, no matter how much better the students learned the subject. One cannot lightly challenge the traditions of a thousand years.

Educating Housewives

During the last war it was imperative to re-educate American housewives to use cheaper cuts of meat. Fashions in foods, however, are more stubborn and much more permanent than fashions in hats and express deep cultural prejudices developed very early. The consumer bureaus of the government were confronted with a serious problem. In one experimental case, directed by Alexander Bavelas and cited in the *Journal of Social Issues*, the advantage of a group decision comes out clearly.

First the housewives were given the standard lecture system. Like college students, they were put into a room, provided with notebooks, and told to pay attention to the professor. As a result of this instructive performance, about 3 per cent shifted their buying habits.

Then another approach was tried. Unlike most college students, housewives were gathered in groups with a competent discussion leader and asked to discuss the war, the food shortage, a balanced diet, vitamins, and the various cuts of meat. As a result, *32 per cent* changed their buying habits, more than ten times the lecture-system figure.

The lecturer told the women what to do and most of them balked.

[3] Since the above was written, New York University has announced group theses for Masters' degrees in public administration research, and the Carnegie Corporation is helping the project along.

In the group program they told themselves what to do, and ten times as many began to act.

Audience and Actors

Joseph Wood Krutch has been reviewing plays for years in the New York *Nation*. He sums up his experience:

A play which one follows in the company of one's fellows is something more than the words spoken, something more, even, than the words plus whatever of special meaning or passion a good performance puts into them. One participates not only in the play but also in the reactions of the audience. One senses, as one can never sense while reading a book, that one is sharing an experience. It is impossible to feel wholly isolated or completely alone. One's fellows are indeed one's fellows—just insofar as they are at any moment being moved by what is moving oneself. . . . The most obvious proof of this is the contagiousness of laughter.

Once driving home from a concert by a local community orchestra, which I found always enjoyable and occasionally moving, I fell to wondering how the identical performance would have sounded on a record or over the radio. I suspected it would not have sounded like the Philharmonic. But because I had been in the company of an audience, listening to real players up there on the stage, something extra had come with the notes, some contact had been established which no relayed music could ever equal.

Pursuing this train of thought, I wondered whether there is a limit somewhere in the human nervous system to music and drama transmitted by radio, television, and records. One gets something, but does he get the full experience of communication—no matter who the performers or the composer may be? Is this one reason why, as people grow older, they go less and less to the movies? (The peak age is eighteen.) Will this limit ultimately check the roaring boom in television? Will only live players before a live audience in the end give the hearer what he needs to be genuinely moved?

Inside an Orchestra

This brings us to one of the most precisely articulated of all human groups, a first-class symphony orchestra. Every player is a skilled performer with years of training, and all participate in producing sound. One member, missing an important entrance or forgetting the key, can ruin the entire output. Tempo, pitch, volume must be minutely co-ordinated, following the intricate pattern set by the composer and relayed by his representative, the conductor. The group has a definite goal, performing a specific composition with every detail in place, and this gives it a special kind of unity. The conductor's discipline may be rigid; and the players, who are often very critical to make up for low fees and other frustrations, love to complain about what a hard taskmaster he is. Yet they will brag that he can hear a wrong sixteenth note in a passage by the second clarinet. One of the most devastating things players can say about a guest conductor is: "All he does is beat time."

A member of the Philharmonic, writing in the *New York Times*, expressed the players' sense of pride by declaring that such an orchestra "can make it virtually impossible for even an inept conductor to give a bad performance." Playing a familiar Berlioz overture, in three-quarter time, a certain conductor—usually a wonderful leader—once forgot himself and beat it out in four-four. "We overlooked his error and went on playing correctly. . . . We give every conductor our best, regardless of whether we agree with him or not." In the last analysis, power lies in the group, not in the leader. Moscow once had a good orchestra without a conductor, but no one would go far to listen to a conductor without an orchestra.

When other groups are at sixes and sevens, and one begins to despair of human nature, it is helpful, I find, to think of a good orchestra. It shows what human nature can do if the goal is clear.

Groups in War

Dr. John C. Flanagan, chief of the Aviation Psychology Program of the Army Air Force, appointed a team of social scientists to make a special study of the four air forces which were bombing Hitler's Fortress Europa in 1943. Their losses were severe: after twenty-five missions only 277 men out of 1,000 were left; a flyer had only one chance in four. Yet morale was high. Why? Good leadership was one reason, good equipment was another, but the outstanding reason was a fierce group loyalty.

A kind of hierarchy of groups was identified by the social scientists. First and fiercest was loyalty to the crew of one's own bomber. Then to the squadron—also a face-to-face group; then to the four-squadron command under a colonel; then to the wing under a general; then to the Air Force—the 9th or 15th or whatever. These outfits all produced strong comradely feelings. Loyalty to the U.S. Army was less strong, to the Allied armies still less so, to the peoples of the United Nations it was barely measurable.

The individual flyer identified himself with his squadron as a kind of extension of his ego. The Quakers would say he was integrated—though they would not approve his task. He took great pride in his outfit and was ready to start a fight with anyone who criticized it. If a boy achieved identification with his face-to-face group, records showed that he was a better fighter than if his loyalty was ideological —"fighting for freedom," or some such slogan, was a relatively weak incentive. He drew his strength from people, not from words.

Samuel A. Stouffer confirms Flanagan in the intensive study already mentioned of face-to-face groups in the army, this time mostly on the ground. Discussing combat teams he says: "The group in its informal character . . . served two principal functions in combat motivation: it set and enforced group standards of behavior, and it supported and sustained the individual in stresses he would not have been able to withstand alone." The group held the individual in line by offering or withholding recognition, respect and approval, and it was far more effective than recognition or censure from the higher-ups.

When the proposition was put to G.I.s: "An enlisted man is more concerned with what other enlisted men think of him than what his officers think"—89 per cent answered yes, while 78 per cent of officers said yes too. The group comes down hard on any member "sucking up" to officers for promotion, hard on "gold brickers" who shirk, on "bright boys" who do a job too well. The army group has rigorous standards of how a job should be done. We shall meet this phenomenon again in industry, where a spontaneous group in the shop can make or break the finest plan of the efficiency engineers.

A combat group provides, too, a fine opportunity to work off aggressions—better than smacking a tennis ball. When a quarrel developed between buddies, the usual comment was: "Save it, Mac, for the Germans."

Said an infantry scout, wounded at Salerno:

You know the men in your outfit. You have to be loyal to them. The men get close-knit together. They like each other—quit their petty bickering and having enemies. They depend on each other—wouldn't do anything to let the rest of them down. They'd rather be killed than do that. They begin to think the world of each other; it's the main thing that keeps a guy from going haywire.

A deep feeling of guilt developed if a G.I. thought he was letting his buddies down. Time and again, men would go AWOL from hospital depots back to their combat units. Guilt arose from leaving one's group, and was always personal, never moral or ideological—exactly as in the case of Flanagan's flyers. The group and its approval "gave the individual soldier the security of belonging."

This evidence of Stouffer's on group solidarity, based on the most extensive public opinion research project ever undertaken, makes one wonder if an army could fight at all without the sustaining force of group relationships. Failing it, the individual soldier would rush from the field. How many battles have been lost because loyalty to officers was emphasized in training rather than loyalty to the team? The evidence indicates that army groups are held together by three main forces: (1) loyalty to one's buddies; (2) pride in the outfit and its equipment; and (3) confidence in being personally taken care of if wounded or disabled—the security drive.

Henry and His Family

The oldest and the sturdiest of all human groups is of course the family, with its prime task of protecting the young. John Bowlby, writing in *Human Relations*, presents some new evidence. People interested in child guidance, he says, must realize that the child cannot be understood apart from the family. Furthermore, "we find a tremendously strong drive in almost all parents and children to live together in greater harmony. . . . Our task is to promote conditions so that the constructive forces latent in social groups can come into play." A surgeon does not mend bones; he creates conditions which permit bones to mend themselves. "In group therapy, and in treating the tensions of groups, the aim should be to bring about those conditions which permit the group to heal itself."

Bowlby tells us about Henry, aged thirteen, a bright lad with a bad school record and in constant trouble with his mother. Two solid years of individual counseling have done no good; Henry is wilder than ever. A group conference is then tried, with the father, mother, Henry, and the counselor. For an hour the air is thick with personal recriminations, as all three vent their accumulated grievances against one another. Then tension suddenly moderates. The family begins to draw together as the deep desire for harmony comes into play, and gradually Henry becomes normal, both at home and in school.

This wise counselor did not try to explain the complex relations between Henry and his parents. Every family, with specialized functions for each member, the deepest kind of emotional and biological experiences, and years of interactions, is beyond the detailed understanding of any outsider—still more any insider. Bowlby's simile of mending a bone suggests the mysterious vitality of this fundamental group. His respectful attitude toward its complexity helped him to understand it. He could not fail to note the pressure of bottled-up resentment in the three people concerned, but neither could he be sure that releasing it would automatically solve the problem.

We shall meet other families as we go on collecting examples of agreement, including one whose unity was so strong that it ruined an experiment. Sensible habits of co-operation, to be sure, could increase unity and improve morale in thousands of homes. Nevertheless, Henry's case should reassure us against current alarms and warnings about the disintegration of the family in America. If the drive for harmony exists, as biologically and logically it should exist, perhaps we do not need to wring our hands and lie awake worrying about disintegration. The American family is certainly in a process of very considerable change, but if it is disintegrating, it will be in defiance of several hundred thousand years of human history and in defiance of a cohesive force as strong as any we know in human relations.

On the whole, the groups described in this chapter bear out the Quaker meeting. There seems to be no reasonable doubt that energy can be released by group action. This raises an interesting question: How many of us are going around like icebergs with eight-ninths of our potential under water?

CHAPTER EIGHT

Clinics and Laboratories

THE study of human groups goes back to Plato if not before, while
the energy they may release has long been recognized, both positive
and negative. It is not always clear which is plus and which is
minus; for example, how to classify the high voltage of a revival
meeting I leave to the reader. Such political scientists as Graham
Wallas have studied group action in the Great Society. Anthropologists have considered a culture and its sub-groups. Teams of social
scientists have made intensive studies of modern communities—for
instance "Middletown," "Plainville," and "Yankee City."

What happens in face-to-face groups, however, is only beginning
to be analyzed scientifically. Group dynamics originates in Robinson's reaction to Smith when they are engaged in some common purpose. This is the reality of human association for most people and
always has been. The state is remote, the culture is taken for
granted like the air, but the people one knows, speaks to, gossips
about, in one's home or village or neighborhood or work place, or
Long House, are the essence of human relations. A face-to-face
group, moreover, used to be the normal unit for food and survival
before the industrial revolution. Chan Kom, a Maya village in
Yucatan, as described by Robert Redfield, shows the immemorial
human pattern with great clarity, the monogamous family firmly in
the center.

Genesis of Group Dynamics

The work of many political scientists, anthropologists, and sociologists has formed a background for the new discipline. So have the careful studies of the conference experts, going back to Mary P. Follett and E. C. Lindeman in the 1920's. Mayo's work covering informal groups in factories contributes an important link, and psychiatrists have furnished both theory and technique, with their experiments in group therapy and role-playing.

Around 1940, the social psychologists broke into the field from three directions. Kurt Lewin and his associates at Iowa State, Douglas McGregor and Irving Knickerbocker at M.I.T., and the Tavistock Institute in London all found that they were sharing many preliminary conclusions about people in groups.[1] Lewin, who died in 1947, has now become the patron saint of the whole movement.

It is today a very active movement, spreading through the universities, the business world, the public schools, adult education. The branch of role-playing is growing like a prairie fire. Another branch, group therapy, promises greatly to reduce the cost of psychoanalysis, which can fill only one couch at a time. The Office of Naval Research has appropriated large sums to aid studies in group dynamics. Meanwhile at Bethel, Maine, the National Laboratory in Group Development has become a focal point for the expanding movement. Devotees go to Bethel as Mohammedans go to Mecca. In the next chapter, we will go to Bethel. But first let us inquire how the science of group dynamics differs from earlier studies of people in groups. We are exploring with our lantern in more or less virgin territory, for no definitive book on group dynamics has yet been published (December, 1950). McGregor tells me that it is too early; not enough has yet been verified. "Give us another five years," he says.

[1] As described to me by Dr. McGregor.

The Scientific Approach

A scientist when he tries to answer a question proceeds in three steps:

1. Careful observation of the available facts covering the question, including canvassing the literature.

2. Formulation of a theory or hypothesis to explain the facts.

3. Experiments and observations to test the hypothesis, which can be repeated by all disinterested and properly trained observers.

The last is what chiefly distinguishes science from philosophy and logical deductions: theories are rigorously tested or else plainly marked: "Unverified, use at your own risk."

The three stages can be nicely illustrated in the way men learned the shape of the earth:

1. Ancient stargazers made observations of the sun, moon, planets, length of shadows.

2. The hypothesis was evolved that the world was round.

3. Magellan continued to sail West until his ship got back to where it started from. Note: You do not always need a laboratory to verify hypotheses.

Designing experiments to test group behavior is not easy. People will not stay still, so the scientist must develop techniques to observe them in motion. This is probably where Lewin made his greatest contribution. The clinic, he said, must replace the laboratory for a good deal of social science research; and he showed how the clinical method can sometimes be used to verify a hypothesis and establish predictability.

Much can be learned, as we shall see in Chapter 11, from the experience of conference leaders over the years. Much can be learned, as we have already seen, from such functioning groups as the Anglo-Saxon jury and the Quaker business meeting. But for the long run perhaps even more will be learned from the patient adaptation of the scientific method to men in motion.

What Is a Group?

Social scientists agree pretty well in defining a face-to-face group as: (1) two or more people; (2) in communication with one another; (3) over a definite time period; (4) committed to a common goal or need; (5) which no member can hope to reach alone; and (6) perhaps as a by-product, affecting each member and his private needs.

Conceivably Whymper could have got up the Matterhorn alone, but his companions on the rope and the confidence they inspired greatly increased the probability. (Some day a student of groups will do a very interesting monograph on the psychological function of the rope in mountaineering. It becomes a kind of extension of each climber's nervous system.)

To be in communication means that members know each other, though not necessarily by name; they see and feel the others' personalities. This implies a face-to-face relation and not too large a number for ready recognition.

Face-to-face groups of strangers, not in communication and having no common purpose, except maybe a transportation point, are called *aggregations* by the experts—people on the streets, in a bus, a railway coach, subway, plane. An intimate example is a packed elevator.

Theater and concert audiences begin as aggregates but may establish a kind of communication if the actors or the music really move them—as Joseph Krutch pointed out. In an emergency an aggregation may become a genuine communicating group very rapidly. When a Bermuda plane crashed in the Gulf Stream, the passengers in their life belts joined hands in a circle in the water and sang through the night until they were rescued.

Beyond the face-to-face relation, as we said before, are large national or sectional organizations with a common purpose but not normally in close communication—the Democratic Party, the Methodist church, the Petroleum Institute, the League of Women Voters, the Elks, the National Association of Manufacturers.

Three kinds of essential groups form a framework for all the others. They are:

1. The local community—the town, village, neighborhood, which we call home.

2. The nation—to which a citizen pledges allegiance and for which he must be ready to give his life.

3. The society—with its common culture and language, in which everyone is embedded from birth.

In primitive societies, the three often merge in a single tribe, band, or clan. "Home" to me is this little rural town in Connecticut where I write. I am also a citizen of the United States. I speak the English language, which binds me to the Anglo-Saxon culture, a group much larger than the United States. On another level, I share the culture of Western civilization with perhaps five hundred million human beings.

Warner and Lunt, studying Newburyport, found the simplest unit of social interaction to be two individuals in some relation to each other. A third individual joining them "increases the complexity of the society, and the difficulty of its examination." When experts say that American society is complex, they mean, technically, that there are many internal groups and thus a vast number of relationship lines.

Looking around and back over the years, I recall, among others, the following face-to-face groups which meet the definition and in which I participated as an active member:

My family
Classes in school and Sunday school
'Teen-age gangs
School athletic teams
A college fraternity
Camping parties
Various boards of directors and business executive groups
Dinner clubs
Many, too many, conferences trying to repair an ailing world.

The reader can doubtless summon from his memory an equivalent list—and join me in regretting how badly some of them performed.

The Groups at Hawthorne

Let us make the rounds of some of the experimental work in this new science, beginning with Mayo's classic experiments at the Hawthorne plant of the Western Electric Company. Mayo and his associates are noted chiefly for their pioneer work in labor-management relations, both at Hawthorne and in aircraft factories during World War II. The same studies, however, with a slight shift in emphasis, illustrate important principles of group dynamics.

Six girls assembling telephone "relays"—a gadget about the size of a pocket whistle—were found to turn out more relays after their group was singled out for attention. They were consulted frequently, participated in minor decisions, and felt recognized and important. Under these conditions, even a reduction in pay did not affect the upward curve of their production.

In another department at Hawthorne, the fourteen men in the Bank Wiring room effectively upset the company's elaborate bonus incentive system. These men had spontaneously formed a group, and leaders had developed. Management was quite unaware of the toughness and strength of this outfit, a social not an economic one. The men could readily have turned out 7,300 wiring connections a day without fatigue, but they held output to a flat 6,000. If some member got ambitious the others slapped him down. The whole plant at Hawthorne was found to be full of similar informal groups, lined up against "rate busters" who worked too hard, "chiselers" who worked too little, "squealers" who told tales.

Thus the results observed in both the Relay room and the Bank Wiring room were in flat contradiction to traditional assumptions about work incentives. They showed how an informal group can cause output to soar or can hold it to an implacable standard well below capacity. These findings not only offered a new challenge to management but helped to lay a groundwork for the scientific study of face-to-face groups.

Kurt Lewin

Lewin was a Gestalt psychologist in Germany and also an ardent believer in democracy. Hitler was too much for him to stomach, and he came to America in 1932. He continued his research work at Cornell, Stanford, Harvard, the National Research Council, the Bureau of Agricultural Economics, and Iowa State, and finally became head of the Research Center for Group Dynamics at M.I.T. This work was tragically interrupted when he died of a heart attack early in 1947. It was a great loss to social science, for above all other experimenters of his day, he knew how to apply the scientific method to problems in human relations.

A group, he says, exists. Let us not talk about it but observe it, measure its changes; how does it function, what can it *do*? He sets a problem for the group to solve, observes it in action, records the results. "Research that produces nothing but books will not suffice," Lewin wrote. He tried to relate his experiments to actual problems of every scale of magnitude, and called on other scientists to include "the whole range of descriptive fact-finding, for both small and large groups, embracing laboratory and field experiments in social interaction and change." Field experiments are not basically different from laboratory experiments.

An experiment, he says, differs from a mere description by bringing about certain changes under controlled conditions. "The objective is to understand the laws which govern the nature of the phenomena under study—in our case the nature of group life."

We described in Chapter 1 Lewin's experiments at Iowa State with the children making masks, which have become social science classics. The groups with democratic structure did better than those with autocratic structure and far better than those organized on an anarchistic basis.

White Bread and Whole Wheat

Here is another interesting experiment at Iowa State. It is early in the war, and the government wants people to eat more whole wheat bread and less white bread. Four college co-operative dining rooms are asked by Lewin to change to whole wheat. The advantages in health as well as national welfare are carefully explained. The boys agree in principle, and continue to devour white bread as before.

Four other eating clubs were then asked to discuss the matter thoroughly before voting on the change. This made it a group decision. Whereupon three of the four proceeded to eat a great deal more whole wheat. But in the last group, a curious and significant thing happened, something the Quakers would appreciate. By a close vote, the boys voted to banish white bread from the table entirely. This extreme was not contemplated in the experiment but was engineered by a flying column of patriotic reformers inside the club. Resentment appeared almost immediately, the pledge was broken, the club thrown into conflict. A supposedly democratic method had been used in an undemocratic way, with ominous results.

Two conclusions came out of the experiment as recorded by Lewin. The first we already know well: a group decision is more effective than any appeal by an outsider. The second is this: if a group decision is based upon strong-arm methods, it may turn out to be no decision at all but rather an invitation to trouble.

We are moving, said Lewin, toward a full-fledged experimental science in the field of group dynamics. It will include problems of group morale, output, leadership, and discipline. All dispassionate observers, I think, must agree with him. It is unfortunate that some of the more enthusiastic disciples seem to be promising more than the research men can yet deliver. It is sad that Kurt Lewin cannot be here to reprove them in his gentle way. He knew how hard it is to measure men in motion, but he knew it could be done.

Bavelas at M.I.T.

One of Lewin's associates at M.I.T. was Alexander Bavelas, a brilliant experimenter with men in motion. I visited him in early 1950, and he told me that he was devoting a good part of his energies to testing Lewin's hypotheses.

At the time he was studying the problem of communication in

groups. He had designed a round table with partitions so that members sitting around it could not see each other. Thus isolated, they tried to co-operate on a common problem or puzzle in the center of the table. His experiments emphasize that the structure of a group, the way members are related, is very important. If the structure is faulty the problem will not be solved, although the same individuals, in a better-organized group, might readily solve it. His diagrams showing relationships between members and leaders, when they are published, are likely to clear up a number of mysteries.

In the *Journal of Social Issues* Bavelas sets forth certain conclusions about change. People in an organization—say a factory—build up through time an elaborate system of habits with many rituals. Thus "McWilliams," the superintendent, must not be called "Mac" except on certain well-defined levels. One man's whole career was ruined because he called him "Mac" three days too soon. These built-in patterns are not easy to change, and they illustrate the tenacity of human culture.

"Much of the anxiety and disorganization which accompanies changes," says Bavelas, "is due to the serious dislocation of this social framework—that serves both as a guide to action, and as a reference system for meaning." If a change comes suddenly, the worker can no longer rely on the stable framework of habits which have safeguarded him in the past. Like a rock climber who has lost his protecting rope, he feels insecure and anxious. He could even become a paranoiac if the change is too violent.

Bavelas describes a company which wants to introduce a big new machine into one of its departments. The machine will shake up a lot of jobs. If the workers arrive on Monday morning to find it all ready to operate, there may be hell to pay, to use no stronger words. But a wise management will consider two courses to help the workers adjust to the new situation.

One course is to make the change seem more gradual, for instance, by putting the machine on the floor but not connecting it with power. Nothing happens for some days; the workers get used to seeing it while supervisors discuss its operation with them. Then power is turned on for a trial period—"See, this is how it works." Finally, after everyone in the department is used to it, the new machine goes into regular operation.

But a still better course, says Bavelas, if it can be arranged, is a *group decision.* The workers themselves, after preliminary investigation and discussion, decide to adopt the new practice or the new machine—"something that the group itself will do, rather than something that will be done to it." This course can transform an impending change "from a misfortune to be resisted or endured, to a positive step to be willingly taken." It offers a measure of security through sharing control and sharing anxiety during a period of transition.

Observe how this conclusion ties in with the story about changing the meat-buying habits of housewives, with the relay girls at Hawthorne, with the Quaker idea of participation, with the college dining clubs. Participation by members in group action is one of the most important principles of group dynamics and a major technique of agreement. The member becomes "involved," deep in his central nervous system, or, as the research men sometimes inelegantly phrase it: "It gets into his guts."

Lewin, in his book, *Resolving Social Conflicts,* makes a similar application. If a person is to change his habits or beliefs, he must change as a whole, and can do it best, he says, through a group. The organization called Alcoholics Anonymous is a case in point, in which members can support one another's resolution, and which is therefore vastly more effective than appeals to logic, lectures, precepts, and arguments.

McGregor and Knickerbocker

McGregor and Irving Knickerbocker, who used to be with Lewin at M.I.T., are now at Antioch College in Ohio, where they are experimenting with group dynamics in classrooms, in faculty meetings and student councils. Their work at M.I.T.—where I used to visit them occasionally in the early Forties—was analyzing human relations in factories and offices, as educational background for young engineers. Also they frequently acted as industrial consultants to firms in Cambridge and Boston. They kept in touch with Clinton S. Golden of the Steel Workers Union, with the Harvard School of Business Administration, with the Tavistock Institute and the Peckham Health Center in England. They brought in Joseph Scanlon to work with them . . . "a growing company of social scientists."

All human behavior is directed toward the satisfaction of needs. This is McGregor's first postulate in group study. These are needs, he points out, not as somebody else sees them but as *you* see them, in your own "perceptual field."[2]

The second postulate follows right behind: *Most human needs are satisfied through interaction with other people.*

If somebody wants you to do something, either he can offer to increase your need satisfactions with rewards or he can threaten to reduce them with punishments. Autocrats operate on the latter principle: Do what I tell you or I will fire you, incarcerate you, make your life miserable. Unless the autocrat controls every alternative form of behavior possible to you—every avenue of escape—the procedure is likely to backfire. The "forced reduction of needs" produces frustration and thus may lead to aggression—to strikes, sabotage, open rebellion.

Far more effective, says McGregor, if you want somebody to do something, is the method of increasing his satisfactions—the reward idea. In industry the best reward is some degree of participation—as in the case of the new machine described by Bavelas. It tends to make the worker feel that his deep human needs are being met, he feels good about his job, and it channels his efforts toward a positive goal. Forcing him to work by threatening to reduce his freedom of action, reducing his pay or his prestige, is still the more usual industrial technique.

Knickerbocker, in his paper in the *Journal of Social Issues,* is concerned with group leadership—again in the factory but again with wider application. He begins by stating the same general postulate as McGregor's, namely, that existence is a continuing

2 See articles by McGregor, Knickerbocker, and others in the *Journal of Social Issues* (Summer, 1948).

process in satisfying needs, relieving tensions, maintaining equilibrium.

The person who controls the means to increase or reduce other peoples' satisfactions is in a position of power. A leader is the man at the control valves. He must give his followers the things they feel they need. All leaders, whatever their personal ambitions, must serve as means for their followers, or their followers will desert, and they will be left generals without an army. A leader by definition is one who has followers and is a product, not so much of his personal characteristics, as of his functional relationship with his followers—a conclusion of very considerable significance.

In a factory the leader's objectives are not normally those of the followers, so the relationship is likely to be non-functional and uncertain. Workers tolerate the boss as a lesser evil than unemployment, but they do not follow him with enthusiasm, and being human they never will until the relationship changes.

In collective bargaining, the union tends to restore the worker's self-respect. Each side now controls valuable means which the other side wants. But the shape is that of battle, not of mutual satisfactions. Only in genuine participation plans between worker and management can a functional relationship be found. We will describe some of these plans in a later chapter, where we discuss labor and management in more detail. Leaders in industry are mostly appointed, and the "dilemma of the appointed leader is simply that he must succeed as a leader despite the fact that he cannot control the conditions in terms of which he leads." Here we are close not only to the dilemma of the boss, but to the dilemma of the whole modern industrial system.

The functional relationship between leader and followers is well illustrated in commando units. Sir Ronald Adam of the British Army set up an experiment with five commandos in World War II. They were well drilled in laying a pontoon bridge under fire or storming a house, but no leader was assigned. Shortly after they embarked on their dangerous missions, a dominant member always took control of the unit—but "only in rare instances did he hold it. After a series of attacks the man who finally emerged as leader had established his position by right of performance." The group had judged and selected their own leader.

Homans at Harvard

George C. Homans of Harvard has written an interesting book called *The Human Group*. It is based on an analysis of five earlier studies. He has tried to dissect out of them certain general conclusions. The range is wide:

1. The Bank Wiring Room at Hawthorne.
2. The Norton Street gang. A sociological study.
3. The Family in Tikopia. An anthropological study.
4. "Hilltown," a disintegrating New England village.
5. An office group of engineers in the Electrical Equipment Company.

Homans constructs a series of hypotheses covering these five groups, and also suggests a method for analyzing any human group. If it is to operate successfully, it "needs some division of labor, some system of communications, some leadership, and some discipline." Groups have an *external* system of rules, goals, functions, he says, but that is not enough to understand them. They also have an *internal* system, which is the network of interactions between members and the resulting sentiments and feelings which arise.

To study a group scientifically, the investigator should begin by evaluating the environment in which the group operates. How does the environment encourage the group to form and then to carry on? The investigator should go on to ask: What is the structure of the external system, and after that, and a good deal harder to dissect, the make-up of the internal system? What about discipline, members' rank, and their relations to the leader? Mr. Homans has not written the definitive book on group dynamics, but he has made an original and useful analysis.

One-way Window

Also at Harvard, in the Department of Social Relations, is Robert F. Bales. He studies groups with an armory of elaborate equipment. Let us observe him in action.

Here is a room about fifteen feet square, looking like a small classroom. It has chairs, a blackboard, tables which can be moved into various arrangements, and a large mirror in one wall. If we now go out into the corridor and enter a kind of closet located on the other side of that mirror we are surprised to find that we can look right through it and see everything that is happening in the classroom. It is a one-way glass. Furthermore, a microphone picks up every sound and transports it to earphones in the observation post. Bales and his staff can see and hear all that goes on, without being noticed.

In the observation post, too, is the "Interaction Process Stabilizer," a machine developed by Bales on which one can record, not words, but changes in the behavior of any group in the classroom. Bales has reduced eighty-seven types of interactions to twelve. The machine will record such things as "solidarity," "tension release," "agreement," "opinion given," "disagreement," "antagonism," and so on. He can make a profile chart of any group by punching the tape on the machine in accordance with these codified responses.

We find the laboratory most ingenious, and it should add valuable knowledge about groups in action. But we are a little uncertain about what might be called the wire-tapping implications, so alien to our culture. We were assured, however, that people are always told when they have been under observation and asked for their permission to use the results. Cambridge is not a very large place, and everybody must know about the room by now. If they *do* know in advance that they are being observed, it makes no difference in their behavior after about five minutes, Bales tells us.

Groups from two to as many as twenty persons have had their profiles taken, including family groups, college classes, union meetings, faculty meetings, nursery school children, group counseling, discussion groups.

The Family Group Again

Here is one of the experiments. A number of married couples are asked in a written questionnaire to comment on the adjustment of their friends to marriage. Are Joe and Dot happy? How good a job is she doing with the children? Does she dress well?—and so on for quite a list. Husband and wife both answer the same questions about Joe and Dot, and of course they do not always agree.

Then they are left alone in the classroom with the one-way window to argue out their differences about Joe and Dot. It has been assumed by the staff that by scoring the "wins" in the family argument, they could determine the dominant partner.

Eight couples take the test, and they make a fine hash of the staff's assumptions. *They take turns at "winning."* "I suppose you are right about Dot and the children. . . ." "Perhaps that *is* the way Joe really feels after all." Then they begin to resist the whole experiment. Something makes them angry and antagonistic.

What happened, apparently, is not too far removed from what happened in the case of Henry, the bad boy, described in the last chapter. The human family is a *tough group* and resists any threat to its solidarity. When people marry they will fight to maintain the relationship against internal differences of opinion—"I guess you're right"—and also against external attempts to separate them—which the experiment in a way sought to do. Thus, as often happens in scientific inquiry, a negative result produces a useful conclusion.

This chapter will not give the reader a rounded view of the present state of the new science of group dynamics. Many competent men and research projects have had to be left out. Only those where I have had some personal contact are included, and not all of them. I have tried to show the kind of questions being asked and some of the experiments being set up to answer them, in the hope that the reader may catch a glimpse of an exciting future. "Give us another five years." . . .

Now, on to Bethel and the most ambitious laboratory of all.

CHAPTER NINE

Groups at Bethel

BETHEL is a pleasant elm-shaded New England town on the edge of the White Mountains. The visitor coming in from the west follows Route 2 through a grove of white birches with the high ranges behind. Across a broad hayfield he looks up to church spires and a group of red brick academic buildings, with an athletic oval in the foreground. This is Gould Academy, which a local philanthropist has given to the town for a combined boarding school and public day school.

The fourth annual summer meeting of the National Training Laboratory in Group Development has overrun the Academy, its classrooms, gymnasium, dormitories, dining room, tennis courts, and library, and has spread out into many private homes. There are about two hundred and fifty people here—"delegates" who have come to learn, some fifty staff members who instruct them, including research people, a few unoccupied wives, and numerous children. As we arrive, we notice a young gentleman of three turning somersaults down the grassy slope toward the athletic field.

People are chatting in groups on the steps of the dining hall, forming a pleasant and colorful picture against the backdrop of deep blue mountains. They have something of the informality of college students, although they average nearly twenty years older. We notice several Negroes, an Hawaiian girl, and one or two foreign faces. Leland P. Bradford, the director, comes up and introduces us to some of the staff. He seems glad to see us, but we feel a slight reservation as he wonders how we are going to fit into the group.

The average I.Q. of those on the steps is undoubtedly exceptional. To get into Bethel requires intelligence, a spirit of adventure, a connection with some suitable institution, or assurance of some other kind that what you learn will be used. It requires patience, as well, for the waiting list is long. It is also a good idea to leave your ego in storage at home, as it is bad form to throw it around here. Celebrities and prima donnas are pulled off their high horses in short order. There is no hearty backslapping, but we shall find a fund of genuine friendliness, toleration, and understanding. We shall find real democracy, too, in the sense of accepting others as having as much to contribute as oneself.

People come from all over the United States and some from abroad, perhaps half of them from American universities. They are school teachers, college professors, graduate students, union officials, corporation executives, personnel directors, public health officers, little theater directors, social security people from Washington, community counselors, Red Cross workers, Girl Scouts, ministers, adult education leaders, conference directors, political scientists, public opinion researchers, hospital executives. There are delegations from the army, navy, and air force, though not in uniform. These, together with the business executives and the labor union officials, give Bethel a different atmosphere from the usual academic gathering. All the social sciences are represented except economics.

The dining room doors open and people stream in. Nobody has a special place; tables are filled in order of arrival and diners talk with everybody around them. It is an important part of the curriculum to have new neighbors at each meal. We find places and presently hear that "our T-group got along fine today, but our A-group fell apart." A tall young man, in a red and green tropical shirt, bangs a water pitcher with a fork for silence and reads a notice: "The X group on role-playing techniques will meet at 3:45 in Hanscom Hall. . . ." The decibels roar up again as conversation is resumed

How It Started

The staff comes early to Bethel, after conferences throughout the year to prepare the ground. The hundred or so delegates spend three weeks, after which the staff stays for a final period of evaluation. Then the town can relax in the midsummer heat. The town, we learn, grows more friendly to its invaders year by year.

Back in 1946 the state of Connecticut was trying to reduce conflict in race relations, with a good committee working on a program. It occurred to someone that social scientists might help, and he picked up the telephone and called Kurt Lewin. Lewin got a team together and went up to see the committee at New Britain. The resulting summer conference was a combination of pure and applied social science—people who had worked on the theory of race relations and those who had a specific job to do in reducing friction.

The combination proved fruitful. After Lewin's death, the team which he had formed stayed together. Next year, in 1947, considerably expanded, it moved north to Bethel. The Office of Naval Research helped with the early financing. The Carnegie Corporation of New York made first a small then a substantial contribution. The National Education Association underwrites part of the budget, and a number of universities do the same. Delegates pay a conference fee of one hundred dollars, plus their board and room. The waiting list is now so long that two conferences are planned for 1951, one following the other. Michigan's Research Center for Group Dynamics provides a good share of the staff, but other leaders come from Ohio State, Cornell, Chicago, California, Antioch, even the Tavistock Institute of London.[1]

What Is the Bethel Idea?

A leader at Bethel was trying to steer his group along what seemed to him a reasonable course, but it did not want to go that way. Later he said, "I felt as if I were wrestling with a healthy bull." The dynamics in a group could hardly be better expressed. But

[1] See partial list at end of chapter.

Bradford reminds us that: "A collection of healthy individuals can easily form a sick group; a collection of mature adults can form a very immature group." The combined intelligence and good will of the members can be wasted unless the structure is such as to bring these qualities out. Alexander Bavelas makes the same point in his research at M.I.T A successful group depends on many variables, and one major task at Bethel is to find out what they are and add to the storehouse of social science knowledge.

Another task is to help delegates do a better job "back home." Most of them are professional group leaders—in conferences, communities, classes, clinics, unions, company personnel departments, squads—and they come to Bethel for a kind of graduate training. Again, as in the earlier Connecticut conference on race relations, we note teamwork between research scientists and practitioners. Ronald Lippitt quotes a practitioner working on a community problem back home:

"Well, no, we don't actually have any good data on what the attitudes and tensions are, or on what effect our present program is having. . . . I guess we do need research, but we can't afford it, and we don't have the personnel."

Bethel is trying to provide such practitioners with research that they can apply. Bethel is also a kind of memorial to Kurt Lewin, carrying on what he so valiantly started.

What Is the Bethel Machinery?

In the previous chapter we looked at Bales in his observation post at Harvard studying groups through a one-way window, and at Bavelas constructing ingenious tables for studying problems in leadership and structure. At Bethel we find a third approach to the same end. It is to organize actual groups from among the delegates, give them a loose structure, including a non-authoritarian leader, and launch them into space. Observers are stationed about to see if they can fly, or how and why they fall. I suspect that each of the three methods is useful, but Bethel is certainly the most ambitious.

The delegates eat their meals, as we have seen, in one vast cheerful pandemonium; they go to "general sessions" just before lunch or after dinner as a total body of one hundred or more. The rest of the time they are weaving from one face-to-face group to another, official in classrooms or unofficial on the grass, in the lounge, the canteen, the corridors, or in each other's rooms. For all I know, they go right on discussing in their sleep.

In the morning the delegate goes to a "training group," which includes an evaluation session. In the early afternoon he goes to an "action group," and more evaluation. Then he can go to "X-groups," which are voluntary experiments of various kinds. If he brings the children there are groups for them, too. In 1950 all delegates took a fearsome psychological test called "Blackie," which will probably not be repeated.

A group may break out at any moment into a charade-like activity known as role-playing, which we will describe, play by play, in the next chapter. It may split into "buzz groups" of four to eight people, forehead to forehead, where discussion is close and easy. It may set up "panels" for intensive analysis of a topic, or even retreat to the canteen, where a disorganized unit may strive to reorient itself.

The Research Machine

All the while trained observers sit poker-faced in the background taking notes. From the observers, the leaders, the testers, and the busy delegates a steady stream of paper flows upstairs to the research and clerical department on the top floor of Hanscom Hall, and a smaller stream flows down. Members of this department range from high-voltage university researchers to local typists from the town of Bethel. Qualified wives are encouraged to fill some of the desks.

The adding machines and mimeographs go all day long, but their sound is rarely heard on the lower floors. The research workers perform their hard, meticulous labor with unobtrusive precision. They shower the delegates with regular and special forms, bulletins, questionnaires, even recreation hints for week ends. I never saw a typographical error in their material or knew of a delay in any activity that depended on paper work.

The usefulness of the figures so meticulously compiled is another question, which I am not prepared to answer. As an old statistical hand, and friend of the devastating Bassett Jones, I am reasonably suspicious of index numbers and numerical ratings in general, and of counts of mental states and attitudes in particular.[2] I am inclined to believe that some indexes, certainly as used in economics and probably in psychology, represent attempts to measure the incommensurable.

Here at Bethel, for instance, is a questionnaire on subjective attitudes, rated on a five-point scale, which has been developed by the statisticians into a percentage table down to tenths of one per cent. It recalls the old warning that no statistical product is better than the data going into it, no matter how many are the decimal places. Mathematics cannot manufacture anything. But I am ready to admit that a large enough number of cases can submerge a few inaccurate unit reports and that in some attitude surveys a dependable trend does emerge.

These attitude studies, psychological tests, sociograms, account for a good part of the Bethel budget. If people just came and sat around large tables discussing and then discussed what they had discussed and went home, the laboratory would not cost so much. But there would be no records, no correlations, no indexes, no opportunity to test hypotheses, and no increase in dependable knowledge about conflict, agreement, leadership, and human relations. Although the research work needs reviewing from time to time, it must go on.

Training Group

I joined a training group for a week to get the feel of the major activity of the laboratory. It was quite an experience. The reader, who has not been through it or had his nervous system mixed up

[2] Mr. Jones periodically berates the wholesale price index people for "adding horses to apples" and so creating mathematical monsters.

in it, can receive only a secondhand impression from the words I write here.

Promptly at 8:45 A.M., twenty-one of us filed into a classroom in Hanscom Hall. Three walls had blackboards covered with technical notations; the fourth had a row of open windows. We took our places around a huge polished oval table. In front of us we set up large cardboard place cards with our first names—"Joe," "Cal," "Pru," "Inez"—hand printed on both sides in large letters. We seldom took the same seat twice—which is harder to avoid than it sounds. We had a leader, "Herb" Thelen, from the University of Chicago, and a co-leader, "Jack," both strictly of the "permissive" type, which means that they gave the group plenty of room to express itself. It took me a while to identify them—in fact, I did not identify Jack as a staff member until the next day.

Two observers sat at a small table at the end of the room. "Fritz" Redl, the head psychiatrist, might prowl in, listen awhile, and go out; a child might tiptoe in to speak to his mother. Our six women members were invaluable in our frequent crises.

The meeting began with a report by a sub-group summarizing the last meeting—a "feed-back" device to keep the main group apprised of its progress or lack of it. On the blackboard were the post meeting reaction—"P.M.R."—figures covering a poll of members at the end of each session. The report that first morning was intelligently discussed. Then I got ready for the main business of the meeting. Now, I thought, our leader will announce the agenda. . . . But he did not announce it, nobody did, and at last I was forced to a surprising conclusion: *There was no fixed agenda!* No problem had been assigned us to solve, no decision to make, nothing specific to do at all. If there were to be an agenda it was up to us to make it. "Ralph" suggested a discussion of group standards, but nobody took him up. Yet the talk went on, largely about how badly we had done last week. There was a kind of confessional atmosphere around the table. I remembered the couplet they had been singing in the dining room:

In T-groups we will bare our souls;
In A-groups we will play our roles.

The "soul-baring" I found strangely interesting, especially because it came out so freely. Nobody, with one exception, seemed to
be trying to show how smart he was; defenses which normally guard
the ego seemed to be down.

Within an hour I felt myself slipping off my perch as a visitor and
beginning to share some of the group's feelings, especially its ap-
prehensions. We were clearly afraid that a new leader from the
ranks was going to force us to do some things which we did not
want to do. We knew very well who he was; he kept interrupting
with objections, suggestions, and dogmatic statements. Once he
called us "Malayan monkeys," in a voice like a steel file. He had
covered a good part of the blackboard with proposals for action—
terrible proposals, they seemed to us, all severely logical. It made
one ill even to look at them. He knew everything about everything.

The group talked against its fear, and the time passed quickly, in
spite of no prepared agenda. Before I knew it, it was 10:30, and the
observers were dealing out paper questionnaires that inquired how
we liked the session today, how we liked our neighbors in the group,
whom we trusted most or least, and so on. This, I recognized, was
an attempt by the research staff to study interactions inside a group,
to find out what leaders were arising, what cliques forming, what
changes taking place. As we left the classroom, exactly two hours
after entering, the questionnaires were collected and carried up to
the machines on the top floor.

The second day at T-1 I felt more at home, though I was still
careful to keep my mouth shut and my ears open. This was a day of
crises. Our leader had intimated earlier that some time he might
leave us for half an hour, an hour. That, we feared, would give our
Napoleon of the blackboard his chance. It was all we could think
about. Every suggestion for an agenda, other than the discussion of
leadership, fell into a kind of Mindanao deep. Tension mounted
until it became almost unendurable. Suddenly our leader closed

his notebook, rose without a word, and left the room. We felt that we had forced him out, because we wanted to get this thing settled. We wanted to know who was boss around here.

We waited in a state of extreme apprehension. After a short silence that seemed endless, Napoleon began to talk about what we ought to do now that Herb had gone. He was trying to move into Herb's role. No one answered at first, but as he went on talking, our fear vanished. Without a word we all rejected him, and we knew it and he knew it. To hell with him! He could not dominate us, for we were stronger than we thought. The healthy bull kicked up his heels, Napoleon subsided and we all felt very good indeed. The experiment we had made so reluctantly, with Herb's help, was successful. We had acted without a leader, refused one, and had none at the moment. We were on our own. Our P.M.R. for the day went way up.

On the third day Fritz, the psychiatrist, came early to give us a play-by-play account in the best Viennese manner of what had been happening to us. We were fascinated by the analysis and would have made him our leader on the spot but he left us. After some discussion we decided to recall our old leader Herb. He returned amiably enough and listened politely to our version of Fritz's diagnosis. We still felt good because we knew that we were strong enough to stop anyone from capturing us. We felt so good indeed that we adopted Ralph's discarded proposal to discuss group standards and went at it with enthusiasm. We had found our agenda. Everybody beamed—even Napoleon—and the P.M.R. that day went through the roof!

By the end of the week I had begun to talk a little and knew everybody's first name without the place cards. I felt sorry to leave such good friends with whom I had gone through so much. I had even begun to appreciate Napoleon, now that he was no longer a threat.

A record of the group's progress in its third and last week was shown me later. I read every word with the deepest interest and felt a generous satisfaction that T-1 went on gaining strength and purpose under Herb's skillful, democratic leadership.

While the machines grind out the measured results, what are the unmeasured ones for a visiting layman, interested in finding techniques for agreement? What could such a visitor learn in a week of participating in a training group at Bethel?

1. He could learn to his considerable surprise that a group of twenty people can consolidate, acquire toughness and strength, without having a formal agenda prepared in advance. Just being together around a table generates an agenda, and this is one of the facts presumably which the research staff is studying.

2. He could learn that such a group can survive temporarily without a leader, block an exceedingly dominant individual from taking command, and in due course find leaders it would follow.

3. He could learn that such a group can tame and incorporate a domineering individual. One's initial impulse is to eject him, but one learns better by watching the group slowly envelop him.

4. Finally, the student could learn something about good structural arrangements for face-to-face groups. They include such things as size, the shape of the table, first names, the virtues of a permissive or democratic leader, the use of observers, role-playing, buzz groups, panels, resource persons, evaluation sessions, "P.M.R.'s."

T-1 was only one of a dozen such groups at Bethel, all developing more or less bull-like powers and continuously raked with statistics. Two other T-groups were sub-divided into four permanent sub-sections, as an experiment by Irving Knickerbocker. Theory was fed to them before, not after, their own performance.

A-group

There were six action groups, or A-groups. The action groups differed from the training groups in that they were asked to choose a specific problem. At least one of these A-groups, which my wife attended, with Bradford as leader, found that this did not necessarily help. A minority formed to oppose the program, and for two days the group was stalemated. At one point no fewer than five observers were in the classroom, furiously taking notes. Someone said:

"When a group is on the rocks the vultures gather!" Ultimately it got off the rocks.

Does this give a hint of what happens in Bethel? I have tried to bring in a little of the atmosphere as well as describe the official curriculum. Time is doubtless being wasted, the right questions are not always asked; nevertheless one feels that something important, perhaps critically important, is going on.

A New Kind of Lecture

As an occasional lecturer, I have long been troubled by the problem of how to get an audience really concerned about the subject under discussion. Most lecturers and their audiences are far apart, while the audience itself tends to be more an aggregation than a participating group.

The staff at Bethel wanted to experiment with a new kind of relationship between lecturer and audience and asked if I would act as guinea pig. I was alarmed by the preliminary plan which they sketched, but I agreed. After all, were we not a "laboratory"?

So one night I got up on the platform in the gymnasium in a general session before all the delegates and staff and even some townsfolk. Max Corey as chairman told us what we had to do.

"Back home," he said, "a visiting speaker is introduced with a variety of rich adjectives. We hear him through, like him or dislike him, and then we go home. Nothing the speaker says affects us much, and nothing we do affects him—unless we walk out on him. Tonight we want to help you in the audience listen more critically; we want to help the speaker get some new ideas. We want you both to operate as a team exploring the topic assigned.

"Stuart Chase, here, is known to most of you through his books. He is going to tell you, in not more than forty minutes, about the book he is working on now, and why he came to Bethel to find material for it. He's going to try and help you, and I hope you will try to help him. He probably needs it."

The chairman then divided the audience of about three hundred into six groups by walking up the aisle and marking off lines with his hands. He gave each section an assignment. On each chair was a mimeographed sheet, sent down from the clerical department, repeating the instructions. They read in effect:

Group 1 was to listen for implications in the lecture which might prove useful to Bethel.

Group 2 was to listen for ideas which the speaker should elaborate later, things he had slurred over. (This was the "probing" team. In an ordinary question period certain individuals in the audience do this.)

Group 3 was to listen for high points of the talk and later emphasize them to the audience.

The above three groups were assigned to *help the audience.* The next three were to *help the speaker.*

Group 4 was to think about additional data for possible inclusion in Chase's book.

Group 5 was to listen to his description of areas of human conflict and see what areas could be added.

Group 6 was to concentrate on suggestions for making the book more readable. Given this subject, where should the emphasis be placed; what treatment would best hold the reader's interest?

I swallowed my dismay and began with an anecdote about role-playing which made us all feel better. Then I told them about this book you are reading, its genesis and its aim. I told about some of the people I had talked to and some places where I had gone for material, like UNESCO in Paris and the TVA in Knoxville. Then I read aloud about half of the chapter on the Quakers, to give them a sample of the approach and the style. Then I sat down, after thirty-nine minutes.

The audience gave me a different feeling from any I had ever encountered. The words did not bounce back as they often do from a bored or indifferent aggregation; they went home, but I was not entertaining anybody. The words went home but were turned around and examined before being taken in. The audience was listening as I never have been listened to from a platform—not agreeing, not disagreeing, neither hostile nor especially friendly, weighing and thinking.

The chairman repeated the instructions after I had finished. The folding seats were loose on the floor of the auditorium in batteries of four, and could readily be moved. Amid a vast scraping, the entire audience swung itself into perhaps twenty small "buzz groups," each separate, like so many campfires. A cloud of sound rose to the ceiling; faces were alight with argument, fingers were shaken, shoulders shrugged; somebody pounded the back of a seat for emphasis. I stood in a corner of the stage watching this extraordinary activity. As there were three or four buzz groups for each of the six divisions mentioned earlier, it took a while to choose spokesmen, compare notes, and get reports ready—say half an hour.

The first report came from the probing group. Spokesmen asked me to tell the audience more about the ethical background of the Quaker meeting and more about Cyrus Ching and the mediation procedure in labor disputes. This I did briefly. Now my evening's talking was over, and I stood and listened as the audience talked through its spokesmen to me. It was well worth hearing!

Why shouldn't Bethel experiment with the Quaker technique of silence?

What can we do about the danger of group dynamics becoming a cult?

The speaker should add *the family* to his area of conflict for especial study.

It is good to know that the study of conflict and agreement is going ahead on so many fronts. The speaker has given us new inspiration.

The speaker should use a great many simple, human cases in his book, so that the reader can readily identify himself with the problems raised. But he must be careful not to oversimplify. He should define the various kinds and levels of agreement early in the book. He should know about research at Berkeley, at Kansas, at Chicago. . . . (Picture me busily taking notes at this point.)

The aftermath took as much time as the lecture—that is, the audience talked through its spokesmen about as long as I had talked. Then we all went home.

I lay awake for a long time, wondering if any other speaker had ever had quite such an experience and thinking how very good for speakers and writers such an experience might be. The P.M.R. report next day showed that the audience had enjoyed it, too. Perhaps, between us, we were making some kind of history in human communication.

A technique had been developed by the staff which gave an audience a real chance to bring a speaker off his usual high ground and down to floor level. It allowed the audience to help the speaker, to correct him, approve him, enlarge his vision. Any staff of experts which can plan and carry through an experiment like this is obviously very competent, knows what it is doing and why. Any audience which can rise to such an occasion is obviously flexible and co-operative as well as intelligent. I am glad to have been a guinea pig, and readers of this book owe something to Bethel for that evening's skilled work by staff and audience.

Driving Home

We took two leisurely days to drive home to Connecticut, while Marian and I went on sorting out impressions of a most unusual week. What had we learned about furthering agreement?

Bethel is engaged, among other things, in training certain faculties which most schools have not often considered, namely, imagination and feeling. Naturally enough, some outsiders, and even some delegates, fail to grasp this purpose and think the course a rather immature performance. Mentally they understand the subject or think they do, and are looking for something more sophisticated.

Again, the daily group meetings at Bethel, with their emphasis on inter-personal relations rather than agenda, are a definite method for making people aware of their feelings toward each other and making them more tolerant and understanding. This is a technique of agreement, and is needed so badly, in so many places, on so many occasions, especially as the planet shrinks, that deliberate, formal training in its use is becoming mandatory.

Meanwhile, research at Bethel, despite some lost motion, will probably increase the possibilities of scientific prediction in certain social situations. The researchers are on the way to conclusions which should bring about:

Improvements in classroom teaching.

Better group productivity in solving problems and making decisions.

Heightened interest by members of discussion groups.

Technical help for conference procedures—local, national, and international.

Improvements in group therapy.

Better personal adjustment to other people and to life generally.

From this list we can readily see why the army, navy, and air force, why corporation managers and union officials as well as educators and social scientists are following Bethel closely.

The gravest danger at the moment, it seemed to us, was that Bethel's popularity might increase and turn it into a kind of cult. People might go about whooping up group dynamics as they once whooped it up for Humanism or Technocracy—the sovereign remedy for all the ills of man. We found no trace of cultism in this Maine village; indeed, the staff was constantly telling us how much it did not know. We found no leaders there who used the techniques for manipulating groups; on the contrary, groups were encouraged to exert their bull-like strength upsetting leaders, as in our T-1.

The danger comes when delegates go back home and are tempted to throw technical terms around—"feed-back," "hierarchies," "goal-directed," "structured," "continuums"—to show that they have drunk at the sacred well. Some outsiders, too, hungry for emotional security, may take up group dynamics as they once took up psychoanalysis, as a mystic solution to their frustrations, without troubling to study it.

Cults and the scientific method have never mixed. It will be far better to spread the word that the knowledge of group behavior is about where biology was before Darwin; it is moving ahead strongly but has a long way to go. The science is greatly in need, furthermore, of somebody with the imagination of a Darwin. Perhaps Bethel will help us find him.

Note:

In addition to those mentioned in this chapter, the staff in 1950 included among others:

Carlo Bos, Royal Victoria Hospital, Canada
Dorwin Cartwright, University of Michigan
Hubert Coffey, University of California
Fred Couey, Air University
Jack French, University of Michigan
Max Goodson, Ohio State University
Franklyn Haiman, Northwestern University
Gil Krulee, M.I.T.
Rensis Likert, University of Michigan
Donald Livingston, University of Kansas
Robert Luke, N.E.A.
Paul Sheats, U.C.L.A.
Graham Taylor, Cornell University
Goodwin Watson, Columbia University
William Foote Whyte, Cornell University
Ben Willerman, University of Minnesota
Alvin Zander, University of Michigan.

CHAPTER TEN

Role-Playing

OUR picture of Bethel in the preceding chapter was deliberately incomplete. The part we left out deserves a short chapter to itself for several reasons: it is important, it is used in many other places besides Bethel, and it has a paradoxical simplicity that makes it hard to explain. Critics have a fine time spoofing it, while enthusiasts tend to regard it as a cure-all.

Examples of role-playing range from a simple rehearsal of a coming experience, to a group solution of a complex problem. It is a way to develop imagination, tolerance, and the power to see yourself from the outside and other people from the inside, and so a way to reduce conflict and further agreement.

An Austrian psychiatrist, J. L. Moreno, came to the United States in 1927 and brought with him something he called "psycho-drama," a method to help people with mental difficulties. He lectured at Columbia and the New School for Social Research, experimented in St. Elizabeth's Hospital in Washington and in Sing Sing prison, established the Psychodramatic Institute, and wrote books and articles on the new technique.

The idea has now been developed and expanded by others and is having a great vogue. Under the name of "role-playing"—sometimes "psycho-drama" or "socio-drama"—teachers, conference leaders, trainers of salesmen, union officials, the staff at Bethel, all sorts of people, have been using this unrehearsed drama to promote a better understanding of human relations. If you have not been exposed to it yet, you will be. Dr. Helen Hall Jennings, an associate of Dr. Moreno's, has been putting role-playing on a New York radio station. It will probably break into television before these words are in print. Your children will sooner or later encounter it in school.

The action groups in Bethel used role-playing to open up their assigned problem. If the problem was how to induce the city fathers to appropriate money for a town playground, one member took the role of mayor, another the chairman of the finance board, others acted the parts of social worker, traffic officer, and so on.

There must be no rehearsal. Role-playing has no point as a psychological aid if lines are learned in advance; a spontaneous, off-the-top-of-your-mind approach is essential. The players can draw up a plan in advance, of course, but no one must formulate exactly what he is going to say. This makes the performance very different from any other kind of theatricals. A good actor may be a poor role-player and vice versa.

Strike!

A high school class in social studies is discussing the big coal strike which is all over the front pages. Some of the children belong to workers' families, some to employers' families. Two parties quickly form in the classroom which view the strikers as either angels or devils.

The teacher tries to break up this two-valued battle by role-playing. She asks Jack to play the part of the strike leader, Betty to play his wife, and seats them at an imaginary dinner table. She gives them no instructions, except seriously to express how they think a strike leader and his wife would feel and behave under the circumstances.

The domestic picture staged by Jack and Betty amuses the rest of the class, but presently the giggling ceases. Betty is telling about the hardships suffered by the miners' families and begging her "husband" to call off the strike. Jack counters by reminding her of the principles involved and how this is a chance to give the miners a real share in determining their wages and working conditions. When these points have been made, the teacher cuts the scene. The class proceeds to ask Jack and Betty serious questions about their roles. The little drama has reoriented the whole discussion.

Next they stage the board of directors of the coal company. Student actors seek to bring out the interests of managers and stockholders in the strike. Again the class has many questions to ask.

The third scene is a street-corner conversation between various citizens affected by the strike. How about federal mediation? Why won't the company accept it? How about the Taft-Hartley Act?

The students are now getting beyond their depth. They begin to realize how little they actually know about the strike and its background, but their interest is higher than ever. So the class begins looking for more information. Some volunteer to consult the local Chamber of Commerce; others will visit union headquarters; someone will look up the provisions of the Taft-Hartley Act. "Assignments are virtually assigning themselves." The ideological deadlock of Labor versus Capital has been completely dissolved. Snap judgments have gone, facts are coming in. The class is really learning about America.

Hunting a Job

Role-playing can help high school seniors who are soon to look for jobs. Here is Nancy who has majored in shorthand and typing, a good student but shy. What shall she say in a job interview? The teacher outlines six rules for getting a position. Nancy promptly memorizes them but they will be of little help. Far better is a role-playing scene in the employer's office with one student as boss, another as his secretary, and Nancy timidly applying for a job.

In the same class is Tom, bursting with self-confidence; no boss is going to faze him! But role-playing teaches him differently. His cocksureness does not impress the "employer" at all, does not impress the class; and to his considerable chagrin he is not hired. But Tom is an intelligent boy and really needs a summer job. So he asks the class to let him act out other ways of approaching an employer. He is not, you see, playing for keeps and can learn by experimenting. . . . A few days later he lands a good job from a real boss.

The National Education Association, one of the organizations that sponsor Bethel, is deeply interested in role-playing as an aid to classroom teaching and considers it particularly useful where ideologies or prejudices block the objective study of a problem, as in the coal strike case just recited. But role-playing, says the National Education Association, can be overdone and become a bore to young minds. The teacher must have a very definite purpose before she tries it and must use it sparingly. No drama should last more than ten minutes; a cut in about three minutes usually gives the best results. The most valuable part, says the N.E.A., often comes afterward, when the class discusses what has happened on the stage.

In the Home

Rosemary Lippitt has used role-playing effectively with her young children—Larry, aged five and Carolyn, two.[1] She spent thirty minutes a day at it for six weeks and kept careful records. "The daily topic for the psycho-drama presented itself through the daily experiences of the children." Ten situations are described in her monograph, including lessons in manners, sympathy for physical handicaps in other children, settling a quarrel between brother and sister, kindness to pets—Larry's rabbit—preparing for the children's first airplane ride, and so on.

In a dramatic episode Mrs. Lippitt cured a strong neurotic fear that might have had serious consequences. Just before Larry's fifth birthday, a number of bad fires occurred in the neighborhood. Children were trapped and burned, and frightening pictures appeared in the papers. Larry was terrified, and it came out clearly in his drawing and painting where the world was going up in flames.

[1] *Psychodrama in the Home.* New York, Beacon House, 1947, Monograph No. 22.

His mother then asked Larry to act out a series of little fire-plays with her and his sister. At first he resisted, with signs of panic. But gradually he became interested. After a fortnight he was taking the role of the big brave fire chief, getting fires under control and saving people. . . . "How is it going, Harry? I think it is safe now. You fellows better come along with me and get back to the station. . . . It's all over now!" The neurotic fear had been completely cleared up.

Larry and Carolyn, like all brothers and sisters, had occasional quarrels over their toys. "I want it." "No, it's mine!" Then a scuffle and many tears. Reasoning, admonitions, even punishment seemed to have little effect. So mother and grandmother put on a show for Larry as spectator. They pretend to be two children playing happily when suddenly both grab the kiddie car. "I want it." "No, I had it first."

Larry laughs. Then one seizes a stuffed animal by the head, the other by the tail, and pull until it comes apart. The first "child" begins to weep. "You've broken my horse."

Larry finds that it isn't a very funny play after all. The scene is cut, and his mother asks how he could help these children to play better. "Well," he says, "they might have taken turns and had fun and not fought. That horse wouldn't have broken." "But," says his mother, "suppose one of us will not take turns?" "Well," Larry replies, "they might have played another game." Then, after a pause: "It's sort of like me and Carolyn, isn't it?"

To say that this cured all of Larry's competitiveness would, of course, be a wild exaggeration. But it did help to reduce quarrels with his little sister and with other children. It gave him a picture of himself which he had never seen before and which no amount of "talking to" would give him.

Salesmen

In the event that the reader thinks that role-playing is all very well for small boys like Larry, even helpful for school children like

Jack and Betty, but rather below the dignity of adults, here is a story from the *New York Times* about training salesmen.

A firm of industrial consultants in Chicago offered a role-playing course originally worked out at M.I.T. by our friends McGregor and Knickerbocker. An impressive list of companies sent their salesmen to take the course, including Ford, Johnson and Johnson, General Foods, Swift, du Pont, Servel, Sears Roebuck, and Diamond Match. There is no script and no rehearsal, of course. Before an audience of a dozen other salesmen, the role-playing salesman is on his own, using his knowledge of the firm's product to sell the "dealer"—who plays the part as realistically as possible with very high sales resistance. To get an order from him is a triumph.

Swift and Company report that the method is far more effective, both for old hands and for freshmen, than any other field training plan. Servel doubled its Minneapolis sales of refrigerators in a week as a result. Furthermore, while orthodox field training costs fifteen hundred to two thousand dollars a man, the role-playing course costs only two hundred and fifty dollars.

Johnson and Johnson is now using the technique for training executives, supervisors, office and research workers. In one subsidiary the whole board of directors took the course! The company reports that role-playing is better than the conference technique for learning new skills; novel ideas are not only accepted verbally, they get into the nervous system.

Rubber Workers

Union officials of the Rubber Workers, C.I.O., who were at Bethel told me they used role-playing to prepare for negotiating a new contract. Several union men take the parts of management representatives while others play union representatives. The rest watch with keen attention. "The truth is we get to see the company's point of view too well, and maybe don't fight as hard. Still, we get on better. It's a fine way to get labor and management together on production. You can argue until you're black in the face about co-operation and get nowhere, but when you have to act out the part of Mr. Big protecting his stockholders, you really learn something about the business you're in."

I have not yet found any cases of management acting out the part of union officials, but I can think of a number of companies where it would be very useful.

Amid the Ashes

My wife and I live in a remodeled barn which has so many old timbers that it could burn to the ground in about twenty minutes! So the other day we did a little socio-drama ourselves.

Here we are out on the lawn, our house and all its contents in ashes. What do we do now? Who will take us in? The car has gone, too. After a few minutes of role-playing, I set off for our safe deposit box in Danbury, call our insurance agent, and tote quite a bit of manuscript and correspondence out to the tool house. My wife orders more extinguishers for strategic spots, rearranges the attic, and takes inflammable matter out of the room where the oil burner operates.

For years we had *talked* about the possibility of our house burning down, but we never did much about it until we pictured, with some emotion, the smoke rising from the ruins. "That's a well-built chimney, anyhow; it's still standing. . . ." We began to wonder if the State Department might possibly role-play the Politbureau.

The National Education Association reports a school superintendent who got ready for a drastic change in policy by role-playing, and a music teacher who uses it at home, the better to face his classes. A mothers' club employs it to examine the possibilities of keeping teen-age daughters at home nights—at least some nights. A mother playing the daughter's role fascinates all members.

A public health official employs it to train his personnel along the lines of the Chicago salesmen's course.

The committee responsible for a big national conference gets ready for the ordeal by pretending to be in the midst of it. As a result, a number of bugs in the plans show up for correction before the meeting, instead of post-mortem.

Balance Sheet

One of the general meetings at Bethel dealt with role-playing and showed motion pictures of psycho-drama in action. Leland Bradford, as chairman, warned us that the technique was good only in specific situations and if misapplied could be more confusing than the problem it was trying to clear up. In favorable situations, however, he said, we might look for the following results:

Role-playing helps us to see what is before us in a more vivid way than is possible by "talking it over."

It gives us a chance to try something *without the chips down*. In real life we have only one chance; in role-playing we have a number of chances with no risk and, like Tom in high school, can experiment with alternatives.

It can help communication, especially when a group stalls because members do not see their subject clearly and talk *past* each other. Role-playing can bring the subject back into focus.

It can break the ice in a group and help members participate more freely.

It furthers agreement by putting us in the other fellow's shoes.

To Bradford's expert testimony I should like to add a few more comments of my own, for what they are worth:

Role-playing has a number of dimensions, depending on whether you are acting or watching and how close the situations and problems are to your own life. The critics who compare it to charades, or a simple rehearsal or a child's game, are seeing it only in one dimension. They also overlook the educational function of these age-old activities.

As a spectator you become more involved, as a rule, than in an ordinary discussion. You see people out there instead of in your mind, and their problem immediately becomes more vivid. As an actor, of course, you identify still more closely.

Trying out contingencies in your own future, as when we burned our house down, may have a clear practical value. Taking the role of somebody else, however, and trying to feel the way he feels, as Jack and Betty did in playing the union leader and his wife, can be a great extension of experience. The group dynamics people are most interested in this approach because of its bearing on social problems. Role-playing comes easy to children as we all know, and adults usually recapture it without too much trouble, unless they are badly inhibited. But children do not think much how other people *feel;* this takes a more mature imagination.

From these demonstrations we can draw up a spiral scale of experience and learning, from words at the circumference to full experience at the center. Reading is a first step, provided one has had experience enough with real things to make the words meaningful. Thinking about what one has read is the next. Writing down the high points of what one has read helps get the subject in. Talking it over with a person who knows the subject helps some more. A group discussion can bring us nearer in many cases. Role-playing, as we have seen, takes us still closer. Best of all is to get one's hands and muscles into it, as well as one's mind and emotions—the whole psychosomatic apparatus.

When one comes to think of it, this is the way that children used to learn to cope with life before we locked them up in schoolhouses.

CHAPTER ELEVEN

In Conference

"I'M SORRY, but Mr. Smithers is in conference."

Assuming that this statement is not a maneuver to allow Mr. Smithers to take an after-luncheon nap, what is he doing in conference? Is he laying it on the line as Chairman of the Board? Is he saying, "That strikes me as very sound," if somebody else is Chairman? Is he in the middle of verbal battle or staring at his fingernails utterly bored?

In short, is Mr. Smithers in the kind of group discussion where the energy said to be locked up in people is getting out? It is doubtful. Outside of a formal debate, there are few better ways to waste human energy than the run-of-the-mine conference, whether in business, government, a faculty meeting, or anywhere else. Here is a summary that would fit a thousand conferences[1]:

The chairman presents the topic, some questions are asked, some objections raised. Old Mr. Meadows goes into a long, rambling reminiscence about the old days when things were better. There is a scraping of chairs. . . . Someone cracks a joke; someone takes a pot shot at the idea of a fellow member . . . Someone says: But we've got to get this thing settled! Someone else says we ought to get down to fundamentals—but nobody is clear about what the fundamentals are. Someone looks at his watch and says he has to go. He suggests that the question be left to the chairman to decide. There is a chorus of ayes and a rush for the door.

[1] By Thomas Fansler, whose description I have slightly abridged and paraphrased. It appears in his admirable book, *Creative Power through Discussion*, on which I have drawn throughout this chapter.

The meeting has taken an hour and half for eighteen people, or a total of twenty-seven man-hours—more than three working days. We are just beginning to learn how to save some of this wasted time.

Parallel with the development of group dynamics, although starting a few years earlier, has grown a somewhat less scientific but more immediately practical study of conference techniques. If the reader wants advice on how to conduct a discussion group in his town, he had better go to these people rather than to Bethel. But Bethel keeps feeding research results to the practitioners. Indeed, it is difficult sometimes to untangle the two movements. We might say the group dynamics people are more interested in theory but do a lot of practical work, while the conference people are more interested in practical work, like adult education, but welcome theoretic contributions which can help them along. There is some conflict between the two schools, but at last accounts they were drawing closer.

Back in the 1920's I happened to belong to one of the early experimental groups, led by my friend Eduard C. Lindeman. He had been working with other pioneers, especially Mary P. Follett and Alfred Sheffield, in the objective study of conference techniques which was just beginning. He wanted to try out some ideas in a cooperative organization in New York in which we were both interested. I remember the meetings as stimulating but a little puzzling. Lindeman also edited *The Inquiry*, a magazine devoted to group consensus.

Harry Overstreet has been interested in conference techniques for many years in connection with his outstanding work in adult education. Other pioneers and leaders include Frank Walser, M. L. Wilson, Louis Brownlow, Winifred Fisher, and of course Fansler. By keen observation, trial and error, and good hard thinking, these students have made an important contribution to the reduction of conflict in face-to-face groups.

Charles W. Ferguson in his book, *A Little Democracy Is a Dangerous Thing*, maintains that discussion groups can become the heart of the democratic process. The cracker barrel has gone, the vast mechanisms of mass communication have all but replaced independent conversation, if not independent judgment, in America. Yet citizens must participate, he says, in forming opinion on public questions if democracy is to survive. He is right.

Here in America, unlike Stalin's Russia or Hitler's Germany, it is not standard practice to be told what to think. Such compulsion from above Lindeman calls a "linear response"—with the wayfaring citizen at the bottom of the line and Der Fuehrer bellowing into a microphone at the top. Discussion in which the citizen can himself participate Lindeman calls a "circular response." The term suggests a round table, with conferees considering public questions—say the Marshall Plan, inflation, the Japanese peace treaty.

Since 1946 there has been a resurgence of community discussion groups. They have been encouraged by various national organizations, for instance, the League of Women Voters. "Discussion," says a League pamphlet, "gives an individual a chance to say what he thinks, to feel that he belongs to his community, and that his opinion counts." . . . And *her* opinion. Discussion groups modify extreme views by finding a median; they demonstrate that experience is often as important as factual information in solving problems. The League is promoting them energetically all over the country, both for clarifying political opinions and for recommending action.

Things go along splendidly, the League observes, until Mrs. Brown gets on her feet and says: "My husband's aunt knows a very fascinating man whose daughter had an experience which isn't exactly pertinent to our topic this afternoon but is very interesting all the same. She went to this hospital. . . ." Nothing short of chloroform can stop Mrs. Brown when she is fairly launched, but a good group leader will be on the alert to forestall personal reminiscences unless they bear on the topic.

A Police Force for the United Nations

My wife has been attending a League discussion group of about twelve women in our Connecticut town. The topic is the plan proposed by the State Department in the fall of 1950 for a standing

United Nations police force ready to stop an aggressor on twenty-four hours' notice—or at least try to stop him.

The members began by exchanging information, with the help of an excellent resource person, about the proposal and its provisions as compared with the original U.N. charter. Questions of fact which no one could answer were assigned to volunteers to look up. The leader then asked for expressions of opinion, and many of these took the form of questions:

"Would we want our sons to serve on such an international police force?"

"Suppose the boys were sent on a mission which the United States disapproved of . . ."

"Couldn't our delegate in the U.N. veto such a mission?"

"Has the U.N. ever made our government do something it didn't want to?"

"Well, why not? Wouldn't it be a useful experience and prove that we could take our own medicine?"

Between individual members there was some polite disagreement but more often a sudden fellow-feeling when one member would answer another's question or express her attitude. A remark that made everyone laugh produced an immediate increase in unity, or "cohesiveness" as we say in Bethel. At times the group would find itself thinking *as a group*—in a kind of spiral rather than the slow progression of one mind—a stimulating and exhilarating experience, with dynamic possibilities.

Ferguson suggests an international experiment. Nearly all the democracies now have machinery for carrying on discussion groups such as the above. Suppose an important topic were selected for *all* democracies to consider—say the very question which our local Women Voters were concerned with, namely a U.N. police force. Suppose a consensus of groups in all nations indicated wide popular support for a specific way to set up the police force and put it in motion. Ferguson would then have this grass roots consensus presented to every government, to the United Nations, to UNESCO, and other international bodies. He would have publicity avenues ready to get it before the people of the whole world—not the democracies alone.

Not all questions could be so handled, but the experiment deserves a trial. A people's solution for a world problem!

Philadelphia Story

Here is another discussion group, mostly men this time, which has been meeting regularly since 1943 in Philadelphia. The first sessions were organized by Standard Oil of New Jersey as an experiment in finding out whether people of widely different backgrounds and points of view could discuss controversial public questions without becoming incandescent. Also officials of the company wanted to get closer to the community.

Bankers, labor leaders, business men, clergymen, a farmer or two, lawyers, educators, government officials, are among the members. Sometimes an outsider is invited to lead the discussion, but usually it is self-generated. It took about two years to make a well-adjusted group, but now members are ready to discuss practically anything. On the agenda we find such topics as full employment, pressure groups, inflation, foreign policy, taxes, budgets, loyalty, public housing, pensions.

At the end of one of the early meetings, a business man pulled the cigar out of his mouth and said: "There's no point in my coming to these things. These professors and these ministers talk over my head, and it all sounds like a lot of nonsense to me." But he stuck it out, and gradually the group found its medium of communication. It was a great day when it was strong enough to welcome members from the C.I.O. and A.F. of L.

Discussion is often hot, but never to the bursting point. Opposing cliques do not form. Perhaps the hottest argument in seven years was over the topic, "What does it mean to be loyal to America?" When the signing of non-communist affidavits under the Taft-Hartley law came up, the room was in an uproar! But nothing broke apart; the group structure held solidly. "We have seen a change come over the feelings of labor and management toward each other," says Charlotte Lochhead, the efficient executive secretary. Early suspicions, she says, have melted out.

At the meeting which I attended, dinner was served in a private dining room of one of the big downtown Philadelphia hotels. The tables were arranged in horseshoe shape with a smaller table inside the enclosure, so that each of the twenty-five diners could talk to at least five people. The leader, at the head of the horseshoe, was a professor of sociology. On my right was a labor man, opposite me a vice-president of a big company, a few places to the left a high city official who happened to be a Negro. As in Bethel, we were on a first-name basis.

The leader introduced old-age pensions as the topic for the evening—a red-hot question in the spring of 1950, when unions were striking more for pension plans than for wage raises. Immediately a corporation executive picked up the ball, with a C.I.O. man close behind him.

For two hours the discussion surged back and forth. All the members took part, as well as a visitor or two. No punches were pulled, but I noted only one emotional outburst when two members got into an argument over joint contributions by company and worker to pension funds. It did not last long and had no hint of personal rancor.

It so happened that I had been making an independent study of industrial pension systems at the time and had spent two months investigating what seemed to be the major points—financial, psychological, historical, sociological. *Every single one of those points came out in that two-hour discussion!* Yet no one there was a pension expert. It would be hard to discover a better illustration of the wealth to be found in group experience!

This dinner and discussion in Philadelphia had points in common with my training group at Bethel. But the latter was a laboratory looking inward; the former, a going concern looking outward. Perhaps Bethel is training leaders to organize groups like Philadelphia and get even more participation out of them.

The Art of Listening

If ten persons are discussing around a table, and the situation is under reasonable control so that only one person is talking at a time, it follows that 90 per cent of all man-hours are spent in listening. If you are there and do your share, you will be listening 90 per cent of your time. Fansler calls good listening the number one rule of human relations. This may be a bit strong; but good communication is certainly close to the number one rule, and that implies two-way traffic: clear talking and good listening. If both parties are talking at once the line will foul. If people stop listening, it is useless to talk—something which has yet to impress itself upon politicians.

One way to test your listening powers—but not in conference, please—is to tell a third person what Mr. Smithers has said. An excellent listening habit in conference is to concentrate on *what* is being said rather than on *who* says it. It is so easy to discount a kernel of real wisdom because we do not like the man who delivers it, or his wife, or his brother-in-law.

Listening can be a powerful weapon in taming a conversational monopolist. Do not contradict him, do not argue with him, do not say a word. Just listen. The monopolist normally runs out of fuel in about six minutes, according to Fansler's calculations, especially if he talks against a fathomless silence. His confidence sapped, his security undermined, he wavers to an unsteady climax—after which he is likely to be a listener himself for a while. This checks with Hayakawa's cocktail argument in Chapter 1, where the labor-baiting gentleman was halted in his tracks and ultimately mollified by polite listening.

Winifred Fisher in early 1950 conducted two "listening clinics" on behalf of the New York Adult Education Council. One member will read while the others around the table concentrate on what he is saying. Later they will summarize what they have heard and compare notes. It seems to do them good. A member reports: "I kept from firing my bookkeeper by taking him out to lunch and listening to him—something I had never done before." A teacher said that the course in listening had enabled him to conduct his classes more interestingly and to bring out more participation. . . . At a rough guess, one hundred million Americans would benefit by attending Miss Fisher's clinics.

Some Helpful Hints

If you want to run a face-to-face conference, the experts, from Lindeman to Fisher, can give you plenty of good advice. They have been testing procedures in thousands of meetings over the years. In what remains of our chapter it is impossible to reproduce all their conclusions. The interested reader is urged to go to the sources suggested at the end of the book, or better still, enroll in a well-designed discussion group and learn techniques at first hand.

We can, however, set down a few outstanding findings, as a sample of what the conference experts recommend. Some of it, you will note, parallels Bethel; some is plain common sense probably going back to ancient Babylon.

Four Goals

Face-to-face groups are a poor way for passing out prepared information rapidly; a lecture or radio talk is much better. They are a poor medium for demonstrating how to do something, like tying an underwriter's knot. The method is useless for staff meetings where Mr. Big has all the answers worked out in advance. Indeed, the conference method is useless if anybody knows all the answers, for a good conference is a machine to find new answers by feeding the cumulative experience of members through it.

Conferences can help in at least four situations:

1. In solving problems where group judgment is superior to individual. *Example:* the Lilienthal-Acheson drafting committee, or a managerial staff.

2. In making decisions after full discussion and fact finding. *Examples:* a jury; a Quaker business meeting; an undominated Board of Directors.

3. In discussing public questions. *Examples:* the Philadelphia group just described; the League of Women Voters' groups; Mr. Ferguson's proposal.

4. In learning new mental skills. *Examples:* listening clinics; many college classes.

Structure of the Meeting

If you decide to organize a discussion group, here are a few points to bear in mind:

In choosing topics, with the help of your members, try to avoid meaningless questions of the type: *Has Democracy Failed? Is Heredity More Important than Environment?* Such questions are meaningless because they are so vague that no operations can be performed to answer them. Argument accordingly can go on forever in a verbalized vacuum. More productive are topics which have answers, of the type: *Do We Need a New School in Our Town? What Steps Might the United Nations Take in Korea? What Are the Available Methods for Controlling Inflation?*

Twenty members are enough; ten to fifteen are often better. Buzz groups of four or five sometimes help.

The more informality, consistent with good manners, the better. Forced good fellowship, however, may boomerang.

It has been found better to be either on a first-name or last-name basis. To mix them invites cliques or the suspicion of cliques.

Members should sit where they can see every other member, preferably with *no* special chair for the leader. Place cards with names, as at Bethel, are useful to begin with. A blackboard may be helpful

Two hours seem to be about as much as the human mind will stand of close conference involvement.

In a deadlock, a ten-minute recess sometimes helps. Some group are also beginning to experiment with a Quaker-like period of silent concentration.

If emotions run high and sides begin to form, the "ice box" idea may be in order. Put the topic—or that particular part of it—in cold storage until the next meeting.

Experience shows that consensus is better than voting. A vote immediately operates to split the group into winners and losers.

Where complicated public questions are being discussed, say "full employment" or "juvenile delinquency," it has been demonstrated that a "resource person" can help. He—or she—should be purely a walking Britannica, *not* a policy-maker telling the group what to think.

And here is a structural hint, apparently serious, from Mr. Ernest Bevin, in London. After a lifetime of conferences he concludes that meetings held in dark brown rooms generally fail, while those in rooms with cheerful yellow walls, generally succeed! I could find no confirmation of this, however, in the monographs of the experts.

Hints for Leaders

The democratic-permissive type of leader is best in most cases. He does not push people around but feels himself a member, learning as they learn. Some authorities say he should be both inside and outside the group, that is, both involved and detached. He must keep members from straying too far from the topic, and foresee trouble coming.

One way to avoid even the *semblance* of autocracy is for the leader to use questions rather than statements. "I wonder if we have quite covered the financial cost of old-age pensions" is better than: "Costs are important; nobody has adequately discussed them."

The leader can make no worse mistake than using ridicule. No matter how erring a member seems to be, to ridicule him will normally cause a group to gang up solidly against its leader. At which point it is a good structural idea for everybody to go home.

There are various signs of approaching conflict which a leader learns to recognize. An increase in formal politeness is one—"Mister Jones" instead of "Ed." Switching from an opinion to a person is another sign, the argument *ad hominem*. A member folding his arms with some ostentation may be another.

Incipient controversies may often be quenched with facts. Quarrels are hard to start on the factual level but burn like prairie fires on the opinion level. But the experts find that a flaring up of argument, a sharp word or two, may prevent an explosion.

A "feed-back" now and then is a good idea: "Let's see where we've got to; could we summarize the discussion so far something like this? Are we agreed on these main points?"

Every leader has three problem cases to watch for: (1) Napoleons who want to take the meeting over; (2) shy people who are too self-conscious to participate; (3) what Fansler calls "persuaders," who want to sell a ready-made package wrapped in cellophane. The classic case of the last is of course the man at the funeral who remarked that if everybody was through talking about the deceased, he would like to say a few words about the Single Tax.

A good leader throws these problem children out of the meeting only as a last recourse. Far better to keep them in and try to involve them, as we did with our Napoleon at Bethel. The listening technique may help. The shy member can be asked a question which is not too difficult and then congratulated on his answer. This may serve to get him interested. Sometimes, the shy member has more to contribute than anyone there.

Hints for Group Members

The conference experts have some general hints for anyone attending a face-to-face group. Never come to the table, they say, with your mind made up. Always expect something *new* to come out of the discussion, something you have not thought of before, something which nobody present had thought of before. It may or may not come, but looking for it may help it come.

Try to get away from "I think" to "we think."

Make a special effort to employ that 90 per cent of your time in the art of good listening.

Come to the meeting expecting every member to contribute something important out of the wealth of his own experience. Expect it to be as important, perhaps, as anything you have to contribute When you can achieve this attitude, you will be getting pretty close to what democracy really means.

Business Men, Union Men, Farmers

These powerful pressure groups in the U.S. are supposed to be locked in eternal conflict, each trying to draw away from the others a preponderant share of the national income. The popular conception is not too distorted, for a pull and haul is actually going on. But the National Planning Association at Washington has demonstrated that it is not irreconcilable and that agreement is possible on some things at some levels.

A series of pertinent and controversial public questions has come before three standing committees of the N.P.A. in joint session, representing business, labor, and agriculture. On all the questions, with one exception, a joint report has been signed by the majority. Sometimes, as in the case of the Supreme Court, a dissenting opinion will be filed, but on the whole, the extent of agreement has been phenomenal.

Here, by way of example, is the contentious matter of social security, the heart of the so-called "welfare state." Early in 1944 the N.P.A. committees gathered to discuss all phases of it. There were nineteen members in the agricultural committee, headed by Theodore W. Schultz and James G. Patton; seventeen members in the business committee, headed by David C. Prince and Beardsley Ruml; twenty-two members in the labor committee, headed by Clinton S. Golden and Marion H. Hedges. Not all members were present, but all went over the agenda.

The atmosphere of the meeting was friendly, a cocktail, a good dinner, no seating in blocs. The meeting began with a cautious statement of principles on which everybody could agree—though hardly so cautious as the famous formula: "We can all agree that the world is round!" An initial agreement orients the minds of those present in a common direction at the very start. After several days of discussion, a statement about social security was finally evolved, including a list of some twenty facts, observations and suggestions. Among them:

The costs of unemployment have to be met by society somehow.

Insecurity is feared by most Americans.

Social insurance applies the sound principle of pooling risks.

Knowledge about the business cycle is still scanty.

A social security program is not a substitute for full employment but it helps.

U.S. social security laws in 1944 are inadequate and revision is in order.

The whole concept needs more attention and more participation by citizens at the local level. "Social security measures are of such vital importance that no democracy can afford to remain in ignorance of the problem, or relinquish control to a bureaucracy."

Only two of the fifty-eight members failed to sign the joint report. A few others put in qualifying footnotes. The whole was a typical case of the National Planning Association's technique. Said Chairman H. Christian Sonne: "In spite of the technical complexities of social security, and differing viewpoints, it is nevertheless possible for men and women of goodwill to weigh the alternatives and work out a realm of agreement."

The N.P.A. three-ply committees prove once and for all that under suitable conditions people of widely opposing views can get together on the most controversial matters. Obviously, something is very wrong with the ways and means by which the Taft-Hartley Act, the farm aid bills, health insurance, are being considered. They, and many similar public questions, have fallen into a dichotomy of Absolute Right versus Absolute Wrong, accompanied by emotions at the boiling point. If we had thousands of local committees all over the country considering such questions after the N.P.A. manner of looking for agreement, the story might be very different. Their deliberations would seep into the stream of national public opinion, into the press, and into Congress, and so we might avoid a good part of the blind emotion while getting much more practical and speedy legislation.

"Feed-back"[2] on the Study of Groups

For six chapters now we have been watching groups of people in action, mostly face-to-face groups where it is possible to call everybody by his first name. We began by going to a Quaker meeting. We watched the Lilienthal committee formulating its famous plan, college freshmen writing themes for their fellows instead of for the instructor, the minute articulation of a symphony orchestra. We looked at the tough, tightly bound squads which form in the air force and the infantry under combat conditions. We glanced briefly at the oldest and toughest of all human groups, the monogamous family.

We followed the development of the scientific school of group dynamics at M.I.T., Harvard, and elsewhere, and spent an arduous and stimulating week with the National Training Laboratory at Bethel. We examined the new technique of role-playing. We watched a discussion group in Philadelphia, the National Planning Association's three-ply conference, and summarized some of the practical conclusions of the conference experts. In the next chapter we shall find additional evidence of the power of face-to-face groups in factories, a power which management is only beginning to appreciate.

We find the whole field in a state of extraordinary activity; even the Quakers are writing monographs on how they do it. We find some absurdities, some danger of cults forming, a good deal of lost motion, possibly too much paper work. But obviously something of great importance is going on. The over all generalization is as simple as it is perhaps profound: *Group dynamics and group study are directing people's attention to the deepest source of human energy: interaction with their fellows.*

In the belief systems of the West, the primary accent is laid on the individual standing alone. His sins and his triumphs have been

---

[2] Norbert Wiener in his *Human Use of Human Beings* gives us this definition: 'The feed-back principle means that behavior is scanned for its result, and that the success or failure of this result modifies future behavior."

judged apart from both his biological inheritance and the culture which has molded him. Such evaluation overlooks his real needs, his drives, and his goals. It is a back eddy. Group dynamics returns the study to the main stream. At the moment we are beating our way out of the eddy in some confusion, but already we catch a glimpse of the broad river beyond.

CHAPTER TWELVE

What Makes Workers Work?

HERE is the American culture today, a seamless web of human relations, changing under the impact of technology but, like all human cultures, fiercely resisting change. Here are a lot of people in the American culture gathered in places called factories. They do not check their culture with their raincoats in the lockers. They take it right in to the bench and the desk—the whole apparatus of customs, habits, and beliefs. And they proceed to adapt to this new and on the whole cramping and unnatural environment, alongside the machines, as best they can. Sometimes with great ingenuity they restrict their work patterns to what they consider right and reasonable, which may not be what their employer considers right and reasonable.

In many shops one is likely to find a tough, competent work group superintending production, as in the Bank Wiring room at Hawthorne, and limiting it to what the group thinks is a fair standard. Of the sixty million persons gainfully employed in the United States, a large proportion are in such work groups. They are the ultimate masters of the plant, for they control the tempo of work. Frederick W. Taylor, the father of scientific management, tells us how he collided with this principle as early as 1878.

Outside this tight, well-articulated organism, informal and spontaneous, a product of both human nature and the culture, stand the worried managers. Without understanding it very well, they appeal to stop-watch men, to industrial psychologists, personnel experts, to work out plans to stop malingering and get out more production.

A great deal of the conflict in factories can be ascribed to assumptions by management about workers and what makes them work, assumptions which may be shaky or sometimes positively untrue. Many of the assumptions of workers, meanwhile, about the company and the boss are equally dubious. The parties often do not understand each other, their minds do not meet. It was his concern about such misunderstandings which led Elton Mayo to say that better labor relations were really a problem in communication.

Russian Factories

From all reports, the Russians do no better in their factories, despite their slogans about the sovereignty of the worker. The management there seems to be as orthodox as that of Sewell Avery at Montgomery Ward. Russia never had a Mayo or a Lewin to analyze a work group or a Joseph Scanlon to organize it on principles of real worker participation.

The Soviet foreman's only job is to see that production goals are fulfilled. He is an agent of the plant manager. The manager must make a profit because his job depends on the books showing it, so the foreman in turn must produce the department quota or lose *his* job. To become a foreman, a worker must be a pace-setter. The training is almost wholly technical. There is no recognition of training in handling men, and no literature to keep foremen abreast of industrial developments.[1]

In handling men, American factories are ahead of Russian factories on two counts: they have begun a scientific study of what makes workers work, and they are also more democratic in their relations between officials and workers. When John D. Littlepage, the Alaskan mining engineer, took the technical job of head of the Gold Trust in the 1930's, he tells us how shocked he was at the behavior of young Soviet engineers. They would not go deep under-

[1] Report by an advisory service, the Labor Relations Institute, *New York Times*, September 12, 1948.

ground, even in a crisis, and get themselves covered with mud and help the miners repair a break, as Littlepage himself would do and always had done at home. No, their gloves must be kept spotless and their white collar status unimpaired. He found a much more rigid line between men and management than in America.

By and large, American, Russian, and all the world's factories have been run on the autocratic system, with orders coming down from above and detailed schedules of rewards and punishments. "Theirs not to reason why . . ." has been the general policy.

Some factory managers in America, however, and to a degree in Britain, have begun to wonder in the last few years if they have not overlooked the most important factor of all in production, namely, a man's interest in his job. Social scientists and practical administrators are on the point of officially recognizing the strongest engine of all for improving human relations, not to mention increasing output, in the energy of a worker who feels that his human wants are being met.

Research for the Navy

We have looked in earlier chapters at some of the work of Mayo, Lewin, McGregor, Knickerbocker, Bavelas. Now let us summarize briefly an ambitious new program of research in human relations in industry. It is still going on as I write, and though conclusions are still tentative, they tend to confirm the earlier work. This project is sponsored by the Office of Naval Research, presumably in the hope that more knowledge about human relations will make a better navy, with better interactions between officers and enlisted men.

The first contracts were awarded in 1947, and the University of Michigan is doing a substantial part of the work through two research organizations, staffed by such scientists as Dorwin Cartwright, Rensis Likert, Daniel Katz, and Angus Campbell. Workers and managers in the following organizations are under study, with the active co-operation of the companies themselves and in some cases the unions, too:

Detroit Edison Company
Studebaker Company
Prudential Insurance Company
Caterpillar Tractor Company
Chesapeake and Ohio Railway
A large government office

Later research will include labor union groups and other voluntary membership organizations. The findings, some of which I was allowed to see in mimeograph, will eventually be published.

The research aims at discovering the causes of group morale and productivity. What things make an organization most effective and yield most satisfaction to its members?

One important conclusion suggested by the work so far is the greater power in the *teamwork approach*, contrasted with the autocratic or man-to-man system. The traditional factory all over the world, as we have just noted, uses the latter. Starting at the top, the manager supervises his subordinates as individuals, and so on down the line of command. Each subordinate tends to identify himself with only *part* of the task, not with the overall job. Team spirit is not as a rule developed by this formal organization, but competition and conflict often are. This requires further precise job definition as functions become rigid and hard to change.

Informal groups may also develop, the Michigan researchers point out, to set goals counter to the formal goals of management. Most workers will not work as lonely individuals if they can help it; groups will form with leaders, rules, goals. If management ignores this need in its formal organization, there will be a boomerang in the informal organization.

"We are all members of the same team," says the vice-president of the XYZ Company at the annual picnic of the drop forge department—and he probably means it. But this amiable stereotype is a long way from the dynamic teams which social scientists are finding in industry. Here are some further conclusions suggested by the Michigan studies:

Clerical Workers

First-line supervisors, in the sections which turn out the most clerical work, were found to be more interested in their men than in production as such—"employee-centered" rather than "production-centered" is the technical phraseology. These supervisors give the people under them a share in making decisions; and they have more initiative themselves and less close supervision from the echelons above. That is, workers and supervisors who have something to say about the conditions of their work turn out more clerical work than those whose every action is prescribed in advance. "When the individual comes to identify himself with his job and the work of his group, human resources are much more fully utilized in the production process."

Most of us believe that free labor is more productive than slave labor, but often we do not extend the principle beyond the removal of the barbed wire or the leg chain. This is not the place to stop, as the Michigan studies show. Better morale and output result if working groups are motivated by impulses *inside* themselves than if they are admonished from *outside*. It helps, furthermore, to give the worker a clear picture of the total job, so that he knows where he fits in. If he only has a picture of a little piece of the job, he does not do well.

Public Utility

In its public utility study, more than eight thousand workers have been included so far by the Michigan scientists. One conclusion was: the higher the skill and the more varied the task, the better the morale. Another: the smaller the group the higher the morale. Morale improved under employee-centered supervisors who welcomed ideas and suggestions. It improved if employees were given opportunity to work at the things they excelled in. It went up markedly if they were allowed to *complete* tasks rather than being interrupted in the middle.

Railroad

Section gangs on a railroad were studied in matched pairs. Variety of work and a chance to use one's skill made for high production. Foremen who bawled out their men got relatively poor production. By and large, the conclusions about this unskilled manual work paralleled the earlier conclusions about clerical and office work. Blue collar and white collar reacted the same way.

These studies all suggest that when supervisors involve employees in the entire task of the work group, when they give general rather than detailed, driving supervision, there is a better chance of achieving high production. . . . This pattern has been recognized in creative work, in the arts and professions, and to some extent in education. It has *not* been recognized in the ordinary work situation. Surely if these results have been obtained with people performing relatively unskilled clerical and manual operations, it would seem reasonable to suppose that the findings will be even more highly applicable in skilled work situations.

It is significant that the five private companies studied are adding substantial amounts to the funds given by the navy. They trust these Michigan scientists and believe that their conclusions will help morale, productivity, and earnings.

Resistance to Change

How can other managers be persuaded to bring their industrial operations closer to these findings? Michigan is also looking into this vital matter of applied engineering. Alvin Zander recalls the story of the TVA agricultural experts who were explaining new techniques to an old farmer up in the hills. He listened intelligently and readily agreed that plowing on the contour was a good idea; so was crop rotation, and so was the use of phosphate. "But," he said, "I don't do it that way."

Human beings often show a granite-like resistance to change, and this serves a very good purpose for survival. If culture were always changing they would have no opportunity to develop automatic habits. Suppose the American culture pattern shifted to driving on the left and using green as a stoplight; suppose that a few months later it shifted back again. We would go crazy—those of us who were still alive! But in spite of this healthy resistance, change is always in process and sometimes needs to be hastened. Scientists are discovering techniques for reducing resistance to industrial change.

Tell Them in Advance

If workers are consulted or at least told in advance about changes which are going to affect them, there is less likely to be a shop explosion. A good example is the story of the new Negro worker in a munitions plant.[2]

Supervisor Powell, who has taken the Job Relations course at the War Manpower Commission, is summoned one day to the front office. The manager says a Negro mechanic has been hired and will report for duty next Monday. There are explosive possibilities here, for no Negro has ever worked in the plant before. Powell swallows his dismay and studies his Job Relations card, which reads: "Tell workers in advance about changes affecting them." He talks to the other supervisors in his department and also to the "natural leaders" among the rank and file. President Roosevelt, he reminds them, has asked for less racial discrimination to help win the war. The company's contract with the government carries a clause for employing Negroes. The new man is a fine mechanic, and the shop, as they all know, is short of mechanics. There is, of course, a storm. Supervisor Powell gives the shop plenty of opportunity to blow off steam—always a good idea and especially when changes are coming.

On Sunday Powell goes around to see the mechanic at his home and carefully explains the situation. The mechanic will be the first Negro ever to work for the company. Will he please remember to

2 Reported in the author's book, *Men at Work*, where the Job Relations program of the TWI is discussed.

be on his best behavior, not only for his own sake, but for the sake of future workers?

On Monday morning the Negro mechanic checks in. He is dignified and careful. The shop, after a few uneasy hours, accepts him; there are no explosions at all. But if he had come in cold, without the skillful preparation by Supervisor Powell, almost anything could have happened.

An even surer way to facilitate a change is to get workers to discuss the new proposal *themselves* and to help directly in its final formulation. Then the change becomes "our" plan, not something which "they" are going to put over on us.[3] The necessity for some kind of group organization, if such proposals are to be discussed, is obvious, and a union is often the answer. If Supervisor Powell could have called a union meeting to ventilate the whole question of Negro workers in war plants, it might have made his task easier and reduced the risk to the vanishing point.

Self-starter Basis

The Michigan work for the navy, confirming and amplifying earlier studies, helps to correct a fundamental misconception about handling men, whether in industry, clerical work, the armed services, your own kitchen, or anywhere else. We might call it the donkey-and-carrot misconception. If people can get on a self-starter basis, they will enjoy the work more and produce more.

The business man or the laboratory head, says Norbert Wiener in his book, *The Human Use of Human Beings,* who "assigns each of his subordinates a particular problem and begrudges him the degree of thinking for himself which is necessary to move beyond this problem and perceive its relevance—both show that the democracy to which they pay their respects, is not really the order in which they prefer to live. The regularly ordered state of pre-assigned functions toward which they gravitate is the state of the ants." Ants are social animals, too, but most of their behavior is instinctive and mechanical.

[3] Alexander Bavelas describes the same principle in Chapter 8.

Hierarchical organizations, Wiener says, such as an army, the Russian state, and many businesses, condemn the human race to move at less than half-steam. They throw away the greater part of human variability. To be chained to the oar of a galley is not only degradation but a terrible waste of good human energy. To be chained to a shop or office where one has nothing to say about the conditions of one's work can be almost as great a waste.

"People Are Lazy"

Other classical assumptions about labor relations are in the process of being amended or refuted by social science research. One widely held doctrine is that most people are inherently lazy; they will not stir a finger unless they have to.

Biologists and social scientists have found solid evidence against this assumption. Man is not only a group animal, he is a working animal. But he likes to choose his work, pick his time, and feel that his labor amounts to something in itself. Few like mining coal underground very well; some cannot take the regimentation of an assembly line.

Here are some oil refinery workers being retired at sixty-five with adequate pensions. Financially they are all right, and within limits they can do anything they want or go anywhere they want—Florida, California. Are they happy? Not according to one of the older employees whom I interviewed:

It's really tragic, you know. So many of the fellows here don't want to think about the future. They'll have to be retired some time, and they'll miss their jobs, and the companionship of the men they've worked with so long. . . . For twenty, thirty, forty years they followed a routine, getting up at a certain hour, going to work, coming home, relaxing, reading the paper. . . . All of a sudden it stops! They get up in the morning and have nothing to do; nowhere to go.

After some annuitants suffered nervous breakdowns, the company began giving passes to let them go back to the old shop and enviously watch others doing what they are no longer allowed to do. It is also recruiting "old-age counselors" to help workers develop hobbies or even small businesses—preliminary to the dreadful ordeal of idleness.

"The weight of evidence from careful study," says Dr. Alexander Leighton, "is on the side of assuming that work is one of the enjoyed and rewarding human activities, and that most people under normal conditions actively seek it." If people won't work—and sometimes they won't—the trouble is probably with the job, not with the men. Instead of cussing the help, managers would do better to find out what causes the abnormal conditions, remedy them, and let the human drive to keep active assert itself.

Economic Man

A kindred assumption is the traditional doctrine of "economic man," which holds that pecuniary gain is what makes people work and get things done. It colors not only classical economics but a good deal of managerial thinking as well. Many labor leaders are wedded to it, too.

Mayo tested the assumption with the girls in the Relay room at Hawthorne, and with the men in the Bank Wiring room. The theory did not stand up. The bank wirers could have made a good deal more money if they had worked as lone individuals under the company bonus plan, but an informal group better satisfied their human wants. Money is only one of a number of motivations, and sometimes a minor one. It is not to be relied on as the sole incentive in running a modern business.

The Class Struggle

This doctrine is cardinal in the account of the world given by Karl Marx and perhaps the chief article of faith in the Kremlin one hundred years later. But anthropologists cannot find a class struggle in most societies. Ralph Linton, for instance, notes that class struggles, like religious struggles or racial struggles, will appear at certain times and places, especially in periods of rapid cultural change, as when the machine displaces hand labor. A more typical society down the ages, however, is one where each member enjoys a stable position, is satisfied with it, and shows profound resistance to changing it.

With the coming of the industrial revolution and the breaking up of old patterns, class struggles have been more frequent. But they tend to be local and temporary—a product of the introduction of the factory system, not a "universal" of human nature. If Linton, Herskovits, and other anthropologists are right about this, Marx is wrong, and the Kremlin has a very inaccurate map to steer by.

There is enough plausibility and temporary validity in the hypothesis of the class struggle to make a powerful appeal to certain people. Workers readily grasp at it when the future looks black and hopeless. In the savage depression of the 1930's, intellectuals all over the world made a cult of it—and have been streaming to the mourners' bench ever since. Labor leaders often base their strategy upon it, even if they have never read *Das Kapital*.

The class struggle is one of those half—no, 10 per cent—truths which have spread enormous mischief in the world, creating conflicts which otherwise might never have arisen. Society is *not* divided into two classes. Right now in America it is roughly divided into six classes, but they are in constant motion, with citizens going up and going down, like elevators in an office building.[4] Too many managers accept the Marxian assumption. They feel unrest and resentment in their workers and conclude it is directed against them, and represents an eternal condition. Workers must work and bosses must boss, and never the twain shall meet.

One of the Michigan studies shows how far from reality this assumption is. It was made in a large automobile plant, and three categories were intensively interviewed, with various cross checks: (1) rank-and-file workers; (2) company foremen; (3) union shop stewards. Says Daniel Katz in summarizing the survey:

The attitudes of rank-and-file workers clearly indicate a substantial basis for industrial peace. The great majority of workers see no fundamental conflict between the aims of the company and the aims of the union. Ninety per cent of them feel that union and management get along

---

4 See the studies of W. Lloyd Warner, especially the "Yankee City" series and "Jonesville, U.S.A."

either *fairly well* or *very well*. The dominant tendency among the men is to give credit both to union and to management for the good working relationship. . . . They see no essential reason why both management and the union cannot achieve their goals, but they recognize that each side may have to give up something in the process. . . . Only one in five says that union and management are not usually pulling together, and only one in five sees management primarily wrong, and the union primarily right. . . . The men in the plant thus show little of the ideology of class conflict.

But the conclusion is not quite so clear cut in the case of those who *lead* the men in the plant. Both company foremen and union shop stewards feel a wider gulf between worker and management than the men feel. "Conflict phases of union-management relations," says the report, "appear more sharply defined in the attitudes of the leadership groups than in the attitudes of the rank-and-file. Foremen are more class-conscious than shop stewards in this particular plant."

It is difficult to overestimate the importance of this study if it truly represents the rank and file of American organized workers. No such conclusion is warranted, of course, from the analysis of only one automobile plant, but it gives us a healthy indication of how a great many union men are likely to feel. We can be confident, furthermore, that if union people are relatively free from the ideology of the class struggle, non-union workers will be even more so. There are sixteen million union members in the U.S. work force and forty-five million unorganized, including farmers and the self-employed.

The Workers Share in Management

One final and comprehensive assumption of management is that workers and their unions have no place in administration. The first big challenge to this assumption came with the organization of the Amalgamated Clothing Workers Union a generation and more ago, when the union began actively to co-operate in a number of functions hitherto reserved to management, such as production quotas. An even broader challenge came with the Labor-Management Production Committees set up at the suggestion of Donald Nelson in

World War II. More than five thousand committees were organized in war plants, and perhaps a third of them really achieved joint responsibility for a number of plant functions. The rest were ceremonial paper plans, because either top management or top union officialdom were not interested. It was found that the plan worked best when high officials on each side became personally involved—a principle, incidentally, which has wide application.

The ice has now been broken. The assumption that workers have no business in helping to set the conditions of their work is on the way out. In the next chapter we will look at a number of cases where active participation by the workers in production has not only reduced conflict but reduced operating costs and increased output.

CHAPTER THIRTEEN

Conditions of Labor Peace

ALTHOUGH informal groups have always existed in factories, with their influence on morale and production, the formal groups called unions have been more conspicuous. Social scientists are at work here, too, and find the modern union often very different from the usual picture. Unions do not necessarily mean conflict—often the contrary.

There seems to be a regular progression from physical violence to accommodation, and then, in some cases, to active co-operation with management. Dr. Benjamin M. Selekman has identified eight varieties, or stations, of union-management relations along this road.

In the long run, he says, relations will be determined by collective bargaining between union and industry rather than by Wagner Acts, Taft-Hartley Acts, or similar legislation. Men and management must work it out together. As matters now stand there are four patterns of relationship where conflict is implicit, ready to break out at almost any moment. To begin on the lowest rung, there is what he calls:

1. *Containment-aggression,* where management accepts the union but tries to limit its activities to bargaining over hours and wages and nothing else. The union is pressing to expand its field of power; tension is always high and can become explosive. Then there is

2. *Class struggle ideology.* Here union leaders act on a Marxian line. They may co-operate with management as a matter of expediency or because left-wing officials tell them to for the moment—as in

World War II—but no real peace is possible. The union leaders, if not the rank and file, are committed by their ideology to the elimination of the managerial class, and the "dictatorship of the proletariat." This category is on the wane as both C.I.O. and A.F. of L. purge their red unions.

3. *Laissez faire ideology*—the class struggle in reverse, though not normally so violent. Many American managers, especially in the South, are committed to the proposition that unions have no place in a free society. Though they will deal with a union if they must, they are always looking for an opportunity to get rid of it, and real co-operation is again impossible. This group also seems to be declining.

4. *Power-bargaining.* By this Selekman means that the parties accept one another as a necessary evil but try to wrest from one another all the traffic will bear. When winter comes and coal is a bitter need, then call a strike! Base your strategy on the market. John L. Lewis, Caesar Petrillo, the dock organizations of the San Francisco Bay area, teamsters in various cities, are in this category— tough leaders on both sides, and tough bargainers. It is the relationship most likely to arouse public wrath, and is often followed by government intervention, as when the army takes over the coal mines.

Still following Selekman, we turn the corner from conflict to agreement. Note that these eight steps are not inevitable. Some can be skipped over.

5. *"Deals."* Here top union leaders and top management make a deal about wages and working conditions. The rank and file never know the details, and of course neither do the stockholders; stockholders are rarely supposed to know anything under our present business system. This is a pretty unreliable kind of co-operation, because if the rank and file do find out about the "deal," they may blow the roof off.

6. *Collusion,* which differs from a deal in two ways. First, the rank and file may know about it; co-operation with employers may

go far beyond the setting of wages and hours. Second, management
and union may jointly seize control of the market, administering
quotas, prices, quality, whatnot, in an airtight monopoly. Collusion
reaches its finest flowering in the building trades, and Thurman
Arnold has given us complete documentation in his *Bottlenecks of
Business*. It certainly reduces labor conflict, but at the cost of the
public—sometimes a very high and fancy cost. The government is
likely to move in here too, under the Sherman Act.

7. *Accommodation*. This term seems to have been invented by
Selekman, and I find it very useful, not only for labor disputes, but
for other conflicts. Perhaps two parties cannot agree completely, but
hopefully they can understand each other's point of view and accommodate their activities. Such a possibility is the chief hope in international relations where there is no immediate prospect of reconciling sovereign states. Such is the hope between Russia and the United
States, as matters stand.

In labor relations, accommodation means that while unions and
management distrust one another, while they still hold rigidly to the
traditional items for collective bargaining, such as hours, wages, and
washrooms, they have become used to one another and "interact
comfortably within a familiar pattern of behavior." Live and let
live. In accommodation, hope has been abandoned of liquidating
your opponent.

8. *Co-operation* or the Promised Land—to which accommodation
has often been the threshold. Gradually the old distrusts melt out,
and each side comes to believe in the other's good faith. They grow
so secure in one another's company that they can go beyond the
traditional items of collective bargaining. They jointly consider
matters of production, solvency, elimination of waste, introduction
of new machines, and so on. "The union accepts managerial problems as being of concern to labor; management recognizes its stake
in stable, effective unionism; together they dispose of problems as
they arise." The needle trades, says Selekman, are the outstanding
example of co-operation. The Amalgamated Clothing Workers
would never attack the Hickey-Freeman Company or Hart, Schaffner

and Marx as "profit-swollen corporations" or "greedy exploiters." The union is pledged to keeping the company solvent, while the employer is pledged to union participation in certain well-defined functions of management. We shall look at some actual cases in a moment.

Selekman warns that stage eight will not arrive tomorrow for most American companies. Given the suddenness of union growth in this country and the enduring rivalry between the C.I.O. and A.F. of L., accommodation appears to be the more realistic and promising objective. We shall do well, he thinks, if we can get accommodation over the greater part of industry in the next ten years—say by 1960.

He has given us a blunt, factual description of how unions and employers interact in America today. "Containment-aggression" is the worst stage, and "co-operation" is the best. As he says, the needle trades, both the International Ladies' Garment Workers and the Amalgamated Clothing Workers, have long operated in stage eight, which they entered soon after World War I.

Various other unions, companies, and social scientists are experimenting with participation plans. Before describing the Amalgamated in action, I should like to tell you about Joseph Scanlon. He has been a business executive, a union leader; he is now a professor at M.I.T. He is a genius at helping unions and managers to work out of earlier stages and reach full participation. He tells me it began in this fashion:

Steel Mill

Here is a steel mill with two thousand workers near Pittsburgh, deep in the depression of the 1930's. The men have recently joined the new steel workers' union, but they are frightened about their jobs and the future. There are brief sit-down strikes, wild-cat strikes, and much turmoil and conflict. The president of the company has spent his life in building it up, has invested all his savings in it, and wants desperately to keep it going. So do the staff, but they are finding it more and more difficult to make ends meet.

The head of the union is a young cost accountant named Joseph Scanlon, who has resigned his white collar work to run a machine. He is deeply convinced that the steel industry needs union organization, but as an accountant he knows that what the president says about insolvency is true. He calls a meeting of the union to give the men the balance sheet facts. He tells them they are wrong when they say that company officials are rolling in wealth because they have big cars. He tells them that management as well as men are in hot water together. He stations friends to guard the doors and make sure that the members stay until they hear all the facts.

It is a wild, stormy meeting, lasting throughout the night. It ends with the men actually voting to take a 25 per cent wage cut, for a three months' trial period, while they co-operate with management in an effort to save the mill. Scanlon has helped them to realize that there is more than the mill to save; their jobs, their families, their homes, are at stake. It is sixty miles to the nearest work, and work is hard to get in a severe depression.

An efficiency program is drawn up jointly by union and management, in which workers actively participate. They soon are personally involved in suggesting ways to keep costs down and output up. Before the trial period is over, costs have dropped below the U.S. Steel Company's average for similar output. The mill pulls out of the red, and in due course the wage cut is returned. The mill is still making money today, with the help of the union.

This was the first, and perhaps the most dramatic, of Scanlon's forty participation plans in many different industries.

Machine Tools

Another of Scanlon's adventures, described by Russell Davenport in *Fortune*, has to do with the Lapointe Machine Tool Company, a tidy concern in Hudson, Massachusetts, which employs about three hundred and fifty workers. It was unionized in 1945, but labor relations were at best in the accommodation stage, with fifteen to twenty official grievances processed a month. There were delays in production, a high spoilage rate, uncertain deliveries of the machines in which the company specialized. The postwar slump in orders for machine tools did not help, and neither did a bitter strike in 1946.

At this point, the union president happened to hear about Scanlon and called on him. In December, 1947, a plan designed for this particular company was put into effect. Almost at once the grievances, trouble, and unrest came to an end. Presently production began to increase, and costs to decline. A new spirit came into the plant as problems were tackled jointly by management and union.

Scanlon's procedure is to take M.I.T. students with him as he moves into a new situation. They act as his assistants and learn his skills. They also receive a thorough grounding in labor-management relations as part of their engineering education. The formula varies with each plant, but the principle is to get workers personally involved in increasing production, with a resulting bonus and a resulting lift in morale.

The first step is to find what are called "normal" labor costs. The second step is to devise a method to reward workers—*all* the workers —when actual operating costs fall below the "normal" level. Normal cost may be expressed in tons, pounds, square feet, gallons, dollars, sometimes in a percentage. At Lapointe normal, set as "the ratio of labor cost to total production value," worked out to about 38 per cent. If the ratio can be lowered, say to 35 per cent, the 3 per cent difference will be distributed as a bonus to the men. There are provisions, too, for various reserves, and for adjusting the normal ratio. Observe that all participants gain when mutually desired goals are reached. No one on the team is happy about losses on the ledger.

It is important to have the cost formula well designed from the engineering and accounting standpoint; but the really significant part of the plan is the *method by which participation is achieved*. It is built around a conference table, where joint production committees, after full discussion, adopt or discard suggestions and ideas for improving plant performance.

Here in *Fortune* is a photograph of the committee at Lapointe, reading suggestions for shop improvements which have come in from the men, discussing business forecasts, company sales, the competitive situation, and various managerial difficulties. (Incidentally, it is hard to tell company managers in the photograph from union managers.)

The minutes of these meetings go back to the rank and file for further discussion, and stimulate further suggestions. Workers used to be told what to do by the stop-watch men; here they tell themselves what to do. There is no "speed up" except as they themselves elect. Perhaps they work harder at Lapointe than they used to; certainly they now work more steadily. They are earning more money and feeling more important and more secure.

Under old-style management, a worker's suggestions were often unacceptable; the worker felt frustrated, and his respect for management declined. There was little communication between the two, no incentive to co-operate. Sometimes the reverse was true, for the worker was afraid to produce ideas lest he incur the jealousy of the foreman. Alfred D. Sheffield tells me of a group of six men in another New England factory who among them invented an excellent boring tool. They kept it hidden under the bench and used it only enough to increase their take-home pay about 15 per cent, without arousing the supervisor's suspicion.

When Scanlon talks about his plan, two terms are frequently mentioned: "maturity" and "participation." Only a union and a management who are willing to act grown up, he says, can make his plan go. Again, everyone from the laborer to the company president must become involved—in the Bethel sense—and deeply desire to have it succeed. It must be "our suggestion," "our responsibility," not something handed to us by management. As Davenport puts it:

Real participation consists in finding a means by which to reward labor for any increase in production, and then in building around this formula a working relationship between management and labor that enables them to become a team. Once a team is established it is found that labor's prime interest, like management's, becomes productivity.

A union official at Lapointe puts it this way: "The most important thing to come out of participation is not the bonus. It is that everyone from top to bottom is working for a common goal."

Improbable Case

Another factory with a Scanlon plan, after operating successfully for a year, called a union meeting. Following a discussion, the men voted to adjust the labor-cost formula, not, if you please, because they thought it unfair to themselves, but because they thought it unfair to the company! Scanlon explains that this was possible because every worker "understood in detail the whole financial picture." Results under the new formula turned out better for workers as well as for the company. A big clock-dial in the yard of the plant showed the daily production with a separate hand to indicate comparisons with the preceding month.

This will sound improbable: when results grew profitable enough, the union voted the president of the company twelve thousand dollars in additional salary! It was one of the few companies which did not go out in the 1946 steel strike, because union demands were instantly met.

No participation plan has much of a chance, says Scanlon, unless the relations between union and management are good before it is tried. You cannot go from the acute conflict stage to the full co-operation stage in one jump. Scanlon is unique in winning co-operation from both workers and managers. People trust him and follow him. His knowledge of cost accounting on the one hand, his years as an official of the steel workers' union on the other, give him a double-barreled approach which is almost unique in American industry. But the fact that he is one in a million should not hide the results, where new habits of participation become permanent. A need was there and he has met it. He knows how to release energy; he does not create it. "The average employer has little conception of the wealth of imagination and ingenuity lying untapped in the heads of the workers."

MEN'S SUITS

The late Sidney Hillman of the Amalgamated Clothing Workers broke into stage eight many years ago on an even broader front.[1] Able lieutenants and farsighted manufacturers worked with him for a generation to bring co-operation between union and management throughout the men's clothing industry.

The Amalgamated was formed in 1914, when Hillman's group split off from the United Garment Workers, A.F. of L. He wanted to replace the craft union with an industrial union where all crafts would be united, from messengers to skilled cutters. At first there were bloody strikes and many picket lines in New York, Philadelphia, Rochester, and elsewhere. Call it stage one, "containment-aggression," on the Selekman scale.

In Rochester, however, the management of the Hickey-Freeman Company, making high-grade men's suits, took a gamble on the future and signed a contract with Hillman in April, 1919. Since that day there has never been a strike in the company! In the last eighteen years not a single grievance has gone to arbitration.

Hickey-Freeman, with about fifteen hundred on the payroll, is one of six large shops in Rochester making men's clothing. It owns a well-lighted, airy factory, with an investment in plant per employee of $1,400. The business was started in 1899, and the stock is closely held, with control in the hands of active management. Profits have been good throughout the period of the union contract, and they average substantially higher than in the industry as a whole. Labor peace has not been bought by "giving the business away."

The 1919 contract was short. It provided for the settlement of grievances, a "labor manager" to be appointed by the company, an open shop, and arbitration machinery. Dr. William Leiserson became the first "impartial chairman" to administer arbitration, a post

[1] This story is based on Study No. 4 of the National Planning Association's series entitled *Causes of Industrial Peace. The Hickey-Freeman Company,* by Donald B. Straus.

which was to win him national respect and honor. Thirty-three cases came to him the first year, but now grievances are settled quickly at the point of origin in the shop.

Over the years the open shop has become a closed shop. A closed shop is dangerous unless the union is thoroughly responsible, and it takes time to acquire responsible habits. Gradually participation plans were introduced, until it became the fixed policy of the Hickey-Freeman management to consult the union before making any major decisions affecting the workers. Such a policy clashes with the traditional prerogatives of the boss and is an acute issue in American industry today. Employers are disposed to fight for what they consider their right to run the business in their own way. Unions are up in arms against what they consider unjust acts of management—rate cutting, speed-ups, arbitrary dismissals. But at Hickey-Freeman "management prerogatives" carry no warlike connotation. Boundaries between managers and workers have been clearly defined and long since accepted.

Plant Chairman

Suppose we look at an actual scene in this drama of participation. Here is the "plant chairman," a union official, whose job is to settle local grievances—the kind which the company personnel department, or the company foremen, try to settle in most concerns. He sits in his own private office, furnished by the company, right in the factory.

A complaint is brought to him. "Julie" is making too many errors in stitching labels, her spoilage rate is way up. He looks over the record. Then he summons the girl, the company foreman, and the union shop steward. He shows them the figures. Nobody questions the high rate of spoilage. The plant chairman looks at the girl and says:

"Julie, the company can't afford to pay you one cent a label to make mistakes and then pay another six cents to have them corrected, can it?"

"No, sir."

"You know, Julie, you just weren't cut out to sit at a machine all day long. After you have been sitting for a while, your attention wanders all over the place, doesn't it?"

"Yes. I guess I'm not cut out for the job."

The foreman speaks up: "She used to be a good messenger when she first came here. We might shift her back into that job."

"How would you like that?" asks the plant chairman.

"I would like it fine," says Julie.

And this grievance, which is an actual case, is settled by a union man, to the satisfaction of the company foreman and of the girl herself.

Style Change

When a new suit is designed, patterns are taken to an operating department of the company for examination. The manager calls in a representative of the union and the company foreman for a joint conference on the new style. Piece rates, quality, the division of work, and many technical matters are thoroughly discussed. Patterns which arouse objections go back to the designer for correction.

When the new style is ready for actual production in the shop, it is a *joint* plan, with all foreseeable grievances and conflicts removed. But that is not the end of joint planning. A few suits are first manufactured in a kind of pilot plant with a special work group. If the workers like the style—not the cut of the vest so much as the conditions of producing it—they tell the rest of the shop, aided by the plant chairman (union) and the labor manager (company). A better way to forestall minor complaints and to encourage production would be difficult to imagine.

Similarly with the setting of piece rates. There are two hundred and fifty job categories in the men's clothing industry, each with its own piece-rate structure. Union and management discuss any proposed changes in rates, so that full agreement can be reached before an announcement is made. Without mutual trust and co-operation, a rate structure as complicated as this one would become a battlefield of incessant conflict. But it has become a traditional and orderly procedure, with the union playing a responsible role.

Depression

Perhaps the most dramatic examples of participation came during
the depression of the 1930's. Clothing firms began to fail under the
pressure of falling prices and shrinking sales. The Amalgamated
Clothing Workers loaned them money out of its treasury to keep
them solvent! Hart, Schaffner and Marx was said to have received
a substantial sum in the nick of time. The Levy-Adler concern was
reorganized by the union to prevent its going out of business. Said
the Rochester Joint Board: "The firm [Levy-Adler] is going to keep
on manufacturing suits as well as overcoats, but the union will have
to face the problem of re-establishing the business upon a sound and
firm footing." That is, the union underwrote the company!

In 1933 the Amalgamated at Rochester negotiated a wage cut—
yes, *cut*—of 15 per cent. Later in that terrible year it negotiated
another cut of 15 per cent. In 1934 came a third 15 per cent cut,
reduced in 1935 to 8 per cent. The union had matured to the point
of choosing the lesser evil—better a 45 per cent wage cut than unemployed. The cost of living was falling too, we must remember.
Co-operation in the needle trades is a two-way street. Workers share
in the high earnings of the good years and in the losses of the bad
years.

Hillman believed that workers could be loyal to both the union
and the company, and thirty years of peace at Hickey-Freeman seems
to prove that he was right. Donald Straus, in summing up this history, says that industrial peace rests on two foundations:

First, the unreserved acceptance by the management of the union
and its functions. Second, the unreserved acceptance by the union
of responsibility for the welfare and solvency of the industry.

The relationship between men and managers at Hickey-Freeman
has been on the basis of "solving mutual problems as they arise, not
of winning arguments." As the relationship developed, says Straus,
increasing reliance was placed on collective bargaining at the local
level, less on arbitration, far less on splitting legal hairs over the
interpretation of the written contract.

The United Nations, by way of contrast, is still in the hair-splitting stage—but it is of course much younger than the Amalgamated.

Conditions of Industrial Peace

Hickey-Freeman is one of a dozen concerns now under intensive analysis by the National Planning Association at Washington—which we met earlier, with its three-ply conference. Instead of studying labor wars, the Association is studying labor peace. In 1946 the American public had more front-page news about strikes than ever before, but even in that turbulent year, nine out of every ten labor contracts were renegotiated without a strike. In the next year, 1947, twenty-four out of twenty-five contracts were so negotiated. The prevailing pattern of American labor is peace, even if the headlines make it look like war. Clinton S. Golden, who heads the N.P.A.'s research committee, said in launching the study: "The time has come when, instead of looking into the causes of conflict that we hear so much about, we ought to try to discover how much peace there is, and what makes peace."

So far reports have been filed and published for the following concerns:

Crown Zellerback Corporation
Libby-Owens-Ford Glass Company
Dewey and Almy Chemical Company
Hickey-Freeman Company
Sharon Steel Corporation
Lockheed Aircraft Corporation
Nashua Gummed and Coated Paper Company

Other studies are in process. Nothing on this scale has ever been attempted before, and already the attention given to it by newspapers, magazines, students of labor relations, has been phenomenal. When the studies are all in, the N.P.A. promises a covering report which will point up the "universals" of good relations, as found in the several companies and unions.

If I were organizing a new business, I would get, first, a checkbook, then a copy of the N.P.A.'s summary report.

CHAPTER FOURTEEN

Maturity in Labor Relations

IN JUNE, 1950, General Motors Corporation and the United Automobile Workers signed a five-year agreement for labor peace. The company agreed to a steady increase in wages, tied to a cost-of-living formula, and the union forswore strikes.

When a Detroit toolmaker heard what Walter Reuther and Charles E. Wilson had negotiated he cried: "That's great! Now I can send my daughter to college and know I can keep her there until she graduates!" Needless to say, this story from the *New York Times* was not reprinted in *Pravda*. It makes a hash of the Communist line, and gives a hint of what relations between unions and managers can be when both sides achieve maturity.

Flint, Michigan, where many General Motors' employees live, began to boom with the signing of the contract. Main Street, like the toolmaker, found the news great. Retail sales rose sharply; there was a roaring demand for new houses, automobiles, refrigerators, washing machines and television sets. A dealer in metal awnings, who had been having trouble moving his stock, suddenly found himself swamped with orders. A proposal for a seven-million-dollar school bond issue, repeatedly voted down, was approved three to one! A banker who had been fearing a strike said that the five-year contract was "like a heavy weight taken off our backs."

Here, again, is a quarter-page advertisement in New York papers, in which an A.F. of L. local asks shoppers to patronize the bosses' store—John Wanamaker's in this case. "Everything for the Ladies; Everything for the Man; Everything for Everybody." The advertisement goes on to say that the union, like hundreds of others, is a good union. "We never had a strike—though we firmly believe in strikes after all peaceful methods fail. We never had a mediation or an arbitration case. All agreements and grievances are settled through our peaceful collective bargaining machinery." This story would probably cause *Pravda*'s presses to disintegrate!

Jersey Standard

In Chapter 1, we sketched the story of the Standard Oil Company of New Jersey, which, following sanguinary battles in the streets of Bayonne, has not had a strike since 1917—a longer record even than that of the Hickey-Freeman Company. How did it happen? The company asked me this question, and I spent several months in refineries and offices, talking to employees and officials and trying to find an answer. My report shows that the major reasons are these[1]:

The persistent, firm recognition by top management of workers as human beings, not commodities. This policy was adopted after a survey by Clarence J. Hicks in 1918.

Collective bargaining with unions, both independent and national, in which men and management have come to trust each other's good faith.

Benefit plans to increase workers' security. Workers are consulted in drafting many of these plans.

A relatively high wage scale.

The encouragement of teamwork.

Recognition of "four publics" with which a large corporation must establish sound relations. The four are: its workers, its stockholders, the consumers of the company's product, and the government, representing the general public. The old philosophy of profits as the only goal has been abandoned.

Jersey Standard workers do not participate in production to the degree which Scanlon's plans call for, or which we found in Hickey-

[1] *A Generation of Industrial Peace,* report published by Standard Oil Company of New Jersey (New York, 1947).

Freeman; but the company has a similar point of view, and a long record of good labor relations. The acid test was that 95 per cent of the thousands of employees who went off to the armed services, in World War II, wanted to work for no other company on their return.

"Vertical Round Table"

The Calco Company, chemical manufacturers, also located in New Jersey, noted a serious lack of co-operation, not only between men and management, but among some seven levels in management itself. One department under M. E. Kilby had excellent co-operation and morale. How could these be expanded throughout the big plant? But "until management was more unified in philosophy it seemed futile to attempt to develop a sense of participation in the rank and file." The company called in Dr. Francis Bradshaw, of the consulting firm of Richardson, Bellows, and Henry, in New York, to see what social science could do about improving it. Applying some of his technical knowledge of psychology and a good deal of plain common sense, Bradshaw set up what he called a "Vertical Round Table."

He took some fifteen members of the management group clean out of the plant to a weekly luncheon at a comfortable inn nearby. They represented all seven levels, from the very top to assistant supervisor. After cocktails and a good meal, he led a discussion of their joint problems, starting with large global matters and gradually coming down to the shop details. Participation and involvement began to work.

The Round Table has been in operation now for many months. The results are being written up, and they are good. Not only has management developed into a better team, with much better communication between levels, but it has noticeably improved its relations with the rank and file of workers.

Then and Now

In the 1920's I was associated with a research organization in New York called the Labor Bureau, Incorporated. We put out our shingle for labor unions, co-operative societies, and other liberal groups which might want economic, statistical, or accounting services. Our largest job was to prepare briefs, buttressed with sound statistics, for unions going into arbitration proceedings. Mass production was coming into its own in those days, but few mass production workers as such had been organized. The South was solidly anti-union. The autocratic pattern of management was all but universal; Hickey-Freeman, Jersey Standard, and a few other companies were oases in the desert.

The labor problem in the 1920's was how to get enough workers to join unions so that they would have something to say about their wages and hours and thus help to reduce wide areas of exploitation. Most mornings before breakfast, this problem seemed pretty hopeless to the staff of the Labor Bureau.

What a vast change as one looks around America today! The problem of organization was suddenly solved by the National Labor Relations Act. The C.I.O. was born and began to organize the great mass production industries—steel, rubber, automobiles, electric appliances, oil, and various others. The number of workers in unions shot up from three million in 1932 to sixteen million. Presently Big Labor was strong enough to take no back talk from Big Business, and even to challenge the government itself.

Instead of pity for the plight of industrial workers, many fair-minded citizens began to feel apprehension. Labor as a whole, they felt, was being harmed by certain union leaders who refused to accept responsibility for the great power which had so suddenly come to them. Today organized labor is a mammoth institution in the American culture, in need of no one's pity or charity, quite capable of taking care of itself. Standards of criticism must accordingly move upward.

One merited criticism, it seems to me, is the reluctance of most labor leaders to take advantage of the new research findings which we have been describing—findings which can be of the greatest value to the rank and file, though not always to the power of the leaders.

Yet in some union quarters, Mayo and his followers are accused of trying to impose speed-ups like the old stop-watch engineers. Nothing could be farther from the truth.

Psychology could be used to bamboozle workers, but the research which we have been examining, from the Hawthorne experiments on, has been worker-oriented rather than dollar-oriented, with a strong accent on democratic rather than on autocratic techniques. As a sometime member of the Labor Bureau, after a good many years of consulting work for unions, I think I can sense a plot to bamboozle the rank and file as readily as the next man.

In the 1920's a big strike meant picket lines, "goons" to beat up the pickets, police with clubs flying and ambulance bells ringing. In the 1949 steel strike the company served hot coffee to workers on the picket lines, while union maintenance squads protected company property from damage! A striker was asked by the *Times* reporter about the likelihood of violence. He said, "Nah, the union has grown up—and so has the company I guess." This story did not make *Pravda* either.

Violence still occurs but is relatively declining. In a steel town the mayor deputized *union workers* to keep law and order during a recent strike; twenty years ago he would have named the company police. We used to have strikes which verged on civil war; now they sometimes verge on the annual picnic of the drop forge department. Congress formerly investigated "industrial unrest"; now the National Planning Association investigates industrial peace. A strange, and on the whole encouraging, transformation.

Balance Sheet

Edwin E. Witte, in a presidential address to the Industrial Relations Research Association, strikes a labor relations balance sheet for us. I am including some comments of my own with his list. The *assets*, he says, include:

1. A decline in violence and in the *bitterness* which is the usual aftermath of physical violence.

2. An increase in functional and necessary labor legislation, such as unemployment insurance, old-age pensions, fair employment practices.

3. The growth of union membership, and the organization of the mass production industries at a rate which nobody believed possible. (In the Labor Bureau we might have admitted the possibility along about A.D. 2000.)

4. The sharp increase in the attention of industry to problems of human relations. Top management now regards them as "one of its major responsibilities." The Job Relations Training course taught to a million foremen during World War II put the new approach into what might be called educational mass production.

5. The progress in developing orderly wage structures—as in Hickey-Freeman.

6. "Fringe benefits," such as pensions, vacations, sickness and accident insurance, which Mr. Witte says are becoming almost universal.

7. Greater stability of employment than in the past, with turn-over reduced, and a growing interest in the annual wage idea and in profit-sharing. (But profit-sharing without union participation can be a blind alley.)

8. Better procedures for grievances, seniority, discharges, lay-offs, transfers, and promotions. New training and job testing techniques.

9. Pleasanter factories to work in, especially those light and airy structures built by the taxpayers during the last war.

Liabilities

Mr. Witte draws up an impressive list of assets, but warns us not to forget the liabilities:

1. Mutual distrust is still widespread in industry. Not many companies have entered the stage of genuine co-operation with their workers.

2. Still far too many strikes, even if they are not so violent.

3. Some legislative and executive action by government which prevents the normal working out of collective bargaining. In a bad

strike the public protest may be deafening and force the government into the situation making natural adjustment more difficult.

In this point we encounter a serious and complicated problem.
It is conceivable that in the next few years the public may come to
the point of refusing to tolerate strikes in such public services as
electric power, telephones, transportation, and even coal. The public
has the last word in these matters. Then, unless labor in such industries is to lose status and self-respect, important concessions will be
called for to offset the loss of the right to strike. One offset that has
been suggested is a guaranteed annual wage.

4. The class-struggle assumption is still too influential on both
sides. Numerous small business men would like to get rid of unions
altogether, while left-wing union leaders treat employers as their
mortal enemies, showering them with special epithets. (As we
said before, however, communist-dominated unions are now practically extinct, owing to the energetic purges by Philip Murray and
others.)

5. Still too much restriction of output, feather-bedding, attempts
to build a monopolistic wall around the job. A recent university
report on labor relations said: "Restriction of output in some form
exists in nearly all establishments, on all sorts of jobs, under all
kinds of payment systems, and in unorganized as well as unionized
plants."[2] It is due to deep-seated fear of rate cutting, speed-ups,
unemployment, and lay-offs—a fear that may remain long after its
reason has disappeared.

Restriction of output is bad for people as well as for production,
but this report shows that it cannot be halted by either exhortation
or penalties. Workers will produce freely when they *feel* free and
secure, and not before. They feel secure when they become personally involved in the success of the enterprise—as at Hickey-
Freeman. It will take a while to inspire this feeling in all the
Americans now on somebody's payroll.

The key to good labor relations is obviously a better understanding of human wants, of human goals, of human behavior. What

2 University of Chicago, Committee on Human Relations, 1946.

conditions in a factory make people feel good there, feel that they "belong"? The key term is, I suppose, *participation*. Said an English laborer in Leeds with some heat, as the company proposed to shower him with benefits: "I don't want to be done good at!" No self-respecting employee wants to be done good at; he wants to help himself, in co-operation with his working group.

Robert W. Johnson, in the *Harvard Business Review* for September, 1949, has drawn up a set of principles for labor-management relations endorsed by an imposing list of business men, economists, and educators. He begins with these six assumptions:

> Management is an ethical as well as an economic problem.
> Modern society is interdependent. "The world is social."
> There is no such thing as "economic man."
> People want the esteem of others; they want association in groups; they want human dignity; they want security.
> Frustrations often result in aggressive action.
> Business is not an end in itself, but only a part of the culture of a given society.

We find plenty of maturity here.

University Research

More than thirty American universities have established departments where scientific research is being applied to labor problems. We have looked at the excellent work the University of Michigan is doing. We have watched Scanlon operating at M.I.T., and Mayo, Roethlisberger, Selekman, and others at the Harvard Business School.

C. Wight Bakke and Charles R. Walker at Yale are heading teams of social scientists to explore such matters as "adaptive behavior," what lies behind decision-making by executives, the problem of the repetitive job. Walker himself published an excellent case study called *Steeltown*, showing what happens to workers and their community when the mill moves out.

At the other end of the country, Clark Kerr heads an important labor research group in the University of California.

Cornell has a State School of Industrial and Labor Relations, directed by Alexander Leighton, who as you know is primarily an anthropologist. He says that the important thing about the new science of human relations is not the very considerable areas which are unknown "but the degree to which what is known is not used."

Working with him at Cornell is William Foote Whyte, who develops an equally interesting line of thought. No economist, he says, has the tools to make a factory survey, that is, a survey of *people* in factories. "The economist cannot operate effectively in this area unless he also acquires some of the tools of the anthropologist, sociologist, and psychologist"—which makes it a task for a social science team. A factory or an office is not primarily an economic organism but a social one, whirling with tensions and powerful group interactions. Furthermore, Whyte points out, you have to study the shop as a whole; it cannot be cut into parts with any hope of understanding men at work.

We noted in Chapter 8 how McGregor, Knickerbocker, and Bavelas at M.I.T. used the factory as a laboratory for working out many problems in group dynamics, industrial incentives, and leadership. Warner, of the University of Chicago, in a dramatic study has traced the industrial and cultural history back of a big strike in the shoe factories of Newburyport. His research covers three centuries of institutional change in New England and throws a strong light on why men sometimes won't work.

All the vital avenues of participation enjoyed under handicraft conditions in Newburyport were closed. Independent little shoe shops had been taken over by a huge holding company; the local market for shoes had become impersonal and worldwide; human skills were replaced by the machine. The function of the workers in the community was lost, most of their roots torn up. They had a great need to belong to something, and they seized the union. Warner draws this lesson:

If business leaders and union leaders, too, are to deal realistically with their problems, they need explicit knowledge of *social change,* and its effects on their own actions. No system of pay, no practical economic method of rewarding managers or workers, can be sufficient to satisfy their emotional needs.

The Tavistock Institute in London, the British Association for Commercial and Industrial Education, nicknamed "Bacie," and various Canadian universities are making scientific investigations similar to those described. Indeed, Mayo began his pioneer work with studies of fatigue in munitions plants during World War I, in England.

If we look around the rest of the world, however, the scientific approach is hard to find. Labor-management committees exist in many European factories, but underlying research in human relations is lacking. Older methods of social science, entangled with philosophy, ideology, and polemics, are still dominant. Wherever the class struggle is a basic assumption it becomes useless to do anything about industrial co-operation. In Russian factories, as noted earlier, after a most appalling interlude in the Twenties of allowing shop committees to run the plant—production often dropped to 10 per cent of normal—the old autocratic system of management was reintroduced, and seems to have remained ever since.

Young Women in Holyoke

Let us end our survey with a story which illustrates participation as well as anything I know. It concerns a clothing factory in Holyoke, Massachusetts, which the Amalgamated Clothing Workers had organized. The social structure was unique, for the boss was a naturalized Jew from Europe, the head of the union a naturalized Italian, while most of the workers were young ladies of Yankee ancestry, with a social status several rungs above either of their leaders.

A few years ago, the shop was running out of capital, with eighty thousand dollars in unpaid loans. It looked like a choice between bankruptcy and a cut in wages. In this crisis, Selekman was called in from the Harvard Business School to act as arbitrator. A look at the books convinced him of a really serious situation; even the union leader was about ready to accept a wage cut, for a strictly limited period.

At this point the young ladies became very vocal and said in effect: "Hold on, why don't you make a more efficient shop before you cut our wages?"

"What do you mean?" said the boss.

"Look," they said, "we're on piece rates, and the conveyor girls are on week rates—no co-ordination between the two. The layout and routing are terrible around here; the waste is terrific."

"Well," said the boss, "we never did lay out this place right; we were in too much of a hurry to get going. What do you girls think we ought to do?"

After some consultation among themselves, the girls offered a series of recommendations. Selekman, as arbitrator, gave them every encouragement and urged the boss to do the same. Even if some of the suggestions seem trivial, welcome them all, he said. The girls originated the idea and should feel it was their plan, their contribution to keeping the company afloat.

In the end, Selekman told me, the morale was extraordinary. Everybody felt splendid. Ben felt so good he remitted his fee as arbitrator! At last accounts the company was still in business.

CHAPTER FIFTEEN

Conciliators and Arbitrators

WE HAVE been discussing techniques of agreement in industry between men and management, aided by modern research. There is another series of techniques where conflict is reduced by the services of outside parties—by "impartial chairmen," by government agencies, a panel recommended by the Bar Association, a conference out of court in a lawyer's office, and so on. These techniques of conciliation and arbitration are important, and we will look at them in this chapter, both in situations where labor is concerned and where the general public is concerned.

The Federal Mediation and Conciliation Service

I asked the famous conciliator, Cyrus Ching, if he would give me an interview. He is an enormous man, with a big nose, a big pipe, big black eyebrows, and keen gray eyes. He swung around in his big chair in his big Washington office and asked me what I wanted. I told him I was interested in finding ways and means for fewer fights, now that we are all jammed up together in the atomic age. Mr. Ching grunted.

"How do *you* do it?" I asked.

"God knows," he said. "You have to sense the situation, feel it out, then you act. Every case is different. There are no set rules."

"How do you break in a new man for the service?"

"We take him along and let him watch. Some get the idea after a while; some don't. I guess you're born with a flair for negotiation. There is a technique all right, but you couldn't put it into words."

"Not at that face-to-face stage perhaps," I said, "but in another sense the Conciliation Service itself is a technique, isn't it? Wouldn't there be more labor fights if we had no service, and no Cyrus Ching?"

"I guess you're right," he said. "We cherish the illusion, at least, that we do some good. We have helped to settle a good many fights."

He was interested now. He relit his pipe and told me about the service. As I listened I realized how lucky the country was to have this wise and kindly man to reconcile crucial disputes. After a while the general counsel, Peter Seitz, came in and joined our conversation. He said that training conciliators was an art, not a science, but they were beginning to experiment with job analysis. Mr. Ching snorted mildly. "It won't do any harm to try it," he said. "I doubt if it does any good either."

Conciliation usually means the same thing as mediation, but arbitration is very different—and often less desirable. The progression in a labor dispute goes something like this.

The *first* and best step is for union and employer to settle the dispute through their own collective bargaining machinery—for instance, using the plant chairman at Hickey-Freeman.

The *second* step, if the dispute cannot be resolved locally, is for both to call on Ching, or some other conciliator. His job is to talk it over with union and company jointly and separately, and try to bridge the gap which separates them. He can be especially useful in helping save face. One side or the other, or both, may be so far out on a limb that they cannot retreat. The Chinese have a phrase for it: "Bring me a ladder to climb down on." Ching—whose unusual name, by the way, is not Chinese—comes to the rescue with a ladder. Usually, of course, he sends an assistant. He could not go personally to thousands of hot spots a year. The service maintains twelve regional offices and several hundred conciliators.

The *third* step is arbitration, which usually is not tried until conciliation has failed to get the parties together. The arbitrator may be an "impartial chairman" serving an industry, or he may be selected from a panel of the American Arbitration Association, or just nominated by the parties without reference to arbitration machinery. His task is very different from Ching's, for he hears out both sides and then, like a judge, renders a decision. The union must do this, and the company must do that. As a rule, somebody wins and somebody loses, leaving the loser sore. The conciliator, on the other hand, tries to get *mutual agreement* so that nobody wins, nobody loses, and nobody is sore. The distinction is very important.

Step *four* is war. If one or both parties to the dispute will not accept the arbitrator's decision, diplomacy ends and the strike begins. Even while war is raging, however, conciliators may be trying to negotiate a peace treaty.

In disputes threatening important public-services, such as coal or railroads, another step has recently found favor in Washington—the *fact-finding board.* The President appoints a group of distinguished citizens to explore the dispute and bring in a public recommendation for its settlement. We shall probably see more of these boards. With a good social scientist or two included, and real impartiality, they can be very useful. They may help us work out a general plan for handling strikes in vital public services—a plan which we must soon have.

The Art of Conciliation

Somebody in the Ching office told me the following story, which I pass on to the reader without comment. A certain union puts an elaborate case with many charts and figures before a conciliator, taking hours to present it. The company also spends many hours, with more charts and tables, proving the opposite. The conciliator accepts all this evidence with a psychiatrist's composure. When the last chart has been hung upon the wall, he says: "Very impressive, gentlemen, very impressive. Now let me sum up the position of the parties to this dispute." He then proceeds deliberately to make a fearful hash of the case. The disputing parties are appalled! They hastily retreat to the corridor and agree in no time at all, lest worse befall them!

A good conciliator must know when to misconstrue the evidence a bit and when to question it; when to interview jointly and when to see each side in separate rooms; when to let them blow off steam and when to calm them down. He must feel the strategic moment to suggest ten cents, after the union has said "twenty cents and not a penny less," and the company has said "we stand on five cents and we do not budge." A conciliator is a broker, acting in the public interest. He must be ready to work all hours in "round the clock" negotiating, for a modest salary, with crisis piled upon crisis. Sometimes the whole country awaits breathlessly the result of his efforts.

Men and management alike know that Cyrus Ching plays no favorites and pulls no punches. He smokes his pipe and probes to find the places where emotion can give way to accommodation. "Even if we help a settlement," he says, "we have not done our duty unless we make a contribution to better relations in the future."

There is an almost dream-like detachment about the Federal Conciliation Service. Ching has no power to intervene; he makes no recommendations, at least in public, cannot settle anything himself, can be thrown out by either side at any moment. Yet he succeeds manifestly and markedly in reducing industrial conflict. How did Congress ever vote the money for such an idealistic enterprise?

Where are we to find another big man who knows so much about human relations when Ching retires? I agree that such men are born, not made. Nevertheless, the science of human relations has advanced to the point where it can offer some real help to the service, especially in selecting and training conciliators. It cannot give them that final spark, but it can start them in the right direction.

Dwight Morrow

"Sometimes," said Ching, "an agreement to disagree is the only possible solution."

"What do you mean?" I asked.

He told me about Dwight Morrow in Mexico in the late Twenties, deeply disturbed by the deadlock between the Catholic Church and the Mexican government. Many essential measures were being held up because of the dispute. Morrow invited high officials on both sides to a conference. They came, for they respected the American ambassador. He asked if they did not agree with him that their ideological differences were irreconcilable? With some surprise at the approach, they did agree; the gulf was too wide to be bridged.

Good, said Morrow, you can never get together philosophically; it is hopeless. . . . Now, how about *practical* matters; how about that business over in Puebla? Whereupon the representatives of Church and State found themselves ready to discuss practical issues in Puebla or elsewhere. Ambassador Morrow succeeded in settling quite a few urgent matters that day, said Ching.

This reminds us of the *accommodation* stage on the labor front, where there is not much mutual trust but a working arrangement for practical problems. I recommend the technique to the attention of the Republicans and the Democrats in all foreign, and even some domestic, policies.

Major Estes' Deep Freeze

One of Cyrus Ching's aides, who has been in the conciliation business for many years, is Charles T. Estes, a bald, genial, fabulously energetic man with a drill sergeant's voice. Actually he was an army major, and the title has stuck. By trial and error, good will, plenty of common sense, and a dash of profanity, Major Estes has developed a remarkable technique for drawing the emotion out of both sides to a labor dispute. Sometimes he dips into social science for ideas about communication, semantics, and psychology. He has been known to imitate the psychoanalysts and get the parties mad at *him*, so they will be less mad at each other.

His idea was born during a big dispute in 1940, involving six unions and a large corporation. Estes, who was working with John Steelman at the time, was asked to help the two sides get together on a new contract. They had been quarreling for years, and emotions ran high. The major eventually calmed them down by an original procedure. He had representatives from both sides take turns reading the contract aloud. Each man would read a section while the others listened. Then they would discuss the document, clause by clause. Controversial clauses were put aside, in two categories labeled: "mild refrigeration" and "deep freeze." Later, after the disputants were calm enough to listen, first the mild items were taken out for action, and finally the serious items.

In two days, says Estes, the lesson was learned. Everyone at the meeting really knew the terms of the contract and went back to bench and office to pass the word along. The listening, the repeating, the taking turns as discussion leader had got the several clauses into the nervous systems of everybody there. "We had conditioned them to communicate." This particular contract has now run unchanged, except for two small amendments, for ten years.

Major Estes went on to design machinery to help foremen and union shop stewards in any factory improve communication and come to agreement on all kinds of shop questions, for instance: how to handle grievances, how to break in a new man, how to correct errors. He had special pamphlets printed in big type with wide margins, dealing with shop problems.

Here is a group in action: ten foremen and shop stewards, pamphlet in hand, sit down around a table. Estes, or some other leader, explains the situation. The man on his left reads aloud page one of the pamphlet, while the others try to listen. The next man reads page two aloud, the next man page three, and so on to the end. Nobody says a word except the reader. Gradually they learn the art of listening.

When the circle is completed, the first man again reads page one aloud, and proceeds to become discussion leader. Does everyone agree with what he has read? If not, the icebox doors are opened and subjects shelved on the two levels—mild refrigeration and deep freeze.

"Controversial material should be discussed only when we are reasonably sure that the group is prepared to think in a serious and unemotional state." We note that the structure of the group is such that members are automatically prevented from emotional outbursts. Oververbalized members have to keep quiet, Napoleons cannot get going, the Caspar Milquetoasts learn to participate. Everybody *must* participate, yet it is almost impossible to steal the show.

Since these problems vitally concern every man around the table, interest is not hard to arouse in the plan. Estes has also tried it out in schools, community discussion groups, and elsewhere. Here the questions may be as hot as in a factory, but the conferees do not, as a rule, know the facts so well. Still, it often seems to work.

Liston Tatum has used the method for a master's thesis at Northwestern University. He experimented with five local groups—two college classes, two community discussion circles, and a Sunday school class. He analyzed their performance carefully and tabulated the results. Among the questions discussed were Palestine, college fraternities, Communism versus Christianity. The Sunday school class of teen-agers ran off the track, which is not surprising. The older groups soon acquired more tolerant attitudes, seemed to learn faster, came to sounder conclusions. The Major's deep freeze system is clumsy in some respects, but is clearly worth following up. Maybe it should be sent to Bethel for testing.

What we have here is of course another experiment in group dynamics, though Estes started it before that term was invented. If the members of a group can begin their discussion with an examination of the facts, then draw inferences, then proceed to solutions, keeping their prejudices and generalizations under control, the chances for agreement are good. This is the order in which scientists attack a problem—facts, inferences, solutions. But most human discussions reverse the order: first, abstractions, principles, prejudices; then some loose facts to "prove" one's prejudices; then a total breakdown of understanding among all present.

Bus Line

Tatum tells a story to illustrate the difference. During World War II, trouble arose at a bus terminal near a large army base in South Carolina. Soldiers coming back to camp would rush for the bus in such a wave it could not be loaded. Civilians were knocked down and trampled on. Two conclusions were presently heard: (1) "You can't change human nature"; (2) "Bring in the MP's and club them into good behavior."

Fortunately, no MP's were available, so the men looked for a more democratic solution. The facts of the traffic were studied. Then some two-by-four timbers were located, and with them the soldiers built a stout hand rail, doubling back and forth to make a queue to the door of the bus. Thereafter soldiers and civilians stood in line and loaded the bus in fair and orderly fashion. Nobody was clubbed; nobody trampled. A simple structural device had transformed a wild riot into a well-behaved military group getting what it wanted, i.e., transportation back to camp. Similarly, says Tatum, Major Estes has provided an effective hand rail for group discussion.

"AMERICAN ARBITRATION"

If two of your friends ask you to settle a quarrel for them, you become an arbitrator. If they ask you to help them settle it themselves by keeping them calmed down, you are a conciliator or mediator. Conciliation is the earlier and better technique on our list for labor disputes, but often in labor disputes and elsewhere, the situation has gone so far that it is either arbitration, or battle on the picket line or in the courts. Fortunately the duel with lethal weapons has disappeared from our culture.

The State of New York enacted the first American arbitration law in 1920. It not only sanctioned machinery for settling current disputes out of court, but allowed arbitration clauses to be written into many contracts, thus cutting down future conflict. "Under this law, agreements to submit to arbitration future disputes arising out of the contract . . . were made legally valid, enforceable and irrevocable."[1] The courts were closed to such disputes until after they had gone through the arbitration procedure. Later, the parties might appeal.

What is the machinery? It is quite simple. Although the state sanctions it, and lawyers usually run it, the procedure itself is

[1] Quoted from Frances Kellor, whose book summarizes the history of the movement. See Bibliography.

voluntary and private. You can use it yourself if you get into a quarrel with somebody and look with apprehension at a trial in court. You can go to the nearest branch of the American Arbitration Association and choose a man from their panel of solid citizens. Arbitrators work without pay as a public service. You and your opponent pick your man, go to his office, taking lawyers if you wish. The arbitrator will hear your stories and render a decision. He will probably be well versed in your particular business, much more so than the average judge or jury. It will be all over in an hour or two, and you pay the Association a ridiculously small fee, saving money, time, and bitterness. Let us look at an actual case.[2]

The Lady and the Cherry

Mrs. Q. was walking outside a fruit market on a rainy day in New York when she suddenly slipped on a sidewalk hatch and had a bad fall. She was in bed for a month and sued the fruit man for one thousand dollars. She said a cherry or a strawberry caused her to slip; he said it was the rain and she should have watched her step. The suit was scheduled to be tried in Municipal Court, where the calendar was some three years behind.

After a year of waiting, both sides decided to try arbitration. They met in an office on Fifth Avenue. The arbitrator they had chosen from the panel of the Association happened to be Watson Washburn, once a ranking tennis player, now a lawyer. He was seated at a desk in a small room and invited Mrs. Q. and the fruit man to sit at a table in front of him. There was no audience, no stenographic record, no publicity. Everything was easy and informal; cigarettes were passed.

Mrs. Q. exhibited her doctor's bill of $51, and another bill of $50 for extra help as she lay abed. The fruit man told his story. The cherry on the hatch did not stand up very well. The hearing lasted an hour and ten minutes; both parties then went home to await the decision.

[2] Following Jack Alexander in *The New Yorker*, April 24, 1937.

Just three days later, Mr. Washburn awarded Mrs. Q. one hundred dollars, which the fruit man was willing to pay. Each gave the Association ten dollars. The arbitrator was rewarded by a sense of civic duty well done.

This procedure is in staggering contrast with what would have happened to Mrs. Q. and the fruit man in the Municipal Court—assuming they had lived long enough to see the case come to trial.

There are hundreds of cases like this. They come to the arbitrator in a non-hostile way compared to a legal trial. There are no fearsome legal documents, not even a "vs." The settlement is usually in money rather than a two-valued judgment of "guilty" or "not-guilty." Many industries now require an arbitration clause in their contracts—shoes, wool, silk, furs, theatrical, insurance, stock exchange brokers. A number of contracts between unions and employers include the standard American Arbitration clause. Meanwhile "those back of the Arbitration Association have a long-range hope that if the movement progresses as it should, it may some day become the basis of world peace."

Refrigerators

A foreign department, opened in 1947 by the A.A.A. and called the International Business Relations Council, is already operating in more than forty countries. In a recent case which it handled, a New York firm shipped sixty electric refrigerators to Singapore. When the importer unpacked them, he found their white enamel streaked with rust and quite unsalable. Before the coming of I.B.R.C., this would have meant an interminable legal brawl with international complications, at great expense. A representative of I.B.R.C. in Malaya promptly inspected the refrigerators and forwarded his expert report to New York. There three arbitrators, skilled in the business, met with the exporter. The importer in Singapore was not even represented. But inside an hour he was awarded two thousand four hundred dollars to refinish the cabinets! Within a month he had sold them all. "Americans," he told his friends, "can be absolutely fair, even with a foreigner ten thousand miles away."[3] It would be nice if General Mao had the same idea. Certainly this kind of co-operation does no harm to world peace.

Settling Out of Court

The British have something they call a "pre-trial conference" with a Master as a kind of official conciliator appointed by the court. The procedure is being introduced in America, but here a judge in chambers takes the place of the Master. He can often halt a quarrel before it becomes irreconcilable. Sometimes a marriage is saved by such a judge without a divorce trial.

Lawyers, too, settle a vast number of disputes in their own offices before they get to court. My friend, Ernest Angell, a New York lawyer and board chairman of the Civil Liberties Union, tells me that most negligence suits are so settled. Criminal cases must go to trial, of course, but not civil cases if someone can catch them in time.

The late Sidney Howard, one of Angell's clients, was threatened with a suit for plagiarism on account of his play, *The Silver Cord*. A certain Mrs. X. had written and copyrighted an earlier play with a similar theme, about the attachment between mother and son—what Freud called the Oedipus complex. Angell set out to learn how Howard had actually built his plot and was told of a parallel story in his wife's family. By means of a good deal of leg work, tact, and plenty of sagacity, Angell got the facts from the relatives-in-law, complete with affidavits. He then invited Mrs. X., her lawyer, and Howard to his office and explained the situation. At the end of an hour's frank discussion, Mrs. X. withdrew her suit, convinced that the close resemblance between the two plots was coincidence, not plagiarism.

Benjamin J. Kizer, partner in a large law office in Spokane, agrees with Angell, and adds an interesting financial note in a letter to me:

Our firm and nearly every first-rate firm of lawyers, settles ninety percent of the disputes which come to us out of court. We could settle a higher

[3] Story from the *Christian Science Monitor*. Reprinted in *Reader's Digest* (November, 1949).

percentage if clients came to us in time, before too much bad blood and misunderstanding is engendered. . . . We succeed because we are professionally cool and patient in probing the problem. Doing so, we discover common ground, which is always there if clients have not become too impatient, or too inarticulate to discover it.

Kizer says the general impression that lawyers spent most of their time locked in forensic battle is false. It arises because the public rarely hears of the lawyer except when he is in the courtroom, making news. A prolonged lawsuit can be a financial disaster for a busy lawyer as well as for his client. "On the other hand, a settlement takes so much less time that the lawyer can be better paid per hour for negotiating it."

This seems to be another situation, like the strike, where the one fight makes the headlines and the nine peaceful settlements are never heard of. One of the worst things about going to court is the frustration arising from endless delays. "Disputes," says Kizer, "are like cancer. If caught early enough, broadly speaking, they can be treated successfully, and the patient will enjoy complete recovery. But if allowed to go too long, they become incurable." We remember Dickens' classic case of *Jarndyce* vs. *Jarndyce*. We think, too, of a cold war that nobody caught in time.

CHAPTER SIXTEEN

Down in the Valley

THE machine age not only puts people under tension, it puts nature herself under tension. Soils, waters, forests, can all be thrown out of balance by the processes of industry and mechanized agriculture. The ecology of a whole river valley can be wrecked by a few decades of forest cutting and one-crop farming, especially when speeded by tractors. Floods, soil erosion, silting, stream pollution, forest fires, dust storms will overwhelm even the gains of mass production. In due course they can send a great watershed into physical bankruptcy—which is a good deal worse than the paper kind. Then the people learn that they too are a part of nature. Eroded soils erode the temper of those who try to wring a living from them; conflicts and frustrations mount with their poverty.

This majestic downward cycle had long been in progress in the valley of the Tennessee River, where one-crop farming was the rule. In 1933 the federal government created the Tennessee Valley Authority and gave it a large appropriation for some mammoth engineering works, to see if the cycle could be reversed. After nearly twenty years of experience the answer is clearly yes. If the conception is wide enough, and the undertaking substantial, it is possible through modern science to check the decay, bring the soils and waters into balance, and increase the well-being and security of the people.

It is only partly, however, an engineering task. Twice the money and twice the engineering talent could not have reversed the downward trend in the Tennessee, except briefly. The people of the Valley had to see a vision and go to work themselves to make it come true. Otherwise the dams might as well never have been built.

The TVA is a success because it has combined superlative engineering with a rare approach to human relations and so, in a way, has joined physical with social science. It won the interest of the people, and it held back on plans until the people were ready to participate; entrusted everything possible to their direction.

The Valley folk were beset with frustrations and problems when the TVA was organized. Their young people were leaving for the big cities; their farming was stagnant and inept. "Crop rotation may be all right, but I don't do it that way," said the old farmer. Malaria was rife in the lower areas; cotton mills were closed down. Thousands of families living in reservoir sites back of the dams began to realize that their homes must disappear under fifty feet of water. It seemed the crowning defeat. Business men, workers, local agencies were skeptical if not downright terrified of what was moving down on them from Washington. Money would be spent in the Valley, which was good, but what was to be the price in freedom and independence? Opposition was widespread.

The TVA staff had a choice between two main policies: authoritarian or democratic. The staff could lay down the law, telling people what they had to do, or it could show the plans to the people first and ask for their advice and help in carrying the plans out. The late Dr. Harcourt Morgan, one of the three original directors, had lived in the Valley a good part of his life, knew the people well, and believed in them. He urged the democratic way.

This approach was chosen and consistently followed with all groups. It undoubtedly has taken longer; it has required great patience and skill on the part of the staff, but it has amply demonstrated its superiority over the authoritarian approach.[1] When Congress threatened an attack on the TVA recently, the entire Valley, nearly every newspaper and business interest, almost every man and

1 See David Lilienthal, *TVA: Democracy on the March,* for a full account.

woman, rose to its defense. It had become *their* project, not Washington's.

Decatur

Suppose we pay a visit to Barrett Shelton, editor and business man in Decatur, Alabama, and ask him to tell us at firsthand how the policy came to his town.

Charles Krutch, who is responsible for many of the superb photographs of the region, introduced me to Mr. Shelton. We had flown down the Valley from Knoxville on a sunny fall day. The crests of the Great Smokies rose cold and blue above the mist. Chattanooga was buried in smoky fog, with only Lookout Mountain visible. The river wound in silver loops, and now and then widened into a tremendous sprawling lake, with the thin line of a dam at its throat.

Recalling this region the first time I saw it from the air, in the early 1930's, I noticed a great change, not only in the water area but in the land. Checkerboard fields have been replaced by sweeping contours over large areas to form an unfamiliar but harmonious design. There are more woods on the steeper slopes, more pastures on the less steep. I noticed farms on flat mountain tops, high roads in white, farm roads in yellow, strings of barges on the river, a sprinkle of white dots for a town—a noble river in a noble great valley, which should support a sturdy people forever.

The town of Decatur, on one of the widening inland seas, was easily recognized by its tall grain elevators. Shelton met us at the airport, a lean, energetic man in a white felt hat, with a fine Alabama drawl. As he drove us around town, he gave us his philosophy: "People are all right; trust them and they will come up with the right answers. But you've got to tell them facts; they have to know the score. We've been operating on this basis for years here in Decatur, and we've made this town over. Now we're working on something bigger, planning along the same lines for the fourteen surrounding counties."

"Who is 'we,' Mr. Shelton?" I asked.

"Why, the Chamber of Commerce, the business men, the solid

citizens of Decatur," he replied. Then he launched into history.

Back in 1933, this town of twenty-five thousand, which now looks so bustling and prosperous, had a population of only twelve thousand and was in very bad shape. Cotton was down to five cents a pound and many farms were being sold for taxes. The railroad shops and the hosiery mill, the only two substantial industries in town, had closed. Seven of the eight banks in the county had failed. Solid citizens were in despair; less solid citizens were hungry.

Into this dismal scene, late one winter afternoon, came David Lilienthal, a director of the newly commissioned Tennessee Valley Authority. Four leading citizens met him. We were almost frankly hostile, said Shelton. We told him in effect: "All right, you're here, you were not invited, but you're here. You are in command, you have the money. What are you going to do?" Lilienthal leaned back in his chair and smiled. "I'm not going to do anything," he said. "You're going to do it."

Thus the keynote was struck early. Lilienthal went on to say that the TVA would provide engineering tools—flood control, navigation, malaria control, agricultural advice, cheap power—but "what you do with these tools is up to you."

Later Harcourt Morgan came with a similar message. The solid citizens wanted to increase prosperity by inviting industry from other parts of the country, holding out the bait of cheap labor and cheap power. Harcourt Morgan opposed the plan and suggested developing the resources around Decatur, putting what local capital there was into home industries.

Our townspeople needed jobs, said Shelton, our farm people needed regular month-to-month income rather than once-a-year income from the cotton crop. The old way of doing things had broken down and had to change. We realized, too, that we had to quit reaching into other sections of the country and trying to bribe factories to come down here. Our job was to diversify agriculture and diversify local industry. Never again must we be dependent on a one-crop, one-industry system.

The TVA gave Decatur physical security by controlling the river

against floods and the rest. It offered the town a broad policy to fit
its resources. But local citizens organized and carried out the new
policy. They made a new way of life on their own responsibility.
Now they take a fierce pride in what they have done. "Look at this
factory . . . and that market . . . and those terminals, did you ever
see anything prettier?" I was particularly impressed with three
modern structures—a flour mill, a high school, and an enormous and
very sightly water tank.

Today there are eighty-seven industrial plants in town, employing five thousand workers and making such diverse products as
bricks, furniture, canned meat, steel ships, aluminum, hats, cotton-
seed oil, fertilizer. The farmers in the surrounding areas, instead of
receiving cash once a year for their cotton, have a daily cash market
for timber, corn, wheat, livestock, poultry, milk, small grains, truck
crops. The consumption of electric power has jumped from twelve
million kilowatt-hours in 1938 to one hundred and twenty million
in 1948, a tenfold increase!

"How about advice from the TVA, as well as tools?" I asked.

"We get plenty—when we want it. The staff will work weeks and
months on some of our requests for industrial and agricultural
advice, but never once has there been any directive to us. They just
say, here are the facts, the policy decision is up to you."

Not all of the TVA activities in the Valley have been so dramatic
as this. A few have been unsuccessful. But all have been informed
by the same spirit, a spirit well stated in the 1936 report to Congress:

The planning of the river's future is entrusted to the TVA. The planning of the Valley's future must be the democratic labor of many agencies
and individuals, and final success is as much a matter of general initiative
as of general consent.

Agreements on Twelve Fronts

Visitors to Knoxville are surprised that such a large organization
as the TVA has such modest headquarters. They are prepared for
another Pentagon instead of some small, rather shabby office buildings. One reason for the lack of ostentation is that most of the ac-

tivities, outside of power generation and flood control, are operated by local agencies up and down the Valley from Kingsport to Memphis. Over the years, by a series of agreements, TVA has energized a vast number of programs, such as the one we saw in Decatur. John P. Ferris, head of the Office of Reservoir and Community Relations at Knoxville, outlined twelve major groups with whom agreements had been negotiated:

1. People displaced by reservoirs.
2. Labor unions whose members constructed the dams.
3. Farmers who agreed to take part in demonstration areas to check erosion and improve farm and forest practices.
4. Rural electrification co-operatives which bought TVA power.
5. Cities and towns which did the same.
6. Public and private health agencies which co-operated on malaria control, river pollution problems, and the like.
7. Business organizations, Chambers of Commerce, Service Clubs. (The Decatur Chamber of Commerce was the first of these.)
8. State agencies. The Valley includes parts of seven states.
9. Other federal agencies in the Valley.
10. Quasi-public associations like the Red Cross, Boy Scouts, and so on.
11. Land-grant colleges—co-operating especially in agricultural and training programs.
12. Special purpose agencies—some of them very large, such as the Atomic Energy Commission's city at Oak Ridge, and the Aluminum Company plants which use huge blocks of TVA power.

All kinds of people with all kinds of interests and points of view are involved—farmers, workers, union members, small business men, large business men, government people, university people, newspaper publishers, doctors, teachers, local politicians, engineers. The TVA must not only avoid disputes with these interests so far as possible, but must conciliate quarrels between rival interests concerning a TVA project. Think of the possible turmoil engendered by the location of just one dam—what it does to highways, railroads, and power lines, to real estate, to business opportunities, to the people going under water, to county taxes and schools, to field and forest, to the fish and game population, the mosquito population, to public health.

Obviously the TVA has been carrying on a large series of experiments in group dynamics without calling it that. Ever since that midwinter day in 1933 when Lilienthal came to Decatur, the experiments have been in progress on a hundred fronts—meetings in country school houses, in city halls, in open fields, in union headquarters, in packed auditoriums, up and down the Valley.

It would be possible to study scientifically the human relations involved—though the social scientist would have to take a leaf from the ecologist, who must face his multiple correlations as they come without benefit of a laboratory. I could find no evidence that such studies have been undertaken.[2] The TVA approach to any given situation seems to have been intuitive, like that of Cyrus Ching, or the Quakers. Once an approach is found to work, it is repeated. Thus a number of useful and practical techniques are now available. There is little theory to explain them, and obviously here is a gold mine for a competent team of social scientists to explore. *Per contra,* I suspect that there are already some dependable principles and techniques at Bethel, Michigan, and elsewhere, which could be useful to administrators at Knoxville.

In these circumstances the reporter must approach the subject by the casework method, describing what the TVA people do rather than the theory or principle on which they operate. We already know *why* they do it, but *how* they do it deserves a good deal more research. First, however, a word on the river itself.

Taming the Tennessee

The mountains of North Carolina, Tennessee, and Virginia form one of the heaviest rainfall areas in the United States. Every winter the white water gushes from their high valleys to spread potentia

2 H. E. Ball of the TVA is thinking hard about making some, however.

disaster down below. Chattanooga used to suffer the heaviest flood damage. Now, however, some twenty-eight great dams have gentled the Tennessee and its tributaries into a series of lakes, while reforestation, contour plowing, crop rotation are holding soil and slowing the runoff. It is the most completely controlled large river in the world, and probably the pioneer demonstration for rivers all around the planet. Engineers and students come from every country to observe it in harness, keeping W. L. Sturtevant and his information staff on the jump. Gordon Clapp, chairman of the Board, recently toured the valleys of the Near East to tell them about the Tennessee.

It is exciting to watch the engineers at their blue and silver control boards, playing the levels of the river as one plays an organ. The order of play is as follows:

First, prepare for flood waters. Reservoirs must be ready to hold back the surplus, especially from December to April along the main river. Correlation must also be made with floods in the Ohio and the Mississippi.

Second, try to maintain a high firm load (steady year-round output) of electric power. A drop of water, coming from the mountains, helps to turn as many as twelve water wheels, one after another, all the way down to the Ohio River in Kentucky.

Third, kill off mosquito larvae by raising and lowering reservoir levels, and so control malaria. Before the TVA came, one person out of four in some areas in the Valley had malaria parasites in his blood. Surveys in 1948 revealed no area in which the ratio was higher than one in two hundred and fifty. A limited survey in 1949 was entirely negative. Dr. E. L. Bishop has headed this fine work. A serious conflict developed at one time between the malaria control experts and the wild-life protection experts. It was resolved by a joint series of experiments which proved that a certain delicate adjustment of reservoir levels would help both situations—another illustration of the way facts can reduce conflict.

Fourth, keep the nine-foot navigation channel, six hundred and thirty miles long, clear from Paducah to Knoxville.

Fifth and last, please as many citizens as possible without interfering with the first four mandates. The engineers try to keep levels adequate for recreation, bathing beaches, fishing, and the like.

A business man, for instance, calls the control room and wants the level dropped two feet so he can drive piles for his new recreation pier. Within ten minutes another business man calls up and wants the same reservoir raised a foot to float a stranded barge. A little later, two farmers want it down so they can get over to an island and harvest their corn. Levels may be shifted to recover the body of a drowned man or even to save a cow. Says the chief engineer, C. E. Blee:

> The operation of the system has been carried out over the past several years as planned. During this time a number of moderately large floods have occurred and have been successfully controlled. No extremely large floods have been experienced, but the planned reservations of reservoir space for flood control have been maintained, and such a flood may be awaited with confidence.

Awaited with confidence. Ah, if we could do that with the floods of human misunderstanding!

The Story of Cash Point

So much for the tools; now let us go back to the TVA approach to people. Here is Cash Point, a community of sixty families in southern Tennessee near the river. In 1935 its eroded cotton fields, tumbledown houses, sagging barns, three battered churches, and three hundred dispirited people did not make it a happy community. With no enthusiasm at all, Cash Point signed up as a demonstration area. This meant that farmers who volunteered could get together with TVA experts to redesign their crop pattern. They would receive some seeds and fertilizer, and could rent tractors and equipment.

Things dragged along with little interest by the community until 1942. By that time a few of the volunteer farms were beginning to show results in increased yields, and one or two local leaders were urging wider use of the new practices.

Suddenly, said Director James Pope—who told me the story and showed me the documentary film which went along with it—this hitherto aimless group surged into life. Woosh! The preacher puts on overalls and learns to run a bulldozer. Every man and boy in town volunteers for the working teams. Woosh! Crews swarm over the landscape, filling gulleys, building terraces, grading and sowing and planting.

The production of corn, hogs, milk, beef, as well as cotton, takes a long jump ahead. People begin to talk about *our* land, *our* community. New houses are built, barns are repaired, a power line appears, followed by electric pumps and freezer lockers. The town acquires a fine new school, a library, even dressmaking classes. The Baptist preacher meanwhile welcomes everyone into his church, the least decayed of the three, as a new "community" church—a move practically unheard of in this region of fierce religious rivalries. Baptists, Methodists, and Presbyterians all begin meeting together. Woosh!

Family feuds cool off as prosperity increases. The whole town turns out to pick cotton for a man who is laid up sick. In all these activities the people do the work, while the TVA and the College Extension Service provide the technical advice.

I wish I had space to tell about Rabbit Creek in North Carolina, where the people set their own goals in a ten-year program and passed them long before that time. Three-fifths of Rabbit Creek has a slope of 25 per cent or better, the kind of land where you have to be careful not to fall out of your cornfield.

I wish I had space to tell how the people of Wayne County brought their woodlands back. Boys fighting in Europe used to ask first of all in their letters home: "How is our school forest getting along?" The TVA when originally set up could have bought large acreages of cut-over land very cheap and put them under strict regulation. A slower and more difficult course was decided upon: show land owners, by demonstration and education, that good forestry practices and private operation can go hand in hand. Such a policy is a little hard on trees but easy on people—until people get the idea. Then it can become the best kind of conservation, because people understand and want it.

Dam Builders

I found a similar approach in dealing with the men who, in yellow steel helmets, build the dams and powerhouses. It corresponds to step eight in Selekman's scale—real co-operation between men and management. As early as 1935, fifteen A.F. of L. craft unions were recognized by the TVA and later seven white collar unions. Contracts were negotiated with these groups under conditions of mutual trust. Strikes have been unknown, except for one or two small jurisdictional walkouts.

In 1942, joint labor-management production committees were inaugurated where workers were encouraged to offer suggestions for increasing efficiency and morale. The war was on, and TVA power was in great demand for war industries. The old standby of the traditional foreman: "You do the work; I'll do the thinking around here," became obsolete. Everybody was urged to do some thinking. There is a photograph in the house organ, *Teamwork,* that shows a carpenter on the Fontana dam receiving an award of merit. He has invented a special tool to clean threads on form bolts and thus speed the erection of the wooden forms which hold the concrete while it sets.

Thousands of suggestions have been received by the joint committees on the various projects. When the matter of a cash reward came up, the workers' representatives decided *against* it. They said cash rewards would emphasize individual instead of group contributions and might start arguments about who had the idea first. The joint committees also make it their responsibility, aided by documentary films, to explain the whole great organization to every employee and show him where his work fits in.

Union representatives meet regularly with the TVA directors, not to discuss grievances, but to talk over all sorts of things of mutual interest. "In all these ways," says George F. Gant, the general manager, "employees take their place with farmers, scientists, business

men, educators, through whose identity of interest and effort the
TVA program is achieved." The program is being built directly
into the culture, like the public school system.

Schools

While building a dam, most workers live with their families. The
lonely single man in a tough construction camp is unknown. When
one dam is finished the family moves on to the next. The TVA constructs a sightly town at each dam site which can be utilized later,
perhaps, as a recreation center. Schools are built for the workers'
children and equipped with the latest in educational facilities and
ideas. Then as rapidly as possible, local authorities are asked to take
over the responsibility and carry on after the dam is completed. The
local people are proud of their new school buildings and new techniques and equipment. These become models and help to vitalize
the whole Valley's public school system.

Power Bills

The cities and towns and rural lines that buy TVA power—one
hundred and forty-five of them altogether—take full charge of dis-
tribution and collect the bills from the consumers. But the contract
with TVA stipulates that any profits go back to the consumer and
must not be reserved for municipal purposes, however useful. There
is a steady temptation, according to Joseph C. Swidler, general
counsel, to snare some profits from power operations for a new fire
engine or swimming pool.

A town which we will call "Chester" built a fine city hall and
office building out of power profits before the TVA caught up with
it. There was no litigation. Swidler went down and talked to the
city fathers of "Chester," explaining that if one municipality started
upon this course, all would follow suit, and the power policy for
the Valley would be wrecked. He suggested a face-saving device
whereby the town power unit took over the new building, rented
offices to the mayor and other city departments at fair rates, and
thus paid back the "loan." Everybody was satisfied.

The policy of co-operation extends even to private power companies in the region. A speech by Eugene A. Yates, president of the five-hundred-million-dollar Southern Company in 1949 "painted a picture of the actual teamwork between the TVA and the private companies," according to the *New York Times*. Mr. Yates said it was quite possible for public and private concerns to "coexist harmoniously." This will be news to power magnates elsewhere, private as well as public.

Graveyards

A book could be written—and ought to be—on the handling of "displaced persons" from reservoir sites. These people are adequately compensated for their homes, but where shall they go after being torn up by the roots? With the first reservoir at Norris, the staff recognized that here was an exceedingly delicate operation in human relations, and lavished great care on it. I knew one of the TVA social workers who was especially skilled in persuading irascible old ladies to cease barricading themselves as the waters rose.

People are told of what is coming far in advance, and consulted about their future plans. Sometimes groups ask for a whole new community to be built to their design. Single families may want a farm on better land; or they may prefer to give up farming and move to town. The whole community is consulted most solicitously when a graveyard has to be flooded. Where shall it be moved; how shall it be arranged? Local committees usually take full charge of the plans, and the TVA sees that the plans are carefully carried out.

Valley Pattern

I have given only a brief sketch of roads to agreement in the Valley, but perhaps enough to indicate a fairly definite pattern. It looks like this:

The most important part is to trust people. Give them the facts. Give them time, all the time they want. If they will not co-operate after that, your idea was probably not much good anyway. Never crowd anybody if it can be helped.

The river should make as many decisions as possible. The water says we must do this, and we must do that. Not human will, but the hydrologic cycle determines action. After all, we are creatures, not of our imaginations, but of this earth.

Communication lines should always be open. Explain and explain the good things and the bad things, day and night. Listen to the people and their needs. Be alert for a call from old man Hitchcock, who wants the level down a foot to save his cow.

The Valley people must be consulted on all plans affecting them, from barge terminals to graveyards. As early as can be managed, put them in charge of operations. Twenty-five of the thirty new navigation terminals, for instance, were built by private capital and are run by local managers. The TVA is negotiating for private operation of the other five.

Finally, make projects voluntary, and encourage local leaders. Educate by demonstration not compulsion. Get one or two enterprising farmers to try the new fertilizer, and let them bring in the neighbors by their enthusiasm. . . . "*You* are going to do it," said David Lilienthal.

Why isn't this a pretty good pattern for the many great conservation projects which lie ahead of us all round the world? Why isn't it a good pattern for any sort of necessary change in habits and institutions? Why isn't it an example on a large and realistic scale of how to tap the energy locked up in groups?

CHAPTER SEVENTEEN

From the Files

ONE of the most difficult things about writing a book is deciding what to leave out. I have used a good part of my space and nowhere nearly all of my material. This is no encyclopedia, as the reader must be glad to realize; it is a journey of exploration.

The cases given in this chapter may not be the most important left in the files, but I think they are too interesting for one reason or another to omit. All are useful examples of agreement except one, and that is a social scientist's demonstration that the American political system should be noted more for its harmonies than for its battles—which may be news to some historians.

"Gripe Week"

Early in 1950, the city of San Francisco announced a "Gripe Week" and asked citizens to write to the mayor about their grievances. In the first three days, six hundred and twenty-five letters were received, covering a wide range of complaints—"sewers and street cars, parking tags and pigeons, bus drivers and B-girls . . . everybody gets into the act." Only three or four of the messages were from crackpots; only thirty were anonymous. The good ones were referred to the appropriate city department for action. Some frustrations of citizens were relieved and conflicts forestalled, and the city administration was improved. Other municipal governments might copy this excellent idea.

186

Protecting the Land

About half of the six million farmers in the United States are now enrolled in groups to protect their land. The groups are sponsored by the Soil Conservation Service, which operates in all but the TVA area. When the Service finds a local watershed or region in danger from erosion, one or two progressive farmers are asked to operate demonstration farms. Methods of crop rotation, contour plowing, gulley control, and so on are tried out, while the neighbors can look over the fence and see what happens. If the neighbors like what happens, they sign up with the Service; if not, they stay out; there is no compulsion. The experience of twenty years shows that most of them come in, and then the country has another action group, personally involved in saving natural resources.

Food Stamp Plan

We find the principle of participation, combined with the principle of "telling people in advance about changes which will affect them," brought out in classic fashion by the Food Stamp Plan. Milo Perkins was in charge of this government project during the 1930's, when ten to twelve million people were unemployed. It was a relief program designed in such a way as to save the self-respect of Americans who were hungry through no fault of their own. It was designed also to give more business to retail food stores—many of them in shaky condition—and while continuing to pay farmers for surplus crops, to reduce the costs of distributing food.

After the plan had been drafted in Washington—Perkins got the original idea while riding in a taxicab—a great many citizens were summoned for consultation. Retail grocers, meat dealers, wholesalers, packers, representatives from all branches of the food industry, also from labor unions, banks, transport services—every group which would be affected—arrived in Washington and went into conference. They were invited to analyze the plan, to show how it could be improved, to make sure that their own interests were considered. Some of the trade association representatives stayed on in Washington for weeks, conferring and discussing, until they began to think of it as *their* plan. And indeed they had made important suggestions for its practical operation. Retailers were especially enthusiastic, for the program brought not only new stocks to their shelves but also customers to buy them. The customers now had stamps in their pockets to pass across the counter, instead of standing in line like charity patients at the door of a government warehouse.

This historic example of agreement—the first great government project on record which was launched *without a single vested interest against it*—was not only a triumph for Perkins, but a case where skillful advance communication brought whole industries into active participation. It functioned with outstanding success for years, until with wartime full employment, customers had real money in their pockets again.

The Conference Committees of Congress

An important new law, like the Social Security Act, let us say, is up for debate in the Senate. After a terrible row, in which sixteen separate amendments are beaten down, a bill is passed. Another terrible row, with many amendments and roll calls, goes on in the House, until a bill is ultimately passed there too, but very different from the Senate version. The two bills then go to "conference," where members from both Senate and House sit down around a table to reconcile the separate views. After listening to the battle-cries on the floor, one might think that the conference room temperature might constitute a fire hazard. On the contrary, all is calm and quiet.

A new draft slides smoothly out of committee, with disputed points adjusted, and in a few days the bill has passed both Houses and been signed by the President. It may or may not be a good law—which is another matter. The point here is that the conference committee provides a technique for achieving agreement in a situation where, to listen to the uproar, agreement seemed utterly im-

possible. If we were not so used to this achievement we would call
it a miracle. How does the miracle occur?

It seems to be due to necessity. Our democratic machinery would
break down without some way of cooling the heat generated on the
floor of Congress. The conference committee provides refrigeration.
Sub-committees in Parliament have a similar function. Both get
away from the battle formation of the floor, with its two-party seating arrangement, to a smaller structure where men talk over the
purpose and practical details of a bill in a spirit of adjustment.
Observe that they are a small face-to-face group.

Such a procedure is good evidence that Congress and Parliament
are not as silly as they often sound. The question remains whether
they should not delegate additional matters to sub-committees,
assisted by experts on the facts, and reduce the sound and fury still
more. Congressmen often have to debate technical matters which
they are no more competent to discuss than I am competent to discuss quantum theory. If they could let men who know the subject
assemble the data and indicate the conclusions which the facts
demand, there might be no reason for argument and debate at all.
As in the case of the TVA, the river would decide. Such a procedure
would let Congress concentrate on its primary and important role
of policy-making.

Parliament has one important advantage over Congress which
well illustrates the critical importance of structural arrangements
in reducing conflict. In the United States the executive, from George
Washington on, has always been engaged in warfare with the legis-
lature, often at a temperature which melts out party lines. Even
Harry Truman, popular in the Senate for years, begins to battle
with his old colleagues almost as soon as he enters the White House.
In England, Sweden, Canada, and other democracies where the chief
executive and his cabinet sit in Parliament, this conflict is unknown.
Clearly it is not the men who cause the trouble so much as the
structure of their relations. Thomas K. Finletter, in his book *Can
Representative Government Do the Job?* offers some thoughtful
suggestions for improving the situation.

Finding Consensus

Public opinion research, though it suffered a setback in the elections of 1948, is an important tool for agreement. The election results made the pollsters re-examine their techniques, check more carefully, and qualify conclusions oftener, so that the tool is now stronger than before. "Sampling theory," on which polls are based, is a sound scientific procedure, allied to the laws of probability; and sampling of popular attitudes on important public questions is far more useful than mere forecasts of who will be elected. Such polls can help communication and reduce conflict in at least two ways:

1. By letting political leaders know what a majority of people want, or do not want. Newer techniques, furthermore, are showing the *intensity* of the want. Polls by George Gallup sampled American consensus in 1950 on these important public questions:

Atlantic Pact—75 per cent of people were for it.

Taft-Hartley Labor Law—majority for revision.

Government Health Insurance—majority against the present bill.

Brannan Farm Plan—Midwest farmers evenly divided.

Federal Aid to Education—64 per cent of people in favor.

Social Security Extension—majority of people in favor.

Registering all communists—majority in favor.

Hawaiian Statehood—80 per cent in favor. Majority also strongly favors Alaskan statehood.

Cabinet post for welfare—majority in favor.

Poll tax—67 per cent U.S. people against it; 53 per cent of Southern voters against it.

Such attitude polls do not necessarily prove that the majority is right, especially where technical information is involved, but they do serve to keep communication open between people and leaders.

2. By informing management what a majority of workers want, or do not want, through factory and office polls. This helps labor-management communication in a substantial way. I have used it with great benefit to check my findings in labor surveys.

3. To aid international understanding by letting the people of

the world know how a majority in this nation and that feel about world events. An actual case in May, 1950, showed that majorities in Norway, Holland, France, Italy, and Western Germany favored a political and economic union of Europe. The European unity movement, headed by Winston Churchill, retained Eric Stern to conduct the survey. Combining the five nations' vote, 64 per cent of the people were in favor, only 9 per cent were opposed, 27 per cent were on the fence. I do not know what the reader thinks, but I find these figures cheering.

London Health Center

A successful experiment in family problems has been made by the Peckham Health Center in London. Families join as a unit and come together to the Center, primarily for recreation. Once there, they scatter to playroom, social hall, gymnasium, swimming pool, nursery, cafeteria, theater, or concert hall, but meet from time to time in the corridors or lounges. The experiment attempts to provide recreation for various ages without breaking up the family unit. Here is a laboratory in group dynamics which would have delighted Kurt Lewin and which is beginning to attract worldwide attention.

Talking with People, Not at Them

Dr. Irving J. Lee, professor of speech at Northwestern University, is working on a research project which combines semantics with group dynamics. Observers compare the behavior of a face-to-face group when it is bogged down with what happens when it is doing well. "We have carried pad and pencil," he writes me, "to such groups as a Parent-Teacher Association, a church Bible class, a Student Council in a small college, an interracial committee in a large college, a foremen's study group, a board of directors in a medium-sized corporation. Wherever possible the observer's notes have been supplemented with sound or stenographic transcriptions."

Already some definite patterns are beginning to appear, although the project is in its early stages. When a group is in trouble, the following characteristics are often in evidence:

Members will be making assertions, not asking questions.

They will be contradicting one another.

They will be impatient of new facts.

They will imply that those who differ with them are untrust-worthy if not worse.

They will be calling names and attacking a person rather than his ideas.

They will mistake strong feelings for objective statements.

They will orate to an unseen audience outside rather than talk to their own group inside.

But when a group is going well, characteristics will be different, often the reverse of the above:

The speaker will talk *to* the group, not *at* them or beyond them.

Flat assertions will be rare, and questions abound.

New evidence will be welcomed.

Members will be "problem-minded," wanting to get the whole picture, rather than "solution-minded," wanting to get this thing settled now.

Ad hominem attacks will be rare.

Lee finds that explaining such distinctions to a group helps its performance. He appoints a member called a "spotter" to look for these telltale signs. We should watch with interest for his full report.

The American Assembly

We should also look for results from a new organization spon-sored by General Eisenhower and Columbia, called the "American Assembly," to offer technical service in forming opinion on com-munity problems. A hundred years ago, the sponsors point out, when a rural community gathered for a barn-raising, every par-ticipant understood clearly what the event meant to himself and his neighbors in terms of the work involved, good fellowship, the de-velopment of the countryside. But how can a citizen pass competent judgment today on such a barn-raising as a great federal housing project or a new steel mill coming into town?

A permanent staff of social scientists, located in a comfortable headquarters called Arden House, will form the core of the Assembly. Businessmen, community leaders, labor officials, plain citizens, who are faced with insistent questions in their communities, may bring them to Arden House for conference and expert advice. The idea is to explore areas of agreement, clear away sham battles, and find real differences, if any, in an atmosphere where politics and emotion are at a minimum. A great deal will depend, of course, upon the corps of experts. They might find some useful hints for reconciling differences in the organization of the Food Stamp Plan.

Trouble on the Border

Herbert Thelen of the University of Chicago, whom we met at Bethel, is one of a group studying race relations on Chicago's South Side. Negroes are much in demand in industry and their numbers are increasing. They must live somewhere, and are forced to invade "white" areas which border the Negro district. Thelen and his group are concerned with this border situation, which could flare into an ugly struggle.

When a Negro family buys a house, a meeting of neighbors is called to discuss the alternatives, which seem to be three:

1. They can throw rocks at the new neighbor.
2. They can ignore him.
3. They can send a committee to talk over neighborhood problems, such as care of the yard, radios at night, and the like.

The third alternative, Thelen tells me, is almost always chosen, and a committee is sent to establish workable relations. There is no attempt to reduce prejudice directly, no argument about "Constitutional rights." The goal is a practical structure for maintaining peace along the border. "But we hope," says Thelen, "after we establish some kind of accommodation, that prejudice will decline."

Lesson from History

A distinguished social scientist, Pendleton Herring, has climbed the heights to command a broad perspective on our democracy.[1]

1 *Pennsylvania Magazine of History and Biography* (April, 1948).

"In studying the basic machinery of democracy, the party system," he says, "we have spent too much energy on the study of conflicts, which to a large extent are sham battles, and have failed to grasp the co-operative constructive side of party power."

A party convention on a hot July night in Chicago is apparently the ultimate in human chaos, but somehow candidates are chosen, a platform is agreed upon, and what needs to be done is done. Political quarrels, such as the struggle over the tariff during fifty years and more, are obviously minor matters. They are not resolved, yet the country goes right on adding population, income, and concrete roads. The present hullabaloo about "big government" has raged so bitterly since Mr. Hoover's day that it is hard to see how it can ever be resolved. Yet the country will go right on adding population, income, and concrete roads.

Our national history as written, says Herring, has been mostly a casebook in conflict—wars, political battles, sectional struggles, who licks whom. But in some largely uncomprehended way our political system has survived, and the nation has prospered, until a single well-knit culture, with a continental market, stretches three thousand miles from coast to coast. How did we do it? Historians should go much further in clarifying the forces which have made possible the United States of America. While history has been largely written around struggle, the real news is union, co-operation, agreement, on a scale no nation has ever before dreamed of! Which is not to say that a number of structural improvements might not be introduced.

When Iceland was first settled from Scandinavia, a chronicler named Njal doubted if a permanent colony was ever possible, so sanguinary were the feuds and killings. One needs only to read a few pages of the Icelandic sagas to see how reasonable was his conclusion. *Yet during the entire nineteenth century there were just two murders recorded in Iceland!* William F. Ogburn, who sends me this story, emphasizes that there could have been no change in the Icelandic genes. People just stopped killing each other.

CHAPTER EIGHTEEN

Danger: Men Talking
Semantics as a Useful Tool

IN EARLIER chapters we have seen some ways in which an individual can use the new discipline of semantics to improve communication and reduce conflicts.

Semantics, which is no mere verbal manipulation, but makes use of physiology, neurology, physics, and other sciences in an extensive system, is aimed at three main goals:

To evaluate the environment more correctly, which means the ability to think straighter.

To communicate more clearly, both in sending and receiving messages. This is of course closely connected with agreement.

To use these corrected meanings in improving mental hygiene. The connection here is less direct, but it exists.

The hypothesis can be advanced, and the semanticists advance it, that many human conflicts are due not to natural cussedness but to failures in evaluation. This is above and beyond the simple misunderstandings that cause quarrels—as when a man goes to meet his wife at two o'clock and she goes to meet him at three.

We do fairly well in evaluating concrete things, but not so well with people whom we know, and very badly indeed with people we have never seen. Most of us are deplorably ill equipped to size up a public question objectively. The semanticists argue that this is not because people are "dumb"—semanticists have a healthy and demo-

cratic respect for the human mind—but because the language structure blocks them from using their minds effectively. We tend to con-
struct wildly inaccurate maps of the world outside our heads.
Semantics might be called a scientific search for better maps—a
simile which the late Alfred Korzybski was fond of using.

Whatever improves these maps and clarifies communication is
sure to help agreement. This book is not the place to explain the
details of semantic method. The reader can find them elsewhere,
and he will be well rewarded. Some sources are suggested in the
reading list at the end of this volume. Here I want to tell you about
some recent studies and describe some cases where semantics could
reduce conflict.

Talk Makes Us Human

Scientists are pretty well agreed today that what chiefly distinguishes humans from all other living creatures is the power to talk,
to communicate in words, to use the words to form abstract ideas,
and so to think. Julian Huxley made the point impressively in his
book, *Man Stands Alone*.

Now some recent experiments, reported in the *Scientific American* (August, 1949), compare dramatically the intelligence of young
monkeys with that of young children. The experiments show clearly
that the power of abstract thought, which of course is not innate
but must be learned, is learned primarily through language. At
first the monkeys' intelligence developed at least as fast as the children's. Only as they began to talk did the children leap ahead.

Talk, in brief, is what makes us human. Talk also allows us to co-
operate in larger and larger groups. At the same time, talk is responsible for many of our conflicts and disagreements: "I am not!"
. . . "You are so!" . . . "You're a liar!" . . . "You're another!"
. . . One can hear it in any kindergarten, or at Lake Success. If we
kept our mouths shut we would seldom quarrel, while organized
warfare probably would become impossible; political leaders could
not inspire patriotism, generals could not give orders. But our in-

tellectual powers might not much exceed those of a smart chimpan-
zee. Says Hayakawa:

Widespread co-operation through the use of language is the fundamental
mechanism of human survival. . . . When the use of language results,
as it so often does, in the creation of disagreements and conflicts, there is
something wrong with the speaker, the listener, or both.

Semantics tries to discover just what is wrong and make suggestions for correcting it. It tries to analyze the process of communication: how to interpret the signs, noises, warnings, coming in from
the world outside, and how to give out signals on which speaker
and hearer can agree. This is precisely what I am trying to do at
this very minute. If communication lines were clear, all around, I
should not need to write a book about agreement, and you would
not go to the trouble of reading it.

Two Kinds of Communication

Norbert Wiener, working with his calculating machines, is
interested in communication, not only as a high-speed modern industry, but also as a set of problems in meaning. He notes that we
can plaster the planet with millions of words at the speed of light,
though the content of the messages leaves a good deal to be desired.
He notes, too, that while many animals besides man live in groups,
no other has man's drive to communicate. Even a person blind and
deaf from infancy will make a desperate attempt to break through
the barrier. If the person is Helen Keller, she will succeed—at what
a cost the rest of us can barely imagine.

"Society can only be understood," says Wiener, "through a study
of its messages, and the communication facilities which belong to
it." We ordinarily think of a message as sent from one human to
another. "This need not be the case at all. If, being lazy, instead of
getting out of bed in the morning I press a button which turns on
the heat, I am sending a message to a machine." If the electric egg
boiler begins to whistle after three minutes, it is sending a message
to me. The thermostat sends messages to the oil burner to lay off the

heat—or lay it on. "Control is nothing but the sending of messages which effectively change the behavior of the recipient."

Wiener describes his alarming new computing machines, costing a million, with vacuum tubes flashing in their bellies, readily capable of playing a game of chess that would be "stiff and rather uninteresting but safe." These machines, he says, are not only ushering in a new industrial revolution, but giving us some startling insights on how the human mind works in its functions of logic and memory as well as message-sending. The machines cannot initiate a line of thought; but once a man "tapes" them and thus gives them something to think about, they can quickly outstrip him in speed, accuracy, and relative freedom from nervous breakdowns—though not even machines are entirely immune.

Super-Semantics

One reason why the study of communication has lagged is that people tend to take language for granted. Like air, it is omnipresent. Who can remember his first words? Many teachers and literary people furthermore feel a vested interest in words and meanings and are seriously disturbed by proposals to analyze them. Meanings, they believe, have been crystallized in dictionaries and good usage forever, except perhaps for technical additions. Semantics has not been warmly received in the colleges, though more than fifty are now offering courses.

All this indicates that language is a function of culture, and the two should be studied together. Fortunately, a small group of social scientists are doing this, developing a kind of super-semantics. They study a language, along with the beliefs and behavior of the people who speak it, and then arrange comparisons with another society speaking a different language. Some surprising conclusions are coming to light.

A Hopi Indian, said the late Benjamin Lee Whorf, "has no general notion of *time* as a smooth flowing continuum in which everything in the universe proceeds at an equal rate, out of a future, through the present, into a past, or in which, to reverse the picture, the observer is being carried in the stream of duration, continuously away from a past and into a future."[1] One can find no words, no grammatical forms, constructions or expressions in the Hopi language which refer to what we Westerners call time, or to ideas of a past, a present, a future, or to something which endures.

Yet Hopi, says Whorf, is capable of accounting for, and describing correctly in an operational sense, all observable phenomena of the universe. Just as it is possible to have geometries other than that of Euclid, so it is possible to have descriptions of the universe, all equally valid, which do not contain our familiar contrasts of time and space.

We are thus introduced to a new principle of relativity, which holds that all observers are not led by the same physical evidence to the same picture of the universe, unless their linguistic backgrounds are similar, or can in some way be calibrated. . . . We shall no longer see a few recent dialects of the Indo-European family, and the rationalizing techniques elaborated from their patterns, as the apex of the evolution of the human mind. . . .

Human languages are very diverse and go vastly farther back than written records. It is a sobering thought to find not only English, but every Indo-European language, handicapped compared to that of an Indian tribe.

Time varies with each observer in Hopi language and does not permit simultaneity—which is so cardinal a concept with us. A Hopi does not say "I stayed five days," but "I left on the fifth day." To study physics in Hopi, observes Whorf, would in some ways be easier and quite different. It is our Western time sense, built in by the words we learn, which trips us up when we try to grasp Einstein's principle of relativity. A Hopi Indian presumably would have little trouble with the fourth dimension.

Research of this type is one activity of the Foreign Service Institute of the State Department, where the Indo-European and other language structures are being analyzed, not only for their syntax,

---

1 Posthumous article in *American Linguistics* (April, 1950).

but for the way they make people think and act. An American will think differently from a Hopi, a Chinese, or a Trobriand Islander. Language, says Dr. Henry Lee Smith, Jr., who with G. L. Trager is directing this research, includes pauses, pitch, accent, emphasis, as well as the words themselves. Sometimes by changing an accent it is possible to reverse the meaning, though the words and their order are unchanged.

Our Western languages, including Russian, are historically connected with Sanskrit, Greek, and Latin. They not only make it hard for us to understand the fourth dimension, but erect a powerful barrier to agreement in what Dr. Smith calls "bipolarization." By this he means dividing things into two, and only two, opposite categories. Semanticists call it the "either-or" choice, or two-valued thinking. We feel obliged to judge events as right or wrong, good or bad, black or white, with no allowance for shades of gray. The Chinese language, among others, does not enforce two-valued judgments. As a result, the Chinese have been known as a tolerant and philosophical people, shy of absolutes, without the religious, racial, and ideological quarrels which rack the West.

If Smith is right about the Chinese language, one begins to wonder if the major ideology of international communism, with everybody polarized between wicked "capitalists" and heroic "proletarians," can be driven into the minds of the Chinese people. If he is right, they may be unable to absorb Marxism unless they first learn an Indo-European language.

Modern scientists studying the space-time world report few absolutes. From Mt. Everest to a glass of orange juice, events, they say, are in a process of change. Our language, however, is constantly fixing absolutes in our heads.

Our language, too, tends to make Westerners, and especially Americans, more competitive than other cultures.

It gives us a convenient way [says Dr. Smith] of judging ourselves against others in achievements in specified periods of time, and actually allows us to compete with our past selves. "Am I more successful now than I was ten years ago?" . . . Our purposive way of looking at life through language is reflected in our behavior and basic assumptions, and seems quixotic to other people.

This school of linguistics has introduced the culture concept into semantics and thus given it a new dimension. They have also suggested that a shift in our language structure toward the Hopi might make it easier to study physics, and a shift toward the Chinese might do away with a lot of ideological conflict. Obviously, research of this kind is very important to agreement. If our young career diplomats are able to absorb some of it, they will be enormously helped in understanding people of other cultures.

Seeing a Dog

The study of semantics proper goes deeper than words and language.[2] It begins with signs reaching the individual from the outside world. Light waves, sound waves are referred through his nervous system to association centers in the brain which give meaning to the signs. Thus the image of a dog coming along the optic nerve is associated with previous canines seen, heard, talked about, petted, or fled from, together with ideas derived from one's culture about the "friend of man." One says "I see a dog," with accompanying emotions.

If one had never had experience with dogs, there would be nothing in the file of memory, and no name would come—though one might say "no such animal," as explorers used to do when encountering a new species. No experience, no file, no savvy. The educators are just beginning to catch up with this tremendous principle. It means—does it not?—that nothing can be learned from words, or from books, unless a person has had specific previous experience to refer to.

The Hanover Institute can push this generalization further. If experience has grooved a pattern in your nervous system, you can

[2] This aspect is documented by Anatol Rapoport, a mathematical biologist at the University of Chicago, in his book, *Science and the Goals of Man.* See also Hadley Cantril, *The "Why" of Man's Experience.*

sometimes see *things which are not there*. Thus Adelbert Ames in his laboratory at Hanover, New Hampshire, asked me to look through the peephole of a screen. I saw a wooden chair, strong enough to sit on, a few feet away. Then he asked me to look over the top of the screen from another angle. Lo and behold, there was no chair, only some unconnected wooden rods hung on wires! When I went back to the peephole, however, the chair reappeared, and by no mental effort could I shake its solidity. Past experience with chairs had worn a groove which enable me to recognize future chairs by a few, not all, of their characteristics.

This whole demonstration illustrates one of the main principles of semantics: Before coming to a conclusion about chairs, or about anything else, try to get *all the major characteristics in*. Look at the event from another angle, from a lot of angles.

Another main principle, also emphasized by the Hanover work, is to talk in terms of the hearer's experience—or as McGregor would say, in terms of his "perceptual field." A great deal of "writing down" is done by advertisers and the compilers of school primers in deference to this principle. Merely shortening the words, however, is often not enough, and may only result in distortion or over-simplification.

Writing in *Fortune*, William H. Whyte, Jr., uses semantics to overhaul the recent educational campaigns by some business men to sell the idea of "free enterprise." He concludes that our canny tycoons have thrown away upwards of one hundred million dollars, because the copy has really been addressed only to other business men. Communication with manual workers, professional people, students, has not really been opened up. The words do not enter their perceptual field, and they are only insulted by the talking-down approach.

The prime obstacle to the confidence the business man must enjoy if he is to be believed, is the prime obstacle of every form of communication. It is simply the fact of *difference*. On this point most students of communication are in agreement; the great gap is the gap in background, experience and motivations. . . .

Though we cannot always close the gap, says Whyte, we can at least acknowledge it. He goes on to quote a profound remark of Dostoevski in *The Brothers Karamazov*, which every student of communication should keep upon his desk:

> If people around you are spiteful and callous and will not hear you, fall down before them and beg their forgiveness; for in truth you are to blame for their not wanting to hear you.

Some Avoidable Confusions

Language grows as the culture grows, and like the rest of the culture it lags behind what is actually happening out there in the space-time world. Probably our language of today would be adequate to evaluate the world of 1750, before Watt's steam engine. It certainly is inadequate for the atomic age without considerable adjustment. Mere technical terms do not bring it up to date; we need more precise ways to express *relations*. Following the normal use, we get involved in some staggering confusions. We have mentioned some and here are a few more:

An alarming amount of our thinking takes a form which can be expressed in the simple syllogism:

My grocer has cheated me
My grocer is a Yankee
Therefore, all Yankees are cheats.

I recently spent hours trying to argue a close relative out of this kind of generalization. She had a maid who had proved unreliable. The maid was a Negro, and therefore the whole race was unreliable. "You can't trust one of them; not one!"

An understanding of semantics automatically corrects such thinking. $Grocer_1$ is not $Grocer_2$; and conclusions applying to $Grocer_1$ cannot be applied to $Grocer_2$, still less to all grocers.

Here is another fallacious generalization:

This book says profits are bad
Business men try to make profits
Therefore, all business men are bad.

Instead of a legitimate protest against profiteering by, say, some wartime speculators in sugar or rubber or other commodities, one damns the whole business group of Western civilization, who perform many useful and vital functions. The semanticist asks: What business man are you talking about? When? Where?

The reverse syllogism is equally unsound:

Adam Smith in his book says profits are good

The Widget Trust makes huge profits

Therefore the Widget Trust is good.

But the facts might show Widgets Consolidated as the most unconscionable band of pirates since Al Capone.

Semantics reminds one to put dates on events before passing judgment, viz:

Brown was a contributor to Russian Relief

Russia is run by communists

Therefore Brown is a communist.

The student of semantics immediately inquires *when* Brown contributed to Russian Relief. He finds it was in 1942, when leading bankers, industrialists, college presidents, senators, were also contributing to Russian Relief, and praying that Stalingrad would hold.

Guilt by Association

The question of loyalty, which covered the front pages in early 1950, was easier to explain with the help of semantics. Many citizens were condemned as disloyal on the basis of guilt by association. As Francis Biddle points out, this means, in effect, that a person is declared guilty of acts committed by somebody else. The fact that he was seen talking to the somebody else, or even belonging to the same organization, was accepted as solid evidence.

Not only people but laws are condemned by association. The National Science Foundation Bill, designed to keep the U.S. in the forefront of scientific research, was bitterly attacked by a great newspaper of the Midwest. Why?

Dr. Harlow Shapley of Harvard is in favor of the bill

Dr. Shapley has belonged to groups labeled subversive by the Department of Justice

Therefore it is a communist bill.[3]

Westbrook Pegler proved himself a master of the art of suggesting guilt by association when he wrote in his column in June, 1949: "Although of course there is no charge of perjury against Mrs. Roosevelt in the Hiss case, she is co-defendant in a figurative sense because Hiss is a protégé of Felix Frankfurter who has been a power behind the throne ever since the New Deal began." Let us unwrap this museum piece:

Mrs. Roosevelt was married to Mr. Roosevelt

Mr. Roosevelt inaugurated the New Deal

Felix Frankfurter was prominent in the New Deal

Alger Hiss was a protégé of Frankfurter

Hiss is on trial for perjury

Therefore, Mrs. Roosevelt is on trial for perjury—"in a figurative sense."

The editor of the New York *Post* punctured this one with a semantic needle a few days later. He cited the Pegler column and went on: "And Westbrook Pegler is a communist because he played poker with Heywood Broun who was called a communist by Martin Dies."

A thorough grounding in semantics for the general population, at about the first year of high school, could pretty well forestall this sort of thing. Campaigns for power and office based on guilt by association would fall flat, if they were even attempted. The nation would enjoy a great deal more internal peace, while the F.B.I. would have time to catch more spies.

Confusions and Abstractions

India, as everyone knows, especially the Indians, is short of food. There is a large district where deer are so plentiful that they have become a pest. Killing them would increase the food supply with their venison, also by saving the crops which the deer now eat. Such

3 Cited by Marquis Childs in his column, September 19, 1949.

a course is impossible, however, because the name of this particular species is *cow deer*. Cows are sacred in this part of India and must not be harmed. There is a legislative proposal to change the name to *horse deer* and thus break the association. But E. C. Lindeman, just back from India, who told me the story, doubted that it would pass.

Here is a case of abstract gobbledegook in a government bureau.

A foreign-born plumber in New York wrote the Bureau of Standards that he found hydrochloric acid fine for cleaning drains, and did they agree? Washington replied: "The efficacy of hydrochloric acid is indisputable, but the chlorine residue is incompatible with metallic permanence."

The plumber wrote back that he was mighty glad the Bureau agreed with him.

Considerably alarmed, the Bureau replied a second time: "We cannot assume responsibility for the production of toxic and noxious residues with hydrochloric acid, and suggest that you use an alternate procedure." The plumber was happy to learn that Bureau still agreed with him.

Whereupon Washington wrote: "Don't use hydrochloric acid; it eats hell out of the pipes!"

Take such a term as "the Welfare State." There is widespread belief that it represents a solid entity. The word is there, so the thing must be there, too. But a little semantic reflection shows that it is only a label for grouping a whole cluster of real things, in this case agencies. One can take a picture of some of the agencies but not of the "Welfare State." Coming down the abstraction ladder to an examination of the Social Security Board, the Child Labor Law, the Red Cross, Workmen's Compensation, the public schools, the TVA, the Public Health Service, the G.I. Bill of Rights, the potato subsidy, unemployment insurance, and the rest—no one outside a mental hospital would approve of all the agencies, or condemn them all. Once I made a list of more than one hundred such federal "welfare" agencies, ignoring those in state and city.

To be belligerently for or against the "Welfare State," accordingly, is to be trapped in a verbal prison. Yet in the year 1950, the high schools of the U.S. had as their official debating topic, "RESOLVED: That the American People Should Reject the Welfare State" . . . which might mean, among other things, repealing the Homestead Act of 1863 and giving some three million farms back to the government.

People lost their tempers all over the country about something which was not there. If we could learn the art of getting down from abstract terms to see the real world, we might agree that old-age pensions are good in principle, but the law needs tightening up, and agree that the potato subsidy is thoroughly bad, in both principle and performance.

A Useful Tool

Elihu Root, arguing the famous Atlantic Fisheries dispute in 1910, admirably summed up the need for semantics:

Half the misunderstandings in this world come from the fact that the words that are spoken or written are conditioned in the mind that gives them forth by one set of thoughts and ideas, and they are conditioned in the mind of the hearer or reader by another set of thoughts or ideas. . . .

In this chapter we have suggested a few approaches to the subject of semantics, perhaps enough to interest the reader in going to sources, and to convince him, I hope, that here is a keen new tool for shaping agreement. Nearly every human quarrel is soaked in verbal delusions. If they could be squeezed out, as one squeezes a sponge, many quarrels would simply vanish.

Suppose we recapitulate some of the semantic principles:

1. Every event and every object is a process; beware of absolutes.

2. Things with the same name seldom have precisely the same characteristics: $Adam_1$ is not $Adam_2$. Beware of treating them as such.

3. Events are always changing. In passing judgment allow for the change. Russia in 1951 is not Russia in 1942.

4. Events usually have many sides, not just two sides. Beware of two-valued judgments.

5. Try to get all the main characteristics in before coming to a conclusion.

6. A fact is not an inference; an inference is not a value judgment. Keep them separate.

7. At some level, agreement is always possible. Keep looking for it.

8. A person with a mature mind—and I think Harry Overstreet will agree—is adjusted to uncertainty, not to fixed verities. Like a good driver at the wheel of his car, he is safe to the extent that he is ready for anything.

Once a person grasps the semantic idea, he is like a man released from prison—a prison of words. Most of us are still locked in. We march endlessly up and down our ideological cells, or round and round a prison yard paved with flint-like absolutes. Semantics helps to open the door and liberate us.

CHAPTER NINETEEN

The In-group and the Out

WE COME now to the most difficult of all problems in human relations, the clash between nations and cultures, our people against their people, the ins against the outs. The very loyalties that help reduce aggressiveness among ourselves often do so by turning it against the outlanders. Some students think this always happens, and leads to an impassable gulf. Must it always happen? Or can the big disagreements be handled like the little ones?

The "Eight Wise Men," a UNESCO office nickname for a group of social scientists from six countries, reported in 1948 that they could find no evidence that war is an inevitable function of human nature. . . . "Men everywhere want to be free from hunger and disease; want fellowship and the respect of their fellows; the chance for personal growth and development. . . ." Peace, they said, is a problem of keeping tensions within manageable proportions—a problem which will require some large changes in social organization.

If war were an inherited instinct, we might as well wait for the ultimate Z-bomb to end it all. An animal which at one time showed considerable promise would then be finished, leaving an extensive ecological mess for nature to clean up.

Loyalty to the In-group is not inherited, however, but taught by the culture. Any healthy baby transplanted to another culture will grow up intensely devoted to his foster land, unless it should treat him as an outcast. Culture—meaning habit, custom, systems of be-lief—is always learned, never in the genes.

Wars, too, are a cultural product. They do not *begin* in the minds of men, UNESCO's preamble to the contrary notwithstand-ing, but are supported there by the patriotism and nationalism which all of us learn in childhood. War-making, the anthropolo-gists tell us, is a widespread practice of governments, from small tribes up—or down. It lies deep in Western cultures, as shown in their budgets, where expenditures for wars, past and present, are anywhere from 50 to 80 per cent of all national costs.

Apparently the only way to get war out of a culture is to build a new institution to replace it—a "moral equivalent," in the words of William James. A super-government to replace the absolute sov-ereignty of nations would be such an institution. This is the effort behind the League of Nations, the United Nations, the Lilienthal-Acheson plan. Many of us hoped that the A-bomb, and later the H-bomb, would add power to that effort, but it now seems clear that the threat of atomic fission alone will not create One World.

The Lilienthal Plan

In an earlier chapter we looked at the method by which this plan was drafted as an example of good group action. The plan finally evolved was, to my mind, the best of all the proposals for inducing sovereign states to co-operate. It was not a political constitution, with executive, legislative, judicial, and voting procedures all com-plete, but an engineer's blueprint aimed at a single function: the control of atomic energy. The international agency which was to do the controlling, however, was so central and so vital that by a process of natural growth other functions might well have been added to it—the problem of world food supply, world epidemic control, conservation, weather information, industrial development in low-income areas along the lines of President Truman's "Point Four" program.

We might have waked up some fine morning to the realization that One World had arrived by functional growth, without any voting at all. The atomic control agency would have been training keen youngsters from all cultures to become in the course of their duties "world men," feeling their major allegiance to mankind rather than to Ruritania.

"If one solves the problem presented by the atomic bomb," said J. Robert Oppenheimer, who helped, as you know, to make it, and later to draft the Lilienthal plan, "one will have a pilot plant for solution of the problem of ending war." Oppenheimer said that his drafting group rejected all proposals exclusively designed for holding the bomb in check as too negative. They wanted positive action and therefore emphasized ways and means to put atomic energy to work in peacetime—power plants, better agricultural methods, cancer research. Their task was to *create* something rather than to *stop* something—a cardinal rule, I suspect, for all international proposals.

Other overall plans, such as Federal Union, United World Federalists, the Culbertson Plan, the Hutchins Committee, and the rest, while often brilliant in conception and informed by goodwill, lack the "process" implications of the Lilienthal plan. They tend to start off One World with a bang. Some advocates cite the American Constitution, which cemented thirteen little jealous nations into one political union. But the thirteen colonies, while jealous enough, and sometimes close to war, had pretty much one culture and one language. The world state is an intercultural problem even more than a political or economic problem.

New York as a Pilot Plant

There are eight million Americans in New York City. On another time scale, and not too long a one, they can be divided into 900,000 Russians, 2,000,000 Jews, 700,000 Negroes, 400,000 Poles, 230,000 Puerto Ricans, 500,000 Irish, 500,000 Germans, and so on, leaving a few Yankees here and there. Says E. B. White:

The collision and the intermingling of these millions . . . representing so many races and creeds, make New York a permanent exhibit of the phenomenon of One World. The citizens of New York are tolerant not only from disposition but from necessity. The city has to be tolerant, otherwise it would explode in a radio-active cloud of hate and rancor and bigotry. If the people were to depart even briefly from the peace of cosmopolitan intercourse the town would blow up higher than a kite. In New York smolders every race problem there is, but the noticeable thing is not the problem but the inviolate truce. . . .

New York thus shows us how diverse cultures can live together if they must. It is encouraging, but we must remember that these people, or their parents, left the old homeland voluntarily to come to America, and were prepared to accept its differences. In any showdown in New York, American culture patterns always have the right of way.

What culture patterns would have the right of way in One World? They will have to be built piece by piece, and that is a tougher task than the one presented to New York's melting pot.

THE FOREIGN SERVICE INSTITUTE

Two hundred and fifty miles south of New York, the searcher for agreement finds a serious effort at toleration and understanding in the Foreign Service Institute of the State Department, directed by Harry G. Hawkins and Frank S. Hopkins. This Institute trains men to understand the culture concept, and so to deal with the Outgroup. Its students are learning to appreciate people whose culture differs from that of Main Street and learning to communicate with them. If it is successful, this could be the most promising technique of agreement we have found in our whole study.

We noted in the preceding chapter the research of the Institute into linguistics, along the lines laid down by Whorf. Why is the Institute so concerned with such a project? To help our diplomats abroad evaluate foreign peoples by analyzing the effects of language on beliefs and behavior. In addition, the Institute operates a year-round school, with an outstanding faculty and a stream of some three thousand students, or trainees, a year, preparing for appointments overseas.

I spent the best part of a day going from classroom to classroom in this school. Here a group of young men were studying Turkish, using a high-speed technique for learning languages developed during the war and improved by the Institute. The technique is based on the principle that men *talked* a long while before they wrote—two hundred thousand years or so.

I also watched a group of forty foreigners, all employed in information work by U.S. embassies and consulates abroad, visiting Washington to study at firsthand the America they were serving. They all spoke English, some with heavy accents, and were full of questions about social security, Negroes, the Marshall Plan, voting procedures. Some could not quite understand why sledgehammer critics of the administration were not summarily deported. After their visit to Washington, the group was to split into three divisions and travel all over the country before going back to Teheran, Rome. or Bangkok.

Trade Treaties

The Institute's director, Mr. Hawkins, told me about his experience negotiating trade treaties for the State Department. Multilateral treaties, he said, were worse than bilaterals. His rules, worked out by trial and error, included: *first,* define the issue clearly and at length, thus saving weeks of argument at cross purposes. *Next,* list carefully all points of agreement, a procedure which will automatically narrow the area of disagreement. *Third,* if you come to the conference with a very strong case, let the solution develop gradually from the discussion. In this way the parties share in the outcome. If you show a strong hand at once, you may arouse so much resentment that your case will be lost.

If enough facts are available for trade treaty makers, said Hawkins, no deep disagreement need ever develop; a Quaker-like unanimity may even be possible. This kind of international solution will stick. But in our troubled and riven world of today, compromise, accommodation, majority-minority settlements may be the best that can be hoped in international dealings.

"How about Russia?" I asked.

"We shall be very fortunate if we can find a basis for accommodation," he said.

Educational Programs

The Institute has a short-range educational program and a long-range one. The first orients new employees in the work of the State Department, especially career men going overseas.

The long-range program among other things offers a course for experienced men. It is concerned with the kind of policy America will need in years to come. Policy-maker for the mightiest nation on earth promises to be quite a role, and one never played before by Americans. In accordance with this long-range concept, a group of foreign service officers of the Department were summoned back in the fall of 1950 for a special course.

What does the course look like? The foreign officers first are coached in social science and the culture concept. Each human society must be understood as a social complex, and this calls for experts in geography, sociology, anthropology, linguistics, social psychology, as well as economics and political science.

Then they study the situation the State Department faces in each major area abroad and are given a number of problem cases to discuss and come to policy agreements about: What should be done in the Philippines? In Palestine? In Yugoslavia? Berlin? Argentina? All main aspects of each area must be considered before a course of action is outlined. This checks with the semantic principle of "getting all the characteristics in."

Finally, before returning to their posts abroad, each foreign officer reports on what he has learned, to the whole group, in a pooling of experience. This checks with a principle in group dynamics.

The "freshmen" at the Institute, men who have not filled posts abroad, study similar courses, though less intensively. In one of their texts we read:

The great problem in international relations and in everyday dealing with foreign people is that most of us tend to identify our traditional ways of meeting problems, of organizing life, and of reacting to situations, as "human nature," whereas all of it is learned. Other peoples have developed different solutions to the same problems, and consequently have different "human natures." . . . Each people tends to regard its own particular culture as the best, furnishing the only proper solutions to problems, and to think of all others as either quaint, queer, or "cussed."

This is obvious enough when applied to South Sea Islanders, the thing is to apply it to ourselves! It is even more difficult to realize that foreigners regard many American customs and beliefs as queer if not downright perverted. The Institute strives to make its career men aware of this foreign attitude.

One course, for instance, studies the assumption of the American culture that every individual is pursuing a specific goal—a million dollars, the vice-presidency of the Stuyvesant Bank, the head of the union—"success" of some sort. But other societies interpret life as a series of activities, each satisfying in itself, without a far goal to keep pressing toward. To such people, American behavior is meaningless and quixotic. They do not understand the excessive competition which goes along with our worship of success. The State Department candidate is trained to allow for these differences in evaluation.

If young men in the Foreign Offices of all nations could be prepared like this, future world wars might never come. For these young men will be the authors of foreign policy tomorrow, the men who can make or break One World. Were I a young man again, I can think of no course I would rather take.

An International Language

Since language difficulties often block communication, why not establish a world language? This hardy perennial is quite logical, but there is a catch in it. Language is a function of culture, and we have as yet no world culture. A synthetic language like Esperanto would save time, money, and earphones at Lake Success, and possibly reduce some of our international misunderstandings. It could help tourists and greatly simplify trade and international transfer of students. But it could not provide the wit, the overtones, the literature, the warm familiar words of one's own language. It would not be talk, as human beings know talk. If we ever have a world culture, then perhaps we can have a real world language; but it may be a long wait.

Norbert Wiener believes that if scholars had not frozen and formalized Latin, it might have served as an international language today. Basic English is similarly logical; psychologically, however, it is impossible. A Frenchman as well as a Russian will bitterly oppose it; and there are enough conflicts in the skyscraper without adding this one.

In its place, the United Nations might ask a panel of experts to help devise an international communication system—perhaps it should not even be called a language. It might well be taught to all the school children of the world, along with the three R's. But do not let anybody try to translate *War and Peace* into it, or *Hamlet*, or *Huckleberry Finn*.

We already have, of course, a number of useful international communication systems, of which the most important is mathematics. A Pole can readily speak to a New Zealander in this language. Scientific findings should be international, and to a large extent they are, as the Nobel Prize and many international societies and conferences demonstrate. A great number of scientific and technical terms are worldwide; so are sporting terms. But sometimes they suffer a sea-change. In Yucatan I traveled a narrow-gauge line behind a gasoline-powered locomotive called a "Kalamázo" because the engine was manufactured in Kalamazoo, Michigan. Its engineer was, of course, a "Kalamazero," and a collision no less than a "Kalamazazo"!

International communication is widespread too in the metric system of weights and measures—though the United States and Britain still insist on rejecting parts of it. We have international systems of botanical and zoological nomenclature and a widespread international system for writing music. A Hungarian, without a word of English, can play in the Boston symphony.

INTERNATIONAL CONFERENCES

A world language would be a help in conferences where delegates must either try to think in a tongue they have not mastered or undergo the boredom and confusion of interminable translation—where meaning, like water in a worn-out pipe, leaks away at every joint. Is there any simpler method for improving international conferences? Why not use some of the principles looked at earlier in this book?

Why not, indeed? UNESCO is now engaged in a comprehensive study of this question. An International Advisory Committee, of which Dr. Walter R. Sharp is chairman and Charles S. Ascher, secretary, includes such eminent social scientists as Gordon W Allport, Dorwin Cartwright, Otto Klineberg, Pendleton Herring, G. Ronald Hargreaves, Rensis Likert, among others. These experts are concerned primarily with international conferences where delegates really want to agree, not with battle formations such as the Security Council—which we will look at in the next chapter.

There are three major communication difficulties in international conferences:

1. Translation failures, where one language lacks equivalent words or terms in other languages. Thus in a debate at Lake Success on the "inevitable" collapse of Nationalist China, a delegate protested that "inevitable" in the French translation carried the idea of "misfortune" and wanted the word stricken from the record.

2. Cultural differences, as already mentioned. Equivalent words may be found, but two nations may attach different meanings to them: "democracy," "compromise," "sacrifice," "loyalty," connote very different ideas to a Russian and to an American.

Take the word *"democracy,"* which in the West means the bill of rights, *habeas corpus,* free elections, the right of the people to depose their leaders. In Russia, however, it has come to mean the right of every citizen to a job and a living for his family, provided he obeys the rules. At the Potsdam conference, the victorious Allies agreed to establish "democracy" in Germany after the war. The negotiators had experts in military science, politics, and economics to help them, but no expert in semantics—who was needed most of all. So the United States went ahead in Western Germany and established its brand of democracy so far as possible, while the Russians, in their zone, went ahead and established their brand.

Before long, of course, the United States began to charge the Russians with violating their agreements about democracy and establishing a police state. The Russians charged the Americans with violating *their* agreements and establishing a capitalistic state. Neither side at Potsdam knew what the other meant by the term "democracy," but both thought that they did. Both sides are now outraged at what seems gross hypocrisy in the other.

3. The third major difficulty in international conferences is that members come as "instructed" delegates, not as free agents. To decide anything they have to get on the telephone to Moscow, New Delhi, or Washington. This destroys at one blow all our principles of conference procedure discussed earlier. We do not have a man at the international round table, so much as we have an alarm clock—all wound up.[1] Sometimes, says the UNESCO Advisory Committee, turning a man into a wound-up machine produces guilt feelings in the man, makes him aggressive, and further complicates the proceedings.

A favorite pastime, at Lake Success and elsewhere, is for a delegate to use the meeting as a sounding board for propaganda, rigging the parliamentary rules so that he can tell his story again and again. On a controversial item it is possible to hold a debate in the steering committee of the U.N., another in the full Assembly, then in the political committee, and again in the Assembly—making four propaganda blasts in a row! Meanwhile, the listening delegates doodle on pads of paper, read the newspapers, wander around the corridors, have a drink, fall asleep.

---

[1] This can happen inside a culture, too. A delegate may come "instructed" to a labor-management conference, for instance.

Diplomatic Emasculation

Ina Telberg, one of the chief interpreters, told me something of her troubles when she was active at Lake Success. Interpreters, as members of an impartial secretariat, not representing Ruritania or any other country, have to keep three balls in the air at once. They must heed all of the U.N. rules; they must try to give accurate reports to the outside world; they must not cause a delegate from any one of sixty nations to accuse them of unfairness. To accomplish this semantic miracle, the secretariat is forced to practice a prose style characterized by what Miss Telberg calls "diplomatic emasculation."

In such tight quarters, the production of gobbledegook is bound to be massive, often misleading to the outside world with its propaganda content, not infrequently choking up internal communication lines, while the official secretariat, to borrow a phrase from Thoreau, leads a life of quiet desperation.

Other difficulties in international conferences, as listed by the UNESCO committee, include overcrowded agenda, "hidden agenda," where real purposes are covered up, too many documents and not enough human contacts, excessive voting with little attempt to find the sense of the meeting.

In recent years there have been more than two thousand meetings per annum at Lake Success, and twelve hundred or so at Geneva. Elsewhere hundreds of international conferences are going on all the time—scientific, religious, commercial, fraternal, athletic. The problem of international communication is obviously immense and of the first importance. Unfortunately, it may be several years before the UNESCO advisory Committee will be ready to report in full.

Meanwhile some helpful suggestions have been given out. Formal rules, the committee says, are important in international conferences because delegates have no common cultural values to fall back upon. Again, find out early whether delegates come "instructed" or as free agents. Be very careful in using humor; a joke in one culture may be an insult in another. Thus "bull in a china shop" is a mildly amusing cliché in English and acceptable in Russian, where it becomes "elephant in a china shop." But on one occasion a Chinese delegate angrily demanded that the phrase be stricken from the record.

The committee believes that many findings about group action can be useful in international conferences. Face-to-face discussion groups should not exceed our old rule of twenty members. An observer trained in semantics, and a resource person ready to supply facts, can both be very helpful. The leader should know something about the culture concept. (Perhaps he ought to take that course at the Foreign Service Institute.) He should stress common functions wherever possible, and try to forestall the "taking of a position" by members early in the meeting. The more fluidity the better. Early agreement on small matters helps build up momentum for agreement on large matters later on.

If communication can be established, an international group has a richer mine of experience to draw upon than any intra-cultural conference has. It may be that face-to-face groups are destined to replace a good deal of the frigid and formal diplomacy of the past. If war is an extension of diplomacy, then diplomacy is a contraction of war, and both are exercises in conflict.

Now we have to exert every effort toward exercises in agreement. Somehow we have to find a road to One World. The International Advisory Committee of UNESCO and the Foreign Service Institute of the State Department are welcome guideposts along that road.

CHAPTER TWENTY

Two Worlds and One

THE television screen is very clear and Jacob Malik of the U.S.S.R. is in the chair of the Security Council of the United Nations. He looks like a successful business man, in a well-cut gray suit, a gray tie, and thinning hair brushed straight back. He is in complete command of himself and the situation, though he knows the Council is solidly against him, and most of the nations of the world, too, since Korea erupted in June, 1950. There are seven million television sets in America, and most of them are probably turned upon him at this moment. Americans in homes, country clubs, and bars are about to have a remarkable educational experience in how not to reach international agreement on anything.

Malik confers with three hovering secretaries and proceeds to describe the situation as he sees it. What he sees is invisible to the rest of the Council. He speaks in Russian, a harsh language to American ears, but we hear a simultaneous translation into English. He is saying the most appalling things: Wall Street instigated the South Koreans to attack the peace-loving North Koreans; President Truman is a warmonger; the capitalists are waiting to follow the army into Korea to enslave the population. He tells these thumping untruths with a straight face but without appearing sincerely convinced of them. Though his voice sounds angry he does not look angry.

Most of the other delegates are very angry. In their wig-like earphones they resemble irate founding fathers. Warren Austin, his mouth in a straight line, looks ready to burst. Little Tsiang of Nationalist China is raging. When Austin gets the floor, he drops all pretense of peaceful discussion and begins to call Russia the worst names he can think of. Naturally, he is no such master of vituperation as Comrade Malik. . . .

As I watch the screen, with its extraordinary technical perfection and its tragic failure in human relations, I cannot help comparing this session at Lake Success with other face-to-face meetings I have attended through the years. I have seen attempts to capture a meeting, verbal skirmishes, jealousy, pretentiousness, sometimes anger, but never anything like this. Malik opens a whole new dimension in conflict—while millions of Americans watch in horrified fascination.

His performance makes no sense in an organization expressly created to keep the peace of the world—no sense to the television audience or to any American. But it must make sense to the Kremlin. Malik, speaking there, seems to care little about the United Nations and nothing about Americans or what they think. He is doing what Ina Telberg told us "instructed" delegates often do. He is using the Security Council as a sounding board for propaganda. If we may venture a guess, Malik is trying to talk to the people of Asia.

It is important that Americans grasp the semantic implications of Jacob Malik and of other instructed delegates from time to time. Never mind the grammar of his words; what does he really *mean?* What is his *motivation;* what have the men in the Kremlin instructed him to mean? To listen only to his words will involve us in endless controversy about the validity of the verbal charges he is making. Malik has no interest in proving the validity of his charges. Neither, unfortunately, has that ragged Burmese peasant listening to him at the village radio and trying to make up his mind.

One thing to grasp is that most Russians traditionally talk, argue and contradict more violently than most Americans, not excepting senators. They can keep it up longer, too, sometimes all night, with incredible endurance. In trying to understand motives, this conventional pattern of what seems to us slander and insult must be allowed for. Beyond this, however, we run into a very complicated situation in trying to understand Comrade Malik. Is he primarily an apostle of Karl Marx or Peter the Great? Is he convinced of what he is saying, or only following the script handed to him? Is the Kremlin leading from strength or from weakness? Despite the vast number of theories about what the Russians are up to, how many of us in America have any real facts to go on; how many of us have paid real attention to all the major characteristics?

Certain groups of social scientists are making a beginning in this direction. I would like to tell you about some facts which Dr. Clyde Kluckhohn and his colleagues at Harvard are discovering about Russia.

Russian Research Center

During World War II social scientists in the Pacific developed what they called "area studies," which can be roughly defined as how to know all about a country without going there. The Japanese army happened to be there—in Leyte, Okinawa, the home islands— and the research men tried to piece together from many sources a summary story to give the armed services as they hit the beaches.

The scientists worked in teams and ultimately evolved a series of very useful techniques. Geographers would get together facts about the land and water; public health experts would get together the facts about diseases, epidemics, endemic syphilis, bugs; zoologists would get together the facts about animal life; economists would examine the resource base of the island; political scientists, the system of government; sociologists would gather facts on population, family systems, urban and rural conditions; while anthropologists would analyze the culture and language of the native peoples.

Such an attack can carry a long way provided its leader can fit the separate facts together and draw reliable conclusions and predictions. The techniques are now being used by a number of American universities to study various nations and cultures around the world. If observers can go into the country so much the better, but if an iron curtain intervenes, social scientists can still learn a great deal.

Kluckhohn is leading a team of some sixty scientists in an area study of Russia. He is one of our leading anthropologists and worked in the Pacific theater with such experts as Alexander Leighton and the late Ruth Benedict. His Russian Research Center is operating on a five-year grant from the Carnegie Foundation. It is not the only university study of Russia now in progress—Columbia, for instance, is doing excellent work—but it is perhaps the best financed and most ambitious. The analysis is divided into three parts: (1) Russian history and politics; (2) the economic situation in the U.S.S.R.; (3) human relations inside Russia.

Politics and the Party

The political analysis deals primarily with the history and performance of the communist party. What is the formal and informal structure; who makes the decisions and so determines the "party line"? This is a fascinating subject. Has the world ever before seen a phenomenon to compare with the Russian party line and its shifts? I doubt it, because only in the last few decades has high-speed communication made it possible to change policy simultaneously around the world. Once the decision is made in the Kremlin, it is passed to communist centers from Union Square to Singapore, and all the faithful hastily reverse themselves. What they held most dear before the phone rang, they now denounce as mouthings of the lackeys of imperialism.

Kluckhohn's center is studying party ideology, major shifts in the line, "deviationist" groups like the Trotskyites. It is studying the impact of the party on Russian society, on government, secret police, army, the church, mass communication, unions, peasants, cooperatives; on Russian literature, music, theater, art, and science. It is studying the Cominform and relations of the Russian party to other parties, to Tito, to Mao in China. It is trying to give an indication of the future of world communism.

Some answers to these questions have already been published, and we are beginning to know more about communism in Russia and what the West must reckon with. At present every Congressman, nearly every American, has his private idea of what communism "is" and how it may be dealt with. Communism is a very large, powerful, and complicated movement, with many of the elements of a crusading religion such as early Islam. It will not be overcome by passing a few hasty laws, quoting slogans about democracy, and threatening to fire clerks in government bureaus. A report by Barrington Moore entitled *Soviet Politics—The Dilemma of Power*, published by the center in 1950, gives us a full-length portrait of Russian communism on which to base a sounder program.

Economics and Human Relations

The center is studying the "ruble circuit" in Russia, a complex subject. What do the Russians use for money; where does it come from and where does it go? How far have they gone in mass production? How do they finance new capital outlays? What about output per man-hour, planning industrial locations, budgets, taxation policy, social security? What has been the fate of Five-Year Plans?

Finally, the center is trying to understand the Soviet concept of man. What are the Kremlin's psychological assumptions? Apparently they have passed through a number of phases since the Revolution. Raymond A. Bauer of the center says that "the model of man used in Soviet psychology changed between 1930 and 1937 from a mechanistic one, which saw behavior as determined by forces outside conscious control, to a purposive one, which postulates the decisive role of consciousness. . . . The mechanistic model failed as a theory for analyzing, anticipating, and controlling the behavior of individuals in Soviet society."

What is the position of religion in Soviet life today? What about "Samo-Kritica," the rite of self-criticism? What has been the effect on the Russian people of the Voice of America? The center has also conducted a kind of "Middletown" survey of a town in Karelia, to find out what people are thinking there.

Across the Border

I asked Kluckhohn if he has men actually in Russia. He said no; the center is doing the kind of job which had to be done with Japan in 1943. I asked him how data is gathered. He said from books, monographs, records, in many languages. It comes from Russians, Americans, and other nationals who had been in Russia long enough to have a story to tell, from Russian publications, such as *Pravda* and *Izvestia*, and from monitored broadcasts. It comes also from a special team of experts, stationed in Germany, who interview Russians escaping over the border.

"Aren't the escapees biased?" I asked.

"Extremely so. But we have worked out a method to discount both their anti-Soviet bias and their pro-Russian bias. We get an interesting, sometimes a significant, residue." Later he sent me a monograph by Merle Fainsod describing a series of interviews with escapees.[1] They included peasants, workers, army men, scientists, civil servants, plant managers, engineers—sixty-four persons altogether. Here is a profile of one of them:

Number 5 was a 36-year-old lieutenant-colonel who left the Army in 1945. His father had been a carpenter. There was no history of repression in his family; he was brought up as a loyal Soviet citizen. He was a party member, an engineer and later a journalist. He served with the Red Army from 1941 to 1945; fled in the confusion of the VE Day celebration. He said that he grew disillusioned with Communism while an engineer, that many of his friends had been arrested during the 1936 purges, and although he was passed over he lived in constant fear. The dominating reason for his flight, he said, was his desire to be free from the fear and suspicion which surrounded him in the Soviet Union.

The small farmers interviewed had become disillusioned because the government had not kept its promises about better life on the collective farms.

Workers interviewed complained of low pay, food shortages, and bad housing. They resented the factory management because of the

[1] *American Political Science Quarterly* (June, 1950).

large number of supernumeraries holding down soft jobs. They resented the Stakhanovite movement, calling it a ruthless speed-up. Workers, they said, had no real freedom to express their grievances. The unions were party-controlled, and secret police were everywhere. "Those interviewed asserted they were practically chained to their jobs. It was almost impossible to transfer."

Soldiers complained of bad food, enforced isolation, stringent discipline, and the special privileges allowed officers. Officers complained of the secret police and the atmosphere of insecurity and fear.

Insecurity and fear were also the chief grievances of the bureaucrats and scientists. The Lysenko controversy had increased uneasiness among the latter by making biology follow the party line. The only favorable report concerned the racial policy, which was said to have been tolerant and decent, though recently it had been deteriorating.

Testimony about propaganda was most interesting. We tend to assume in the West that because the Soviet regime controls all sources of mass communication, its hold on the loyalty of young people must be complete. But conversations with a number of escapees cast some doubt on that assumption. A teacher who had taught for twenty-five years in Soviet schools pointed out the wide difference between a cause which appealed to the idealism of youth and an official dogma which insisted on conformity. In late years communism has become such an official dogma, dinned into the children day after day, till many of them grow bored and turn with relief to literary, athletic, and technical interests. A former Komsomol leader, who had worked professionally with youth groups for many years, said it was a mistake to assume that all youngsters come off the Pioneer and Komsomol assembly lines as unthinking tools of the regime. He said even very young children pose embarrassing questions. Crowded home conditions, food shortages, arrests of friends and relatives, compulsory labor service, planted doubts which this informant found difficult to handle when teen-agers came to him with their problems and questions.

Youngsters who came of age in the early 1930's, with the first Five-Year Plan, had a vision of the future and a consequent idealism and constructive energy which he said has now been lost. Today the "Komsomol and party organizations are much more of a bread and butter affair." Morale was low when Hitler struck in 1941, and young Russians surrendered in great numbers. After the Nazis began killing prisoners, however, their deep strong nationalism asserted itself. They rallied to the In-group.

Fainsod emphasizes that his sample of escapees is too small to warrant generalizations valid for all of Soviet society. "It is a record of how some former Soviet citizens in diverse walks of life reacted to and appraised their environment."

However much we may qualify, nevertheless these are significant reports from inside Russia; they form, of course, only a small part of the total fact-finding of the Russian Research Center. As monographs and books are published, they should help us to see Russia and communism more objectively and so to draw intelligent conclusions about possible causes of action. The reports can serve as a valuable check on the assumptions of the State Department, the Defense Department, Congress, editors, columnists, commentators, and the rest of us.

Areas of Agreement

We learned earlier that listing all possible items of agreement between two belligerents sometimes helps to narrow the conflict. It is not improbable that most Americans and most Russians would subscribe to the following list:

Both peoples want peace, and especially security from atomic attack.

Both want a brisk development of atomic energy for peacetime uses.

Both want comfortable living standards. (But Russians may be envious of American standards.)

Neither wants widespread unemployment.

Both want epidemics and pests controlled, and good health, especially for children.

Both want high production of food, and ways and means to exchange raw materials between the Have and Have-not regions.

Both want conservation of natural resources.

Both peoples welcome an exchange of non-political art, music, literature, films. Both need the exchange of scientific information.

Both want the international postal union maintained, and S.O.S. wave bands. Civilians probably want free communication and transportation services generally.

Both want weather information, standard rules for navigation, lighthouse services. (Russia is still in the international weather information exchange, as I write.)

Both want the narcotic trade controlled.

Both want international labor standards, as set up by the I.L.O. at Geneva.

Both enjoy Olympic games and other international sporting events. The Russians are particularly keen on chess tournaments, which gratify their superiority feelings.

This list is enough to show that the area of agreement between the Russian and American people is a wide one. Note the word *people*. Indeed, the two countries have almost nothing to quarrel about so far as their own territory and raw materials are concerned. There are no serious clashes of economic interest—such as Americans have with the British—over oil, rubber, and foreign trade.

Differences between the two populations are largely on the ideological level, but so were the differences between the American democracy and the absolutism of the Czars. With no severe economic cleavages, the ideological differences could probably be bridged, as in Czarist days, when Russians and Americans, while never too friendly, were ready to live and let live.

Power Conflict

The real difficulty is of course a power conflict. The Kremlin, whether through fear or arrogance, is in a dynamic phase, carrying on the territorial expansion of Peter the Great. The United States is the most powerful nation ever known, now producing half the industrial goods and consuming half the inanimate energy of the planet. The United States is in no mood to be pushed around by anybody, no matter how dynamic.

These two nations are now the chief world powers, where in 1940 there were seven—Britain, France, Germany, Italy, Russia, Japan, and America. The two are now in collision in Berlin, Vienna, Yugoslavia, Turkey, Iran, Korea, and other points in Asia. They are engaged in an arms race, spearheaded—quaint phrase—by the stockpiling of atomic bombs. How this power conflict can be resolved I do not know. This book could hardly presume to answer such a question. One or two modest suggestions, however, can be advanced:

First, one hopes that the West will try to base its strategy and decisions in this critical period on facts rather than hunches, slogans, and passions—the type of facts which the Russian Research Center is collecting.

Then, as our "psychological warfare" is developed, there are perhaps some hints to be found in this survey. The Voice of America, for instance, is appealing to people all over the world, telling them that democracy is better than totalitarianism. Remembering McGregor's advice, and asking, "What do they want?"—not what do we think nice for them, but what do they want in their own lives and feelings—the Voice might reach them better. What do the majority of the Chinese people want, the Indian people, Iranians, Koreans, Burmese? There is good evidence—Mr. Justice Douglas has just collected some—that millions of them want (1) relief from landlords, (2) relief from moneylenders, (3) relief from white men bossing them around, (4) technical help in raising living standards. The Kremlin seeks to capitalize on these wants, and therefore has had so far an inside track.

Rensis Likert at Michigan, working out new methods of public opinion research, says that it is not enough to tell the people of the world about U.S. democracy, U.S. sincerity, and the awful powers of the H-bomb. "It is not what people are told that counts—it is what they accept. To be convinced people need to participate or be involved." If we try to sell "freedom" in the usual manner, we shall fail. But if we can invite people to join us in discussing freedoms of various kinds, we may really gain acceptance. We should try to create opportunities for the peoples of the world to express their needs and help solve problems—even to the control of atomic energy. Participation once more.

Another hint: U.S. statesmen would do well to take note of what the Foreign Service Institute has to say about cultural and linguistic differences, in dealing with people on both sides of the iron curtain. They would do well to ask themselves in all candor how the international policy they are promoting sounds to other people. If it is based primarily on the American belief system, it may be misunderstood and resented, even by our friends and allies.

Finally, how well do the statesmen of the U.S., and the U.N., remember the primary goal of the atomic age, namely One World? Eyes cast backward to nineteenth-century nationalism, old balance of power concepts, can lead only to defeat and disaster. There is no longer any hope of victory for one nation or a few nations. Friends and enemies survive or go down together. Our bed was made at Alamogordo, and we must lie in it.

United Nations

The sardonic face of Malik returns on the television screen. For all his tough talk, he was talking in the chamber of the United Nations in New York, a long way west of the iron curtain. He was an accredited member of that body, with dues (I think) paid up. He was unarmed, and broke no rules except those of courtesy.

The day that war broke out in Korea, June 25, 1950, may turn out to have been the signal for World War III or it may have been that great day in history when One World at last came to birth!

It may be that the United Nations, despite Malik's performance, despite discouragement, delays and inefficiencies, is destined to become the mediator for the power struggle between America and Russia. It may be that the United Nations can provide the machinery for accommodation between them. It may be that both governments, preferring peace to war, can use the United Nations to save face and even engineer solutions in matters for which, on a two-power basis, there are no solutions.

It may be. The hope is dim as I write, but it is still there. The United Nations may fail in this test and disintegrate, as the League disintegrated. But where else can the world now go? It will have to try again with another model—perhaps a better structure, perhaps worse.

We have something now, something unprecedented, when fifty-three nations stand together to resist a violent seizure of territory in Korea. One hopes, indeed one prays, that we can hold onto that something, and not have to retreat, through the fearful perils of a two-valued world, and begin all over again for the third time.

CHAPTER TWENTY-ONE

The Road Is Open

OUR journey in search of agreement is nearly over. We have covered a good deal of territory and observed many different people, from the Arapesh natives in New Guinea to the T-groups of Bethel, Maine. We have seen numerous conflicts resolved and noted the methods in the hope that they might be useful in other cases. If a technique works with children or with factory girls or with Congressional committees, may it also be used with town meetings or sharecroppers or a conference at Lake Success? Have the various methods anything in common?

We have been optimistic in applauding any case where conflict has been resolved or avoided and have implied that disagreement is homogeneous enough to be added up, so that reducing the total would in some way reduce the intensity and the threat. This implication is partly justified by the vicious spiral which often grows out of a petty quarrel. Take for instance a simple case of a child punished in school, for whatever reason, who then picks a fight with a playmate and has a temper tantrum at home, which upsets his mother so that she complains to the school board, which tells the superintendent to reprimand the teacher, and so on. One man's aggression often becomes another man's frustration, in a kind of chain reaction. It is also clear, as applied to children, that harmony and co-operation can become good habits and help to form the child's character so that he grows to be a co-operative and friendly adult, an asset in any town meeting, union local, or board of directors.

Round-up

We began our study with a pitched battle between strikers and managers in New Jersey, succeeded by a generation of industrial peace. We then pictured an eighteen-story building with a quarrel on every floor, and proceeded to dig under it, to find that many of the quarrels were due to something other than their apparent cause —some frustration, tension, competitive pressure, which put people on edge. We glanced at certain stereotypes about human nature and recoiled a little. It is hard to find a human without his cultural clothes. But we can remember that the human young take at least twelve years to mature, which necessitates protection by the group, if children are to survive. We are also willing to admit that all normal people are born with a kind of fuse in them which can very easily flare up. The psychiatrists have some sensible advice here about control and safety valves.

Most of our space and time, however, were spent on specific cases and situations where agreement has been reached, or conflict reduced. We gave a chapter to the Quaker meeting and one to the National Laboratory at Bethel. We observed many cases of group performance, such as the drafting of the Lilienthal-Acheson plan, combat groups in the army, the Anglo-Saxon jury system, role-playing, the research work of Lewin, Bavelas, Bales, and others. We noted a steady advance in the study of conference techniques. Group dynamics is growing rapidly—so rapidly it is in some danger of becoming a cult—and it contributes many insights about how people react in face-to-face groups.

Next we inquired at some length into conditions of labor peace, and paid special attention to Joseph Scanlon's participation plans and to the Amalgamated Clothing Workers Union, which shares responsibility with employers for the well-being of the whole industry. We also inspected some pioneering work by scientists at the University of Michigan.

We interviewed Cyrus Ching about the conciliation of labor disputes and took a look at Major Estes' deep-freeze technique for
adopting a contract. We noted the astonishing growth of the
American arbitration movement. We inspected human relations in
the TVA and wondered if their engineering, in the long run, might
not be as important as the engineering of the dams. So far, however,
it is unformulated.

Finally, after a chapter on the danger of men talking—and being
misunderstood as they talked—we looked at agencies for agreement
in international relations, where In-group meets Out-group. We
found some encouraging beginnings, such as UNESCO's analysis of
international conferences, Kluckhohn's area study of Russia, the
program of the Foreign Service Institute at Washington. But we
did not find enough to convince us that One World was immediately assured. It is still a race between the inventors of ever
more lethal weapons and the inventors of international techniques
of agreement.

Five Principles of Agreement

In the course of our inquiry we found many useful methods, rules,
and suggestions to reduce conflict. Some of them kept coming back,
like recurring decimals, in situation after situation. I would like to
underline five of them:

The principle of participation.
The principle of group energy.
The principle of clearing communication lines.
The principle of facts first.
The principle that agreement is much easier when people feel
secure.

Participation

This principle of agreement comes out most dramatically perhaps
in labor-management problems, where workers become actively involved in keeping their industry functioning, their morale and output high. We also found participation a key to the success of the

TVA, of the Quaker business meeting, of any good conference, of college classes, all sorts of things.

As the cases pass in review, it becomes clear that we are looking at democracy in its deepest sense. Let the people into the act—all the people. Consult them, involve them, make them responsible. This is a procedure considerably beyond the mechanics of voting and the tyranny of majorities. The Quakers never vote, but all members participate in a unanimous decision. The keynote is doing things *with* people, not *to* them.

Group Action

It is possible to analyze the energy which comes out only through group interaction. The more we examine the idea the more important it becomes. A major concern of group dynamics is how to release this energy, but it can be seen at work without benefit of scientific study in the army, in conference and discussion groups, in some boards of directors. We see its negative power in mob violence or a theater panic.

As a group creature we do not make sufficient use of our heritage. The failure to do so not only costs society a great deal of constructive energy but probably increases individual loneliness, tension, and conflict. Group dynamics has already gone far enough to show that amiable sentiments about the brotherhood of man and the rewards of co-operation are not enough. Much more spontaneous energy will come from a group where the structure has been designed to encourage the process. It is beginning to look as if Lewin's democratic-permissive type of leadership serves this end best. It is beginning to look as if well-structured groups can solve certain types of problems better than can any individual.

Clearing Communication Lines

This necessity came out in the first chapter, in the case of the man who said "all labor unions are rackets," and on every floor of the skyscraper of conflict. Opening two-way communication is now a major concern of both management and unions. It is a major rule in personal relations. A group leader can be pictured as a switchboard operator in a telephone exchange, with lines to every member. His task is to make connections and keep the lines from jamming. Cyrus Ching exerts his greatest efforts to prevent the severing of negotiations. While there is communication, there is hope.

Semantics, too, is largely concerned with understanding and clarifying communication. The chasm between In-group and Out-group can be spanned only by improving communication techniques. Propaganda can be reduced to impotence when enough listeners understand the principles of communication; semantics is the demagogue's worst friend. The finest way to increase conflict is to snarl the lines, and it is well illustrated by the editor of the communist paper who says, as he tosses a news story to the desk of the rewrite man: "Class-angle that, Joe."

Facts First

Facts traveling over open communication lines can help agreement. We see the intellectual side of this principle in the scientific method, where facts precede deductions and verify theories. Emotion often varies inversely with knowledge. On nearly every floor of the skyscraper, a little pause while the facts of the situation are gathered and brought in might prevent the quarrel. The spectacular case of Captain Saunders' chemical paper pellets applies over a wide area in human relations. Agreement on facts can serve a warm human purpose too.

Mark Twain in *Huckleberry Finn* tells a story which seems to me to illustrate the principle as well as anything I know. You probably remember it.

Huck and Jim are floating down the Mississippi on their immortal raft when Jim begins to talk about his little daughter Elizabeth and the injustice he had done her. He cannot get it out of his head.

She had had scarlet fever but seemed well again, and standing in the cabin he asked her to shut the door. She did not move. He asked her again more sharply but she didn't move. So he slapped her hard and left the room.

When he came back she was sobbing and the door was still open. Suddenly the wind closed it with a great "Ker-blam!" Elizabeth never moved.

Then Jim knew what had happened and saw how he had misunderstood the facts. "Oh, Huck, I grab her in my arms. . . . Oh, she was plumb deef and dumb, Huck, plumb deef and dumb—and I'd been a-treat'n her so."

The Feeling of Security

This principle, though often quite personal and subjective, is too important to ignore. If an individual feels well adjusted and secure, he is not so ready to pick a quarrel, is more inclined to live and let live. Security seems to depend on a sense of belonging, of being wanted; and both conditions are elements in a stable culture.

Security does not necessarily mean economic competence, although that may help. A beggar in India—like the holy man with his bowl in Kipling's story *Kim*—may feel more secure, more at peace with the world, than an American banker in the top bracket. A secure person is not afraid of what life may bring.

The principle also fits in with the frustration-aggression cycle. Back of frustration often lie personal insecurity and fear. We might hazard the guess that if most people *felt* secure—whether they are or not is another matter—the toll of conflict would be enormously reduced. How much conflict between the races is due to insecurity? How much of the truculence of the Russian government today is due to fear of a rearmed Germany and Japan?

The Road Is Open

These five principles are only the highlights of many conclusions and suggestions which our journey has revealed. The cumulative effect is, to me at least, profoundly hopeful for the long range. The science of human relations is gathering momentum. Every year there is more knowledge to add to the storehouse, and it grows, as William F. Ogburn has noted, at an exponential rate. Every year new applications are made, and if even our present knowledge could be fully applied, the effects might transform society. We have already transformed it through partial knowledge and understanding of the physical world, and now to complete the adjustment we must use knowledge to understand ourselves and one another.

With improved understanding, some of the dreadful things anticipated by writers with vivid imaginations—like *Brave New World* and *Nineteen Eighty-four*—lose their probability. Collective tyrannies like these do not square with what anthropologists are finding out about human culture or what psychologists know about frustrations or what biologists have to say about group survival. Such vivid expectations, however skillful the verbal logic, fade before more realistic and on the whole happier probabilities.

It is encouraging to realize that people have much more ability and constructive energy inside them than normally comes out—a first principle in group dynamics. Great men are not so great as advertised, and little men are bigger than advertised—as well as being the kind the Lord must love because he makes so many of them. Greatness lies in the strength of the whole society and its capacity to adjust to changes, external and internal. Social science now makes plain the futility of struggling to beat society.

It is encouraging to realize, at the same time, the uniqueness of individuals. What I see out there is not quite what you see out there, but depends upon our separate experiences. This concept helps us to respect the contribution of others, helps us to appreciate what pooled experience can mean in solving problems.

With these new tools to aid us, life becomes more simple while it takes on new meanings. It becomes happier in a way, or so it seems to me. Our whole apparatus for judging people and events becomes more acute and at the same time more tolerant. Our minds may be no better, but the tools give them a sharper cutting edge. We are better prepared to meet the two chief tasks which have always faced mankind: coming to terms with nature, and coming to terms with our fellows.

The two tasks in a sense are one, for as knowledge and understanding grow, and bring with them more humility toward the universe, we see more and more clearly the interweaving of all nature, including human nature. We grow more intensely aware of our dependence on this planet we inhabit, and of our interdependence on each other.

SELECTED BIBLIOGRAPHY

Adorno, T. W., and associates, *The Authoritarian Personality.* Harper, 1950.

Allport, Gordon, and Postman, Leo, *The Psychology of Rumor.* Holt, 1947.

American Friends Service Committee, *The United States and the Soviet Union, Some Quaker Proposals for Peace.* Yale University Press, 1949.

Barghoorn, Frederick C., *The Soviet Image of the United States: A Study in Distortion.* Harcourt, 1950.

Barnard, Chester I., *Organization and Management.* Harvard University Press, 1948.

Bettelheim, Bruno, and Janowitz, Morris, *Dynamics of Prejudice: A Psychological and Sociological Study of Veterans.* Harper, 1950.

Cantril, Hadley, *The "Why" of Man's Experience.* Macmillan, 1950.

Cantril, Hadley, and Sherif, Muzafer, *The Psychology of Ego-Involvements, Social Attitudes and Identifications.* Wiley, 1947.

Chase, Stuart, *Men at Work: Some Democratic Methods for the Power Age.* Harcourt, 1945.

Chase, Stuart, *The Proper Study of Mankind: An Inquiry into the Science of Human Relations.* Harper, 1948.

Chase, Stuart, *The Tyranny of Words.* Harcourt, 1938.

Clinchy, Everett R., *Intergroup Relations Centers.* Farrar, Straus, 1949.

Comfort, William Wistar, *Quakers in the Modern World.* Macmillan, 1949.

Community Service Society, *The Family in a Democratic Society.* Columbia University Press, 1949.

Cooke, Morris Llewellyn, and Murray, Philip, *Organized Labor and Production: Next Steps in Industrial Democracy.* Harper, 1940.

Copelof, Maxwell, *Management-Union Arbitration, a Record of Cases, Methods, and Decisions.* Harper, 1948.

De Huszar, George B., editor, *New Perspectives on Peace.* University of Chicago Press, 1944.

Derber, Milton, editor, *Proceedings of the First Annual Meeting.* Champaign, Ill., Industrial Relations Research Association, 1949.

241

Dietz, Walter, and Kirkpatrick, Frances, editors, *The Training Within Industry Report, 1940-1945.* Washington: War Manpower Commission, 1945.

Dollard, John, and associates, *Frustration and Aggression.* Yale University Press, 1939.

Dollard, John, and Miller, Neal E., *Personality and Psychotherapy: An Analysis in Terms of Learning, Thinking and Culture.* McGraw-Hill, 1950.

Duffus, R. L., and Krutch, Charles, *The Valley and Its People, a Portrait of TVA.* Knopf, 1944.

Fansler, Thomas, *Creative Power Through Discussion.* Harper, 1950.

Ferguson, Charles W., *A Little Democracy Is a Dangerous Thing.* Association Press, 1948.

Finletter, Thomas K., *Can Representative Government Do the Job?* Reynal & Hitchcock, 1945.

Follett, Mary P., *Creative Experience.* Longmans, Green, 1924.

Follett, Mary P., *The New State.* Longmans, Green, 1926.

Foulkes, S. H., *Introduction to Group Psychotherapy.* London: Heinemann, 1948.

Frank, Lawrence K., *Society as the Patient. Essays on Culture and Personality.* Rutgers University Press, 1948.

Fromm, Erich, *Escape from Freedom.* Farrar & Rinehart, 1941.

Gardner, Burleigh B., *Human Relations in Industry.* Chicago: Richard D. Irwin, 1947.

Golden, Clinton S., and Ruttenberg, Harold J., *Dynamics of Industrial Democracy.* Harper, 1942.

Hader, John J., and Lindeman, Eduard C., *Dynamic Social Research.* Harcourt, 1933.

Hayakawa, S. I., *Language in Thought and Action.* Harcourt, 1949.

Herskovits, Melville J., *The Economic Life of Primitive Peoples.* Knopf, 1940.

Hicks, Clarence J., *My Life in Industrial Relations. Fifty Years in the Growth of a Profession.* Harper, 1941.

Homans, George C., *The Human Group.* Harcourt, 1950.

Huxley, Julian, *Man Stands Alone.* Harper, 1941.

Inkeles, Alex, *Public Opinion in Soviet Russia. A Study in Mass Persuasion.* Harvard University Press, 1950.

Jennings, Helen Hall, *Leadership and Isolation.* Longmans, Green, 1943, 1950.

Johnson, Wendell, *People in Quandaries. The Semantics of Personal Adjustment.* Harper, 1946.

Kellor, Frances, *American Arbitration, Its History, Functions and Achievements.* Harper, 1948.

Klapman, J. W., *Group Psychotherapy, Theory and Practice.* Grune and Stratton, 1946.

Kluckhohn, Clyde, *Mirror for Man. The Relation of Anthropology to Modern Life.* McGraw-Hill, 1949.

Kornhauser, Arthur, editor, *Psychology of Labor-Management Relations.* Champaign, Ill.; Industrial Relations Research Association, 1949.

Korzybski, Alfred, *Science and Sanity.* International Non-Aristotelian Library, 1933, 1948.

Krech, David, and Crutchfield, Richard S., *Theory and Problems of Social Psychology.* McGraw-Hill, 1948.

Lee, Irving J., *Language Habits in Human Affairs: An Introduction to General Semantics.* Harper, 1941.

Leigh, Robert D., *Group Leadership.* Norton, 1936.

Leighton, Alexander H., *The Governing of Men.* Princeton University Press, 1945.

Leighton, Alexander H., *Human Relations in a Changing World: Observations on the Use of the Social Sciences.* Dutton, 1949.

Lever, E. J., and Goodell, Francis, *Labor-Management Cooperation, and How to Achieve It.* Harper, 1948.

Lewin, Kurt, *Resolving Social Conflicts: Selected Papers on Group Dynamics.* Harper, 1948.

Lilienthal, David E., *TVA, Democracy on the March,* Harper, 1944.

Lindeman, E. C., *Social Education.* New Republic, 1933.

Linton, Ralph, *The Study of Man: An Introduction.* Appleton-Century, 1936.

Lippitt, Ronald, *Training in Community Relations.* Harper, 1949.

Littlepage, John D., and Bess, Demaree, *In Search of Soviet Gold.* Harcourt, 1938.

Locke, Alain, and Stern, Bernhard J., *When Peoples Meet: A Study in Race and Culture Contacts.* Barnes & Noble, 1950.

Lundberg, George A., *Can Science Save Us?* Longmans, Green, 1947.

Maier, Norman R. F., *Frustration, The Study of Behavior Without a Goal.* McGraw-Hill, 1949.

Masserman, Jules H., *Behavior and Neurosis.* University of Chicago Press, 1943.

May, Mark A., *A Social Psychology of War and Peace.* Yale University Press, 1943.

Mayo, Elton, *The Human Problems of an Industrial Civilization.* Macmillan, 1933.

Mayo, Elton, *The Social Problems of an Industrial Civilization.* Harvard University Graduate School of Business Administration, 1945.

McBurney, James H., and Hance, Kenneth G., *Discussion in Human Affairs.* Harper, 1939, 1950.

Mead, Margaret, editor, *Cooperation and Competition among Primitive Peoples.* McGraw-Hill, 1937.

Mead, Margaret, *Sex and Temperament in Three Primitive Societies.* Morrow, 1935.

Menninger, Karl, *Love against Hate.* Harcourt, 1942.

Miller, Delbert C., and Form, William H., *Industrial Sociology.* Harper, 1951.

Montagu, Ashley, *On Being Human.* Henry Schuman, 1950.

Moore, Barrington, Jr., *Soviet Politics—The Dilemma of Power: The Role of Ideas in Social Change.* Harvard University Press, 1950.

Moreno, J. L., *Who Shall Survive?* Washington: Nervous and Mental Disease Publishing Co., 1934.

Murphy, Gardner, editor, *Human Nature and Enduring Peace.* Houghton Mifflin, 1945.

Nichols, Osgood, editor, *Partners in Production.* Twentieth Century Fund, 1949.

Northrop, F. S. C., *The Meeting of East and West.* Macmillan, 1947.

Overstreet, Harry W., *Influencing Human Behavior.* Norton, 1925.

Overstreet, Harry W., *The Mature Mind.* Norton, 1949.

Pear, T. H., editor, *Psychological Factors of Peace and War.* London: Hutchinson, 1950.

Pollard, Francis, Beatrice and Robert, *Democracy and the Quaker Method.* London: Bannisdale Press, 1949.

Rapoport, Anatol, *Science and the Goals of Man: A Study in Semantic Orientation.* Harper, 1950.

Redfield, Robert, *A Village That Chose Progress.* University of Chicago Press, 1950.

Robinson, James Harvey, *The Mind in the Making.* Harper, 1921.

Roethlisberger, R. J., and Dickson, W. J., *Management and the Worker.* Harvard University Press, 1940.

Rogers, Carl R., *Counseling and Psychotherapy.* Houghton Mifflin, 1942.

Schultz, Richard S., *Wartime Supervision of Workers: The Human Factors in Production for Executives and Foremen.* Harper, 1943.

Selekman, Benjamin M., *Labor Relations and Human Relations.* McGraw-Hill, 1947.

Sheffield, Alfred D., *Creative Discussion.* Association Press, 1925, 1936.

Slavson, S. R., editor, *The Practice of Group Therapy*. International Universities Press, 1947.

Slichter, Sumner H., and associates, *Report of the Governor's Labor-Management Committee*. In Robert F. Bradford: *Addresses and Messages*. Boston, Commonwealth of Massachusetts, 1948.

Snygg, Donald, and Combs, Arthur W., *Individual Behavior: A New Frame of Reference for Psychology*. Harper, 1949.

Stouffer, Samuel A., and associates, *The American Soldier*. 2 vol. Princeton University Press, 1949.

Tead, Ordway, *The Art of Administration*. McGraw-Hill, 1951.

Tolman, Edward C., *Drives Toward War*. Appleton-Century, 1942.

Utterback, William E., *Group Thinking and Conference Leadership*. Rinehart, 1950.

Walker, Charles R., *Steeltown, An Industrial Case History of the Conflict Between Progress and Security*. Harper, 1950.

Walser, Frank, *The Art of Conference*. Harper, 1933, 1948.

Warner, W. Lloyd, and associates, *Democracy in Jonesville*. Harper, 1949.

Warner, W. Lloyd, and Low, J. O., *The Social System of the Modern Factory. The Strike: A Social Analysis*. Yale University Press, 1947.

Warner, W. Lloyd, and Lunt, Paul S., *The Social Life of a Modern Community*. Yale University Press, 1941.

West, Ranyard, *Conscience and Society*. London: Methuen, 1942. New York: Emerson Books, Inc., 1945.

White, E. B., *Here Is New York*. Harper, 1949.

Wiener, Norbert, *The Human Use of Human Beings*. Houghton Mifflin, 1950.

Williams, Robin M., Jr., *The Reduction of Intergroup Tensions*. New York: Social Science Research Council, 1947.

Pamphlets

National Planning Association, Washington: *Causes of Industrial Peace under Collective Bargaining*. Case studies reported in pamphlet series, 1948—

Periodicals

ETC: A Review of General Semantics. Quarterly. Chicago: Vol. I, 1943—
Harvard Business Review. Quarterly. Boston: Vol. XX, 1941—
Human Relations. Quarterly. London and Ann Arbor, Michigan: Vol. I, 1948—
Journal of Social Issues. Quarterly. New York: Association Press, Vol. I, 1945—

INDEX

247

Leiserson, William, 144
Lever, E. J., 243
Lewin, Kurt, 7-8, 69, 70, 74-75, 77, 85-
  86, 124, 125, 191, 234, 236, 243
Lewis, John L., 14, 137
Lie, Trygve, 12, 13
Likert, Rensis, xiii, 98, 125, 217, 230
Lilienthal, David E., 57, 173, 175, 178,
  185, 243
Lindeman, Eduard C., ix, 69, 109-110,
  115, 206, 242, 243
Linton, Ralph, 34, 132, 133, 243
Lippitt, Ronald, 7, 86, 243
Lippitt, Rosemary, 102
Littlepage, John D., 124, 125, 243
Livingston, Donald, 98
Lochhead, Charlotte, xiii, 113
Locke, Alain, 243
Locke, John, 46
Loring, Mrs. Russell A., xii
Low, J. O., 245
Lucas, Scott, 12
Luke, Robert, 98
Lundberg, George A., xiii, 243
Lunt, Paul S., 72, 245

McBurney, James H., 244
McCarthy, Joseph R., 12
McDougall, William, 23
McGregor, Douglas, xiii, 69, 77-78, 104,
  125, 157, 202, 230
Magellan, Fernando, 70
Maier, Norman R. F., 23, 243
Malik, Jacob, 221-23, 231
Mao Tse-Tung, General, 170, 224
Marquand, John, 37
Marx, Karl, 132, 133, 223
Masserman, Jules H., 24, 243
May, Mark A., 243
Mayo, Elton, x, 7, 69, 73, 124, 125,
  132, 153, 156, 158, 243, 244
Mead, Margaret, 36, 42, 244
Menninger, Karl, 244
Miller, Delbert C., 244
Miller, Neal E., 22, 242
Montagu, Ashley, 41-42, 244
Moore, Barrington, Jr., 225, 244
Moreno, J. L., 99, 100, 244
Morgan, Harcourt, 173, 175
Morrow, Dwight, 163-64
Mowrer, O. H., 22

Murdock, George P., 55
Murphy, Gardner, 244
Murray, Philip, 155, 241
Mussolini, Benito, 33

Napoleon, 50
Nelson, Donald, x, 134
Nichols, Osgood, 244
Njal, 194
Norris, Alfred, xiii
Northrop, F. S. C., 46, 244

O'Conor, 12
Ogburn, William F., xiii, 194, 239
Oppenheimer, J. Robert, 57, 211
Overstreet, Harry W., 109, 208, 244
Owen, Robert, 50

Patton, James G., 119
Pear, T. H., 244
Pegler, Westbrook, 6, 205
Penn, William, 45, 50, 55
Perkins, Milo, xiii, 38, 187-88
Peter the Great, 223, 230
Petrillo, Caesar, 137
Plato, 68
Pollard, Francis, Beatrice, and Robert,
  4, 46, 47, 49, 52-53, 54, 244
Pope, James, 181
Postman, Leo, 241
Prince, David C., 119

Rapoport, Anatol, 201, 244
Redfield, Robert, 68, 244
Redl, Fritz, 89, 91
Reuther, Walter, 149
Robinson, James Harvey, 244
Roethlisberger, R. J., 156, 244
Rogers, Carl R., 244
Roosevelt, Eleanor, 205
Roosevelt, Franklin D., 129, 205
Root, Elihu, 207
Roper, Elmo, xii, 4
Ruml, Beardsley, 119
Ruttenberg, Harold J., 242

Saunders, James, 8-9, 10, 237
Scanlon, Joseph, xiii, 78, 124, 139-43,
  150, 156, 234
Schultz, Richard S., 244
Schultz, Theodore W., 119